SAM WALKER

THE
CAPTAIN
CLASS

The hidden force that creates the world's greatest teams

EBURY
PRESS

1 3 5 7 9 10 8 6 4 2

Ebury Press, an imprint of Ebury Publishing
20 Vauxhall Bridge Road
London SW1V 2SA

Ebury Press is part of the Penguin Random House group of companies
whose addresses can be found at global.penguinrandomhouse.com

Copyright © Samuel Walker 2017

Samuel Walker has asserted his right to be identified as the author of this
Work in accordance with the Copyright, Designs and Patents Act 1988

This edition published by Ebury Press in 2018

First published in the USA by Random House, an imprint and division of
Penguin Random House LLC, New York.

www.penguin.co.uk

A CIP catalogue record for this book is available from the British Library

ISBN 9781785030291

Waltham Forest Libraries

Please return this item by the last date stamped. The loan may be renewed unless required by another customer.

may 18		

the greatest teams of all time – and quickly has the reader reexamining long-held beliefs about leadership and the glue that binds winning teams together.'

—**Theo Epstein, President of Baseball Operations for the Chicago Cubs**

BY SAM WALKER

Fantasyland
The Captain Class

For Sylvie

My ego demands—for myself—
the success of my team.

—BILL RUSSELL

CONTENTS

PROLOGUE

The first time I stepped through the looking glass into the private sanctum of a professional locker room, I had just turned twenty-five. I had a notebook jammed into the back pocket of my college khakis and a press credential looped around my neck. If I didn't look like I knew what I was getting into, that's because I didn't. This locker room belonged, as fate would have it, to Michael Jordan's Chicago Bulls.

Since that March evening in 1995, I have seen Tom Brady's Patriots win their first Super Bowl and mingled with an FC Barcelona team steaming toward a Champions League title. I have watched cyclists storm up Mont Ventoux at the Tour de France and been doused with forty-nine-dollar champagne by the New York Yankees as they celebrated a third straight World Series victory.

For a reporter, all of this was exactly as charmed as it sounds. Every championship brought with it the guarantee of good play and a generous word count in the newspaper, not to mention the chance to tell everybody who'd listen that yes, I was there.

Behind the glamour, however, there was one persistent problem with my career choice. Every time I watched some group of euphoric athletes collecting its trophy, I had an intense personal reaction that surprised me. I felt jealous.

Every summer, throughout grade school, I played second base for a neighborhood baseball team called the Burns Park Bombers. For the most part, there was nothing remarkable about this team. Our pitching was decent, our hitting was serviceable, and our coach was a taciturn guy with oversize glasses who conducted practices with a cigarette bobbing between his lips. We usually won about 50 percent of our games and played just well enough to earn the coveted postgame trip to Dairy Queen.

In the summer of 1981, however, something changed. The nose-pickers who used to let balls roll between their legs started making competent plays. When hits were needed, hits materialized, and our pitchers threw just enough strikes to hold the lead. All of us seemed to have escaped the confines of our eleven-year-old bodies: We floated above the diamond in awe as these children who looked suspiciously like us transmogrified into a formidable team.

We finished the season 12–0.

What I realized about this glorious experience, years later, is that it had forever modified my expectations. The Bombers gave me a taste of what it was like to play on an excellent team, and this had rewired my brain to believe it was my God-given right to experience the same sensation many times over. As the years passed, however, it became painfully clear it was not. The 1981 Bombers were the only championship team I ever played for.

As I started writing about a multitude of sports, and parachuting in to cover some of the world's best teams, the memories of that summer kept bubbling up. Feelings of disappointment and longing took possession of a modest apartment somewhere at the back of my brain. If it's true that our lifelong obsessions stem from seemingly mundane events in our childhoods, then I suppose this is mine. I ache to be part of a great team.

Behind the scenes with these elite groups of athletes, I always paid rapt attention. I studied how they spoke to one another, noted their mannerisms and body language, and observed their pregame rituals. When they offered theories about what made their collaborations successful, I jotted them down in my notebook. No matter the sport, I always heard the same handful of explanations—we practice hard, we play for each other, we never quit, we have a great coach, we always come through in the clutch. More than anything, I was struck by the business-like sameness of these groups and by how nonchalantly their members spoke about winning. It was as if they were part of a machine in which every cog and sprocket was functioning precisely as intended. "You do your job so everyone around you can do their job," Tom Brady once said. "There's no big secret to it."

In 2004, I took a leave from my job to write a book about competing in America's toughest fantasy-baseball expert competition. My strategy was to spend many days and nights with real major-league teams collecting inside information. The club I followed most closely was the Boston Red Sox.

The Red Sox franchise had a long and glorious history of failure and heartbreak dating back to 1918, the last time it had won a World Series. The moment I met them at spring training in February, I found little evidence that this season would be any different. Despite a sprinkling of stars, the roster was largely composed of misfits and castoffs— oddly shaped and sloppily bearded party animals with unconventional skills that other teams didn't value. Behind the scenes I found them to be candid and funny, unpredictable and hopelessly undisciplined— a profile that would earn them the nickname The Idiots.

When Boston fell nine and a half games behind their rivals, the dynastic New York Yankees, I wasn't the least bit surprised. I believed my first impression had been spot-on. The Red Sox were nothing like the dominant teams I had known. They weren't championship contenders.

In early August, however, the Red Sox—like that youth baseball team of mine—seemed to fall under the influence of a spell. The Idiots started playing with confidence and ferocity, keeping cool under pressure and projecting a sense of unity and purpose I hadn't seen in the spring. After clambering back up the standings and sneaking into the postseason, the Red Sox met the Yankees in the American League

Championship Series and promptly lost the first three games. Before Game 4, the bookmakers put their odds of survival at 120 to 1. They would come within three outs of being eliminated.

Yet the Red Sox didn't fold. They not only battled back to win Game 4 in extra innings, they defeated the Yankees three more times, capping the most dramatic postseason comeback in baseball history. Next came the World Series, where they swept the St. Louis Cardinals four games to none.

To Bostonians, who had endured one of the severest dry spells in sports history, this championship felt like deliverance. Three million people jammed the streets for a victory parade. There was even talk in the sports world that these Red Sox deserved a place among the greatest ballclubs of all time.

Here was a team that had been left for dead in July—and yet somehow the players had pulled together to form a brilliant, resilient whole. I wouldn't call the Red Sox a dynasty—it would take them another three years to win a second title—but out of nowhere, they'd been gripped by a contagion that allowed them to play like every other magnificent team I'd observed. What I wanted to know, but couldn't fathom, was *why* this happened. What provided the spark?

The following spring I started reporting an analysis piece for the *Wall Street Journal* that I hoped to call "The Secret Lives of Elite Teams." My plan was simple: I'd come up with an objective formula for identifying the ten most accomplished dynasties in sports history, then trace their performances back to the moment they made the "turn" toward greatness to see if there were any similarities. Maybe these teams had all hired an inspiring coach, or drafted a standout player, or developed an innovative strategy.

The fact that this article never ran in the paper is not an indication of flagging interest. In fact, I developed the opposite problem. The deeper I dug, the more complex and engrossing the subject became.

Just deciding how to define a "team" turned out to be a major undertaking requiring several weeks of spadework.

As I type this sentence, I've been working on the same line of inquiry for almost eleven years. I have reviewed and researched the accomplishments of more than twelve hundred teams across the world in thirty-seven major categories of sport since the 1880s. I have ripped through hundreds of books, articles, documentaries, scientific papers, and statistical analyses. I have tracked down interview subjects in Auckland, Barcelona, Boston, Chicago, Havana, London, Los Angeles, Madrid, Melbourne, Montreal, Moscow, New York, Paris, Perth, Rio de Janeiro, and dozens of sleepy hamlets in between.

When I started out, I never expected to reach one emphatic conclusion. I assumed the fingerprints of these elite units would have many of the same whorls and ridges yet no perfect matches. In the end, I was shocked to discover that the world's most extraordinary sports teams didn't have many propulsive traits in common, they had exactly one. And it was something I hadn't anticipated.

The Captain Class is the culmination of a lifetime of watching sports, two decades of spending time in the orbit of world-class teams, and my own lengthy investigation into what drives the dynamics behind a surpassing collective effort. It's not the story of one team's triumph, although there are many triumphs recounted here. It's not a biography of one transcendent star or coach, although many legendary figures will be discussed. Though it uses sports as its source material, it's ultimately a book about a single idea—one that is simple, powerful, and can be applied to teams in many other fields, from business and politics to science and the arts.

It's the notion that the most crucial ingredient in a team that achieves and sustains historic greatness is the character of the player who leads it.

PART I

GREATNESS AND ITS ORIGINS

The Birth of a Freak Team

LONDON, 1953

On a chilly Wednesday afternoon in northwest London, one month before Christmas, a procession of football fans filed toward the gates of the Empire Stadium, Wembley, in a calm, purposeful manner. The women wore long woollen coats with modest heels. The men wore ties and overcoats with the collars turned up, flat caps and trilbies raked just so. Several carried briefcases, having slipped out early from the office.

These ticketholders had every right to feel confident. In the previous thirty years, the national football team of England, which they'd come to cheer for, had amassed a sterling home record of nineteen wins and two defeats against visiting teams, outscoring them by an average of four goals to one. In fact, in the eighty-one years since England had begun hosting teams from outside the British Isles, it had never lost at home.

The only visual record I found of the scene outside the stadium before this match came from an old eight-millimeter home movie. There was no audio, the focus was spotty, and it lasted just fifty-two seconds. What it did show, however, in surprisingly vivid color, were the final moments of a world order that was about to be stood on its head.

On the docket that day was an exhibition match known as a friendly—the results of which would have no direct bearing on the qualifying process for the quadrennial World Cup. England's opponent was expected to show a bit more fight than most. It had earned a pugnacious reputation by winning a gold medal at the Olympics the summer before and remaining unbeaten for twenty-three matches, albeit against relatively weak competition. The London papers, never known for their restraint, had taken to calling it "the match of the century."

The central flaw in this narrative was the origin of the visiting team. It did not come from one of the world's traditional football empires. It hailed from bloody Hungary.

In 1953, Hungary was a nation of roughly nine million, about one-quarter the size of England. It was not moving in a prosperous direction. The prime minister and party general secretary, Mátyás Rákosi, and his Communist planners had seized control of every aspect of life. They'd collectivized the land and forced masses of people into manual labor. Personal income, which was two-thirds below the European average before World War II, had fallen by 20 percent since 1950 as military spending and "socialist construction" bled the treasury. Conditions in the country bordered on primitive: Barely 10 percent of homes had bathrooms, and fewer than 20 percent had running water. Heat came primarily from coal- or wood-burning stoves.

The members of the Hungarian national football team lived far better than most but were hardly insulated from the poisonous politics and its deprivations. The best players had been conscripted into the army in large part to discourage them from defecting, and secret police traveled with them to away games to monitor their activities. Some were under suspicion for harboring "dangerous" ideas.

To this point, the Hungarian football team's finest achievement, beyond its 1952 gold medal, was a trip to the final of the 1938 World Cup, where it had been soundly beaten by Italy. But since most of the world's top professional players hadn't competed in the Olympics, and many of the world's best teams hadn't participated in the '38 World Cup, the English public didn't take either of these accomplishments seriously. Fattening up on teams from nearby countries like Austria, Bulgaria, and Albania didn't make Hungary a proper rival.

The English believed that the brand of football played on the Continent, while lovely to behold, was lacking in force and rugged directness. When England played at home and squared up with their opponent, they believed, losing was all but impossible. Despite the exhortations of the London papers, the oddsmakers at the betting house William Hill had installed the Hungarians as underdogs at the astonishing odds of 500 to 1.

"This was [supposed to be] a 2–0, 3–0, 4–0, maybe 5–1 demolition of a small country who were just coming into European football," said Bobby Robson, a future England manager who attended the match as a twenty-year-old fan. "We thought we would demolish this team. England at Wembley: We are the masters, they are the pupils."

The English players sauntered onto the field in their traditional billowy white-collared tops, their sleeves rolled up to the elbows, looking regal and relaxed, as if they'd just spent the morning trimming hedgerows. England in 1953 was finally feeling itself again. Postwar rationing had all but ended. A youthful new queen had been crowned in June. Researchers at Cambridge had discovered the structure of DNA, and a party of explorers organized by the Royal Geographical Society had summited Everest.

As the Hungarian players filed out of the tunnel from the dressing rooms, they were not an intimidating sight. Markedly smaller than the English, they wore tight-fitting cherry-red tops that clung to their torsos, making them look even less substantial. Their shorts were higher cut than the English versions, and their low-rise shoes, handmade by a cobbler in Budapest, looked more like loafers than proper football boots. The numbers on their backs were laughable, too, in that they didn't correspond to their positions on the pitch. As he watched the Hungarians make their entrance, England's Billy Wright chuckled to a teammate that their opponents "haven't even got the proper kit."

If the Hungarian strip struck the English fans as the setup for a joke, the punch line was the team's twenty-six-year-old captain and top scorer, Ferenc Puskás. At barely five foot seven, Puskás had stumpy calves and meaty thighs that rubbed together as he walked, making his shorts ride up awkwardly at the crotch. Puskás would struggle with his weight during his career—at one time ballooning up to two hundred pounds. At home he was known as Öcsi (Kid Brother), but the English simply referred to him as "the little fat chap." More surprisingly, Puskás had holes in his game. He hated heading the ball and had never learned to shoot or even dribble with his right foot.

In the opening frames of the English television broadcast, the Hungarian players twitched with nervous energy. As they waited for the referee's whistle, they seemed ready to leap out of their tiny shoes. Just before kickoff, Puskás did something odd. He scooped up the ball with his left foot and, as the players on both teams watched, juggled it for a few seconds with his feet and knees. Although ball juggling was something the Hungarian players often did before matches to settle themselves, it was a feat the English were not familiar with. It also provided the first glimmer of what was to come. "Now, there's an exhibition of ball control," said the English commentator, Kenneth Wolstenholme, as Puskás performed his trick. "If we see a great deal of that I think we're going to have an awful lot of trouble holding these unbeaten Hungarians."

As I settled in to watch the match, I remembered something a football historian had told me—that the best way to appreciate what I was about to witness was to have a stopwatch handy. So at the moment the referee blew the whistle, I clicked Start.

The Hungarians opened play by stringing together four precise passes, one of them a pretty backheeler, playing the ball all the way down the right side of the English half until a defender cleared the ball. I glanced at the stopwatch. Twelve seconds had elapsed. After a pair of throw-ins, Hungary recovered possession and drove forward again. England's defenders cleared the ball a second time, but the Hungarians, who seemed to be playing at an elevated tempo, recovered it near midfield. Thirty-four seconds had gone by.

The Hungarian forward Nándor Hidegkuti received the ball and charged directly at the nearest English defender, Harry Johnston. Without breaking stride, Hidegkuti dragged one leg back behind his body as if preparing to shoot, prompting Johnston to spring into the air, stiffening for impact. Hidegkuti deftly recovered his stride and whipped past him.

Since he wasn't known to be the team's striker, football orthodoxy dictated that Hidegkuti shouldn't be attempting to score. If he'd been playing his role by the book, as the English would have preferred, he would have been scanning the field for a passing opportunity. Instead he kept advancing as if *he* were the striker.

As my stopwatch reached thirty-nine seconds, the English player with the best chance to stifle the attack was Jimmy Dickinson. But Dickinson did not seem like a man with a plan. He looked bewildered. Unable to decide whether to challenge Hidegkuti for the ball or to focus on patrolling the back, he froze on his heels. Hidegkuti, now working with a cushion of space, had a clear look at the goal from the top of the penalty box. In a flash he launched a screamer at the upper-left corner.

Gil Merrick, the English keeper, dived lamely but the ball hit the back of the net. As Hidegkuti leaped in the air to celebrate, I clicked the button on the stopwatch. Hungary had scored against the invincible English in 43.2 seconds.

Wolstenholme, the typically phlegmatic match commentator, couldn't contain his amazement. "It's a goal!" he shouted. A silence followed, stretching from two seconds to three, then to five. On the pitch the English defenders glared at one another in disgust. "My word," Wolstenholme finally said. "If that's a sample of what we're going to have this afternoon, then England are going to be in dire trouble."

The final score at Wembley that day was Hungary 6, England 3— which sounds less disastrous than it was, given that the home team was outshot 35–5. After the match the English fans were so awestruck by what they'd seen that they applauded the Hungarians and even showed up at Victoria Station to watch them board their train. An editorial in the *Times* the following morning billed the English defeat as "Agincourt in reverse." By any standard, it was the end of an era. According to English bookmakers, Hungary's 500-to-1 upset of England remains one of the longest-odds sports bets ever to pay out.

As the English began rehashing the match, it became clear that every assumption they had made about the Hungarians had been faulty. If the players had seemed laughably small, it was because the team's selectors prized quickness. Their low-cut boots had been de-signed that way to allow for greater lateral movement. And their gar-bled shirt numbers were a deliberate ruse to keep the English players guessing about who was playing in what position. This hadn't been football at all, really, but a demonstration of advanced strategic ops.

The tactics of the Hungarian team, as dazzling as they were, told only part of the story. On that overcast Wednesday afternoon, in front of a hundred thousand hostile spectators in one of the biggest matches of their lives, the Hungarians had conquered their own considerable anxiety. In the face of the blunt force of England's best team, whose players were larger, stronger, and more experienced, they had man-aged to play with astounding grace. As any athlete will tell you, the first thing nerves interfere with is fine motor control. Every touch becomes hundreds of times more difficult with a gallon of adrenaline coursing through your bloodstream. But the Hungarians had not collapsed. From Puskás's juggling display to the final whistle, they had played with lethal precision.

The Hungarians would not have to wait long to prove that their victory wasn't a fluke. A few months later in Budapest, the English were given a chance to redeem themselves. This time, Hungary trounced them 7–1.

The following summer, at the 1954 World Cup in Switzerland, the Hungarians continued their run, humiliating West Germany in the group stage by the hard-to-fathom score of 8–3 and then beating the mighty Brazilians 4–2 in what football analysts describe as one of the hardest-fought matches in history.

The World Cup would not end the way the Hungarians had hoped. In the final match, an ugly mud-caked affair, the so-called Golden Team blew a 2–0 lead and lost to the same Germans they had soundly beaten two weeks before. On the heels of that defeat, however, the Hungarians launched a second undefeated run that lasted for another one and a half years. Overall, between June 1950 and February 1956 this team played a total of fifty-three matches, including international friendlies, and lost only twice.* When asked about the Hungarians, the English player Stanley Matthews left no doubt about their place in history. "They were wonderful to watch, with tactics we'd never seen before," he said. "They were the best ever."

In sports, any team that achieves this sort of dominance will have an extraordinarily difficult time sustaining it. Unlike the business world, where innovative new products and technologies can be developed in secret, sports does not allow teams to hide their techniques. They can hone them in practice, but they must display them during matches in full view of their opponents, who can keep rewinding the tape until they find vulnerabilities.

Moreover, sports competitions are restricted to fields with set dimensions and are often governed by a clock. In this constricted, pressurized environment, the outcome can be determined by a fraction of a second or a gap no wider than an inch. One small mistake made by a single person can overwhelm an hour of otherwise flawless play.

Because the margins are so thin, it's fair to say that any team that takes on the world's toughest opponents and wins abundantly is doing something remarkable. But what are we to make of a team that wins almost every game it plays for six straight years?

Whether it's the introduction of the forward pass to college football in 1906, the attacking style of rugby pioneered by the Welshman John Dawes in the early 1970s, or Joe Montana's touchdown pass to Dwight Clark in the 1982 NFC Championship Game, it has become an authorial cliché to suggest that one game, one season, one team, or even one play was the catalyst that changed a sport forever. But when it comes to international football, this spark of transformation really does exist. The sport's Talmud, the sacred text that altered its course forever, is

* Many historians disregard one of these defeats, to the Soviet Union, because they suspect the team lost for political reasons.

that grainy footage from Wembley in 1953. The ability of the Hungarians to open up spaces in which to attack the English defense would go on to influence the tactics of every other football dynasty since: the Brazilians from 1958 to 1970, the Scottish club team Celtic in the 1960s, the Dutch dynasty of the 1970s, and the dazzling Barcelona squads of the 2000s.

Before Hungary, football teams were thought to be collections of individuals with specific orders to do distinct things. A left-winger was supposed to patrol the left-hand touchline, for instance, while a striker's job was to play forward at all times with an eye on the goal—no more, no less. The Hungarian Golden Team destroyed this notion. It didn't respect rigidity. It was fluid. Players switched positions and dispositions all the time, depending on the circumstances.

There was nothing about the physical ability of Hungary's players, or the poor, repressive nation they came from, to suggest they should be great, much less that they should be better than every other team before or since. What distinguished them was a style of play that erased specialization, forced players to subordinate their egos, and coaxed superior performances out of unlikely characters. "Imagine the best team you've ever seen," said Jackie Sewell, who scored one of England's three goals in the Wembley match. "That Hungarian side is easily as good, if not better. They were a group of individuals who were unremarkable alone, but together—potent, magical. It wasn't just us who were baffled by them. Everyone was."

At the time there were two romantic explanations for Hungary's brilliance. The country's Communist leadership viewed it as a testament to how a centralized command-and-control system that deemphasized the individual could conquer the world—a Marxist propaganda coup. The team's coach, a party stalwart named Gusztáv Sebes, called it "socialist football." Opponents of the regime, meanwhile, took it as a sign of the irrepressible creativity of the Hungarian people peeking out from the blanket of oppression.

If there was something about being Communist, or Hungarian, that supported the execution of tactically beautiful football, it has not expressed itself since. No Communist state has ever won a World Cup, and since 1960, Hungary has struggled just to maintain a place among the top fifty major football-playing nations. It has qualified for the World Cup only three times since 1970. The truth is that neither explanation holds up. The moment these particular players disbanded in 1956, the greatness vanished with them.

Dozens of football teams throughout history have been described as dynasties. As I examined Hungary's six-year winning run, however, it was such an outlier among its peer group, such a freak, that it inhabited a category of its own.

When economists stumble onto some entity that doesn't conform to the usual trajectory of things and can't be easily explained, they often describe it as a black swan. In Silicon Valley, the land of infinite possibilities, a tech company that emerges from its founder's basement to earn a valuation in the billions of dollars is called a unicorn. This sort of thinking holds sway across the entire spectrum of the sciences. When researchers gather a sample of test subjects, one of their first steps is to eliminate the outliers. The logic is that these anomalies, with their exaggerated results, can't be relied upon to reveal any universal, practical truths. In science, there is no point in trying to understand soaring excellence unless it's repeatable.

It would be easy, then, to label Hungary a unicorn and lump it into the same discard pile. One could say that this team's achievements must have come from some sui generis convergence of events and that its dominance was an accident of randomness.

Yet while the Golden Team might have been an outlier, international football is only one team sport among dozens played throughout the world. In all of these sports, at some point over the decades at least one team has posted a record that beats everybody else's hands down. What would happen, I wondered, if you canvassed the histories of each one of them, starting with the first clumsy professional associations of the nineteenth century, plotted their performances on a scatter chart, and drew circles around the ones whose performances have never been matched? If there are five of these standout teams like Hungary—or ten, or even thirty—wouldn't it be interesting to see what they had in common?

This book is divided into three parts. Part I will explain how I developed the criteria to identify the top 10 percent of the top 1 percent of teams in history and the process I used to zero in on their similarities. Part II will draw upon the stories of these freak teams, and a survey of scientific research, to explore the one component they shared and why it enabled them to make the turn toward greatness. Part III will examine why so many teams make poor decisions that impede their ability to create and sustain a winning culture, and how these mistakes can be avoided.

ONE

Alpha Lions

Identifying the World's Greatest Teams

There is no better, faster way to start a barstool argument with another sports fan than to trot out a list of the world's greatest teams. Once you go down this road, God help you. You're in for a long night. The only redeeming quality of this line of debate is that by the time it finally ends, you won't be sober enough to remember it.

I had never written any of my own half-baked opinions down, but I knew that others had. So I launched my study by gathering up every such list that had been published anywhere in the world, from the pages of prestigious newspapers to the most homespun websites, to see if they had come to any consensus. I found about ninety of them.

After I spread them out on my dining room table and attacked them with a yellow highlighter, it was immediately clear that this species of sports-page punditry had some flamboyant empirical weaknesses. Some of the lists didn't bother offering a methodology—their conclusions were based on the collective opinions of a bunch of guys in the office. The ones that did use numbers were often statistically dubious.

The most common procedural error was something known as "selection bias," a gaffe which has long plagued all kinds of polls, surveys, and scientific experiments. This occurs when researchers base their studies on samples that aren't large enough, or random enough, to offer a representative cross section of the whole. The telltale sign was that most of these lists had a suspiciously regional flavor. Rankings from England, for example, were clogged with the names of football clubs like Liverpool and Manchester United, while those from Down Under went heavy on rugby, cricket, and Australian rules football.

What this told me was that these list-makers had failed to cast a wide enough net. In many cases, they hadn't even considered teams from outside their own national borders.

Another problem was that the same gangs of standbys kept showing up over and over. In the United States, for instance, the 1927 New York Yankees, the 1972 Miami Dolphins, the 1990s Chicago Bulls, and the New England Patriots of the 2000s made nearly every list. The only difference was the order in which they were ranked. This suggested that my fellow analysts had probably allowed themselves to be prejudiced by the candidates other people had already anointed.

To build a proper list, I realized, I would have to ignore all the others, put on blinders to block my own assumptions, and start fresh. I would have to consider every team from every major sport anywhere in the world through the fullness of history.

The first step was to locate reliable historical records for every professional or international sports league, association, confederation, or annual tournament, from Australia to Uruguay—and to isolate every team that either had won a major title or trophy or achieved an exceptional winning streak. This process, which took months to complete, yielded a spreadsheet of candidates that ran into the thousands.

To set some parameters for my research and filter this group down to a more manageable number, I set out to answer three fundamental questions.

Question 1:
What qualifies as a team?

Most of the rankings on my dining room table neglected to deal with one vital issue: What constitutes a team in the first place? A sport like ice dancing, where two people perform together in front of a panel of judges, was often given the same weight as a sport like rugby union, where two groups of fifteen athletes compete head-to-head. The members of Olympic boxing teams, who enter the ring alone, were lumped together with volleyball players, who compete side by side.

The dictionary definition of "team" is about as bare-bones as it gets. It's defined as any group that works together on a task. When it comes to horses or oxen, a team starts with two and goes up from there, but there is no conventional view of how many humans are required. Is a group of two people a team or a partnership? And do three people make up a team or a trio?

To settle the matter, I decided that a group of athletes can only be considered a team in the fullest sense of the word if it meets the following three criteria:

A. It has five or more members.

One thing we can say with certainty is that the smaller a team, the more its results depend on individual performances. If a team has two members, for instance, each person's contribution should account for something close to 50 percent of the outcome. If one athlete performs spectacularly, or chokes miserably, there's a strong possibility that they might single-handedly determine the result.

To limit my sample to teams where the collective performance of the group will nearly always matter more than the contribution of any one member, I decided to eliminate all teams that involve dyads: doubles tennis, doubles luge, Olympic beach volleyball, pairs skating, and ice dancing. I also eliminated curling, which involves teams of three. Only polo teams have four members, but that sport was nixed for another reason (see Question 2, Section A). In the end, the smallest units

I included were basketball teams, which field five members, and where the average contributions of the players at each position should theoretically account for about 20 percent of the team total.

B. Its members interact with the opponent.

A big part of the mysterious alchemy of a team is how well its members respond in real time to another set of athletes that is trying to clobber them. This kind of synchrony is obviously a big part of American football, football, basketball, water polo, and ice hockey, where the athletes spend the whole game engaging with their adversaries on both offense and defense. But there are some sports in which teams don't interact with the other side. A few examples of these discards: rowing, team cycling, judged competitions like synchronized swimming, and timed events like running and swimming relays.

C. Its members work together.

In some so-called team sports like Olympic wrestling, boxing, gymnastics, and skiing, the athletes show up together wearing the same uniforms but compete individually. In golf and tennis team competitions like the Ryder Cup and Davis Cup singles, the players also contribute to an aggregate score but compete as individuals. Because the athletes on these teams never physically interact with their teammates, I eliminated them.

This rule put two major sports on the bubble: baseball and cricket. In baseball, pitchers and catchers will interact throughout the game, and fielders often work together to make plays—but that's about it. In cricket, there's even less direct engagement. One teammate might relay the ball to another while stopping a boundary, and run-outs are often achieved by one player throwing to another at the stumps, but the most crucial things players do, whether they're batting, fielding, pitching, or bowling, are generally done alone without any direct assistance from teammates. It's impossible to say that direct, physical interaction between athletes is the key to success.

There is one aspect of both baseball and cricket that distinguishes these games from other low-interaction sports, however—the amount of teammate *coordination*. In cricket, for instance, players running between wickets have to keep close tabs on one another. The positioning of the fielders and the approaches taken by the batsmen, who work in partnerships, are all determined by a larger collaborative plan. A cricket bowler and wicketkeeper don't exactly play catch, as baseball pitchers and catchers do, but they sometimes do strategize together on what deliveries to use for specific batsmen. In both sports, the importance of coordinating effort, and making split-second mental adjustments, overrides the fact that the players don't physically engage very often. I decided to let both games play on.

Question 2:
How do you separate the wheat from the chaff?

Question number one cut my list of candidate teams down by roughly a third, but there were still thousands left to analyze. My next job was to figure out some criteria to use to decide whether a team's accomplishments belong in the highest echelon.

If the threshold for greatness in sports is simply winning lots of games over a lengthy period of time, then there is nothing distinguishing a multiple Olympic champion from a neighborhood beer-league frisbee team. To make sure only the most exceedingly credentialed teams were considered, I applied the following three rules:

A. The team played a "major" sport.

No team can claim freak status if it played an obscure regional sport with a modest fan base and a relatively limited talent pool. This rule led to some easy cuts, most of them involving non-Olympic team sports such as Brazilian footvolley, Scottish tug-of-war, Finnish pesä-pallo, Japanese bo-taoshi, and American professional lacrosse.

Another group of relatively small non-Olympic sports was more difficult to judge. Australian rules football, Irish hurling, Gaelic football, Argentine polo, and netball in the Commonwealth nations are not globally popular, but they all enjoy huge followings somewhere, either in terms of spectator interest or participation. The trouble is that the countries that adore them just aren't very big. To decide which ones to include, I resorted to looking at television ratings. Unless a sport's premier matches attracted many millions of viewers, it was axed. The only sport that passed this test was Australian rules football.

The final six cuts here were the trickiest. When it comes to handball, women's football, volleyball, field hockey, water polo, and rugby union, the international teams—the popular and prestigious ones you see at the Olympics or at World Cups—qualified for inclusion in my study. The professional teams in the same sports, which compete in relatively obscure domestic leagues in different countries, generally have smaller followings and less talent. They did not.

B. It played against the world's top competition.

There's an old saying in sports that to be the best, you have to beat the best. While many teams on my list regularly took on the fittest thoroughbreds of their sport, there were more than a thousand who faced a level of competition that paled in comparison to that found in a richer, more prestigious league somewhere else.

By culling these lesser leagues from the herd, I eliminated Canadian football, professional ice hockey in Russia and Sweden, and all European men's and women's domestic professional basketball associations, among others. This rule also disqualified intercollegiate team sports in the United States, where the player pool is limited to currently enrolled students and the quality of play is inferior to that seen in professional leagues or at the Olympic level.

C. Its dominance stretched over many years.

Anyone who witnessed Argentina's "hand of God" goal in the 1986 World Cup quarterfinals, or David Tyree's fluky "helmet catch" that allowed the New York Giants to win the 2008 Super Bowl, knows that luck plays an essential role in sports. No team has ever won a championship without benefiting from a few favorable bounces. But while some luck is essential, too much of it can camouflage the truth about a team, making it seem exceptional when it really isn't.

Statisticians acknowledge the role of luck, and they have tied themselves in knots for years trying to develop formulas to account for it. They have calculated historical averages that can tell you whether a team is winning or losing more often than it should based on how many goals or points it scored versus how many it allowed. These kinds of statistics can make a convincing case that a team's performance is unusual—but they still can't tell you whether the culprit was luck or some other kind of anomaly.

The first assumption we can make about luck is that some teams probably owe their accomplishments to an extraordinary abundance of it. At the same time, we can assume that a handful of teams out there managed to win multiple titles despite having suffered more bad luck than good. It's also possible that some teams control their own destiny by putting themselves in enterprising positions where a little luck goes a long way (have fun trying to measure that!).

The principle of regression to the mean tells us that if you wait long enough, any overheated level of performance, good or bad, is likely to fade. For example, if an NBA team makes ten shots in a row, the laws of probability suggest that after two hundred shots, its success rate should even out to the league average—about 45 percent. The safest assumption is that luck is randomly distributed and that its influence should even out over time.

I have no doubt that a surplus of good luck can carry a team to a championship, or possibly even two. But from there probability will begin to gang up on it. The likelihood of flipping a coin and getting heads three times in a row, for example, is 12.5 percent. The odds of getting four heads in a row are just 6.25 percent.

To correct for the influence of luck, and to put the focus of my study on a team's ability to sustain its winning ways primarily through its talent and teamwork, I set a floor based loosely on the odds of coin flipping. No team would be included in my sample unless it played at an elite level for a period of at least four seasons.

Many of the teams that flunked this test were one-year wonders like the Arsenal "Invincibles" of English football, which finished the 2003–04 Premier League season undefeated, and the 1985 Chicago Bears, which only won a single Super Bowl. It also nixed Don Bradman's undefeated Australian cricket team from 1946 to 48, England's World Cup winning rugby team from 2001 to 03, and championship three-peats achieved by the NHL's Toronto Maple Leafs (1961–64), the NBA's Los Angeles Lakers (1999–02), and Manchester United (2006–09), all of which failed to extend their dominance into a fourth season. In all, this test knocked more than three thousand teams out of contention.

Question 3:
What qualifies as freakish?

After applying Questions 1 and 2 to the field, only 122 teams survived the putsch, a group I will call my "finalists."* All of these candidates had fairly muscular arguments for ranking among the elite. The next task was to distinguish the freaks from the garden-variety dynasties.

The chief problem with trying to judge teams across all of the world's various leagues, associations, cups, and confederations is that their formats and scoring mechanics are often vastly different. Some teams partake in a handful of competitions per year, while others play seemingly endless regular seasons, followed by lengthy postseason tournaments. This makes it tough to find any one statistic that's a fair point of comparison.

The first metric I considered was winning percentage. Many famous teams, including the 1950s Hungarians, have fared well by this yardstick. But winning percentage has several liabilities. It doesn't account for the strength of a team's opponents, for one. It also favors teams that play fewer games. In Major League Baseball, for instance, where teams play 162 games per season, the win rates of the best teams

---

* A complete list of the "finalist" teams can be found in the appendix.

will flatten out into a narrow range not too far above 60 percent, while the winning percentage for a top Olympic volleyball team that plays only a few dozen matches a year might skew closer to 85 percent.

Another problem with winning percentage is that it's not always relevant. For teams that play in leagues like the NFL, the goal isn't to win the most games or even to capture the division title. It's to win *enough* games to qualify for the postseason playoffs and the right to compete for a championship. If an NFL team wins the Super Bowl, for instance, nobody cares if it finished the regular season 8–8.

A fairer way to judge a team's win rate is by its standard deviation from the mean, which measures the magnitude of how superior its record is in relation to those of its competitors. This number is more meaningful than raw winning percentage, but it also fails to factor in the quality of the opposition. By this measure, a team that fattens up on cupcakes while losing all of its marquee matches might still come out ahead.

The next group of statistics I considered don't bother with a team's record at all. They gauge a team's success by underlying measures of its performance, such as how many more points, goals, or runs it scored relative to opponents. Some statisticians will wrap several of these metrics into a "power rating" that rewards teams for their overall efficiency, regardless of their records. There are two problems with this concept: First, it can fail to account for the difference between playing well in crucial games and running up the score on patsies; second, if a team dominates everyone statistically all season but fails to win a championship, does anyone really care about its power rating?

The deeper problem with averages, rates, percentages, and coefficients of all kinds is that none of them tells the full story of every team's accomplishments. In fact, there's an argument to be made that a team's success is just as impressive, if not more so, if it won lots of trophies without being statistically exceptional.

The thing that ultimately distinguishes a freak team isn't how impressively it won—only that it did.

The best statistic available for isolating a team's ability to win, especially in consequential matches, is the Elo rating system, which was first adapted to sports in 1997 by a California software engineer named Bob Runyan. As a lifelong fan of World Cup football, Runyan had always wondered which historical soccer teams would rate the highest if their performances could somehow be fairly compared across time. He had grown weary of the official team-rating system of FIFA, the sport's governing body, in which a team received three points for a victory and one point for a draw in any FIFA-recognized match, regardless of its importance. He found this method to be hopelessly imprecise.

As a chess enthusiast, Runyan was familiar with an evaluation system designed in 1960 by a Marquette University physics professor named Arpad Elo. The formula ranked elite chess masters by giving them running point tallies based on the outcome of every match they played, plus the weighted quality of the opponent and the weighted significance of the event. A win against a highly rated master in a major tournament, for example, would add more points to the tally, while a low-stakes victory against a weak opponent in an exhibition wouldn't matter as much. "I remember looking at the FIFA rankings and seeing they were really bad and thinking the ones in chess were really good," Runyan told me.

After gathering all the match records he could find, Runyan wrote a program that evaluated each team by the Elo method. After fiddling with the weights, he examined the final results. As he'd suspected, the list was thick with celebrated teams from England, Spain, Brazil, and Germany. But the team with the highest score, by a fair margin, was Hungary, circa 1954.

Since Runyan unveiled his study, the Elo method has become something of a darling to the most forward-thinking sports statisticians, who have adapted it to rank teams in dozens of sports, from the NFL to cricket. Though far from perfect (it requires the compiler to make some subjective judgments about the importance of matches), it was the metric I decided to lean on, in a few cases, as a tiebreaker.

In the end, however, I decided to keep the statistics at the periphery. While I knew that Elo ratings and other available measures might be useful from time to time, I wouldn't be able to rely on any one metric exclusively. I decided that to identify the genuine freaks among this pool of 122 finalists, I would have to take a more holistic approach.

To determine my winners, I came up with two simple claims any team must be able to make if it is, in fact, one of the best of all time.

Claim 1:
It had sufficient opportunity to prove itself.

All of these finalist teams, no matter the sport they played, were exceptional dynasties. Yet there are some aspects of a team's competitive résumé that are beyond its control. The era when it played, the format of its league, and even the occasional intrusion of politics: They all can weaken a team's accomplishments by limiting the chances it had to prove its supremacy.

Many of the finalists, through no fault of their own, played in the earliest days of organized team sports when they rarely had chances to play in formal multinational competitions. Some sports, like water polo and field hockey, barely existed outside of the Olympics. In other cases, some of the world's top teams simply didn't choose to participate in every major event. When Italy's national football team won two World Cups in a row in the 1930s, for example, many of the world's best teams didn't show up. As a result the Italians, like several other finalists, finished their run with some unanswered questions about their true ability.

England's Arsenal and Italy's Juventus, which dominated their respective domestic professional football leagues from 1930 to 1935, were the exemplars of a different problem. Because they played before the inception of international club competitions like the European Cup, they never met on the field. It is therefore impossible to declare that either team belongs in the pantheon of the greats.

The saddest outcomes in the study were those occasions when a team's streak was interrupted, ended, or otherwise minimized by politics. The Homestead Grays of baseball's Negro National League won eight titles in nine seasons, along with 68 percent of their games from 1937 to 1945, but because of the strict segregation of the time they were not allowed to take on the leading all-white teams of the major leagues. The Cold War claimed a prominent victim, too. From 1977 to 1983, the Soviet Union's men's volleyball team won two straight World Cups, all four European Championships, and two World Championships. But when it won its only gold medal at the 1980 Moscow Olympics, many nations had boycotted the event. That fact alone prevented it from achieving undisputed freak status.

This test knocked out 28 of the 122 finalists.

Claim 2:
Its record stands alone.

To make a case to be one of the greatest in history, a team must have put together some exceptionally long or concentrated burst of success that can be defined by cumulative wins or titles, and that goes beyond the accomplishments of every other team that has played the same genre of sport. In other words, its achievements have to have been unique.

In some sports, such as international ice hockey and women's volleyball, there was really no contest. The team with the best record had lapped the field. In a few cases, two teams in the same sport achieved peerless results in different ways, forcing me to include both of them (Hungary, for example, was joined by a second men's international football team that stood out by winning two consecutive World Cups against all of the world's top teams). In a handful of sports, including cricket and rugby league, the margins between the most-decorated champions were so narrow that it was impossible to say for certain that any one team was the best of all time.

The list of teams that narrowly missed making this claim includes a Murderers' Row of sports dynasties. They include: Michael Jordan's 1990s Chicago Bulls; various iterations of the New York Yankees; a host of professional football teams that competed under the banners of AC Milan, Liverpool, and Real Madrid; and several historic international dynasties such as German football, Brazilian volleyball, and women's field hockey in the Netherlands. Among the most difficult and controversial cuts were the outstanding cricket teams from Australia and the West Indies, and two celebrated NFL teams—the 1981–95 San Francisco 49ers and Tom Brady's 2001–17 New England Patriots (for a full explanation of these omissions, please see the appendix, page 277).

Overall, this method of analysis eliminated sixty-six of the remaining ninety-four finalists.

A Quick Word About Professional Football

Nothing turned my hair grayer than trying to identify the world's best club football team from a list of thirty-six finalists. Because every football-playing nation has its own domestic professional league with its own slate of annual titles, the sport is maddeningly fragmented. While teams from top leagues in England, Germany, Spain, and Italy attract most of the attention, clubs from smaller countries like Portugal, Scotland, and Uruguay sometimes put up similar numbers. The formats of a few leagues, in particular Argentina's Primera División, have been so historically chaotic that a team has only rarely emerged from any season as an undisputed champion. Worst of all is the fact that club teams from different nations don't meet with any regularity, which makes it difficult to tell whether a unit was truly exceptional or just a big fish in a small pond.

Over the years, multinational competitions like Europe's Champions League, South America's Copa Libertadores, and the Intercontinental Cup have increased the opportunities for cross-border competition. But it's still difficult to know, year to year, whether the best standard of play can be found in England's Premier League, Spain's La Liga, Italy's Serie A, or even Germany's Bundesliga.

The majority of the thirty-six professional football teams among the finalists were eliminated from the top tier for the same two reasons I noted above: They either lacked sufficient opportunity to prove themselves or their achievements didn't stand out. But after applying those filters, and considering their winning percentages, winning runs, total trophies, and Elo ratings, there were still thirteen professional clubs

that refused to die quietly. All of them balanced home-league domina-
tion with success on the international stage, and many could boast of
being the best professional team a country had ever produced.

To whittle the list down, I took a closer look at the overall quality
of the domestic leagues these thirteen teams played in and whether
they dominated the table during their dynasties without suffering
some significant losses. I also factored in the results of a handful of
matches in which two of these thirteen teams actually met on the field.

In the end, this exercise eliminated twelve of the thirteen remaining
professional finalists, which are listed here in chronological order: Real
Madrid (Spain) 1956–60, Peñarol (Uruguay) 1958–62, Benfica (Portu-
gal) 1960–65, Santos (Brazil) 1961–65, Internazionale (Italy) 1962–67,
Celtic (Scotland) 1965–74, Ajax (Netherlands) 1969–73,
Bayern Munich (Germany) 1971–76, Liverpool (England) 1975–84,
AC Milan (Italy) 1987–96, Olympique de Marseille (France) 1988–93,
and Manchester United (England) 1995–2001.

These cuts knocked out every club team except one.

The World's Most Elite Teams

After I had evaluated every team in sports history, only sixteen stood
up to all eight of these various questions, tests, subtests, rules, and
claims. They represent the best of the best, and they belong in a group
I'll call Tier One. The 106 other finalists, who failed to meet one or
more of these criteria, are grouped into Tier Two.*

There is no shame in a berth in Tier Two. Many of the teams that
finished there came within a few inches of Tier One. They were arguably
just as impressive as the Tier One teams and, as I would later discover,
had most if not all of the same characteristics. Once again, to be perfectly clear about this: I didn't make these designations just for the sake
of settling one of the world's most radioactive sports debates. I won't
pretend that my calculations are the final word on the subject. My only

---

* For a full list of Tier Two teams, see the appendix.

goal was to create the purest possible sample of laboratory specimens—
a group of empirical freaks that had so few blemishes of any kind
that I could feel comfortable using them to explore the question I was
really after: What do the most dominant teams in history have in common?

The sixteen teams in Tier One, which are listed below in chronological order, were unambiguously outstanding. They achieved bursts of
success that were unique to history in some way and needed no qualifi-
cation. Together, they represent the apotheosis of sports excellence—
they are the alpha lions with the loudest roars.

Here is the list:

The Collingwood Magpies, Australian rules football (1927–
30): Known as the Machine, this Aussie rules team from
Melbourne won a record four consecutive Grand Finals in
the Victorian Football League, the predecessor of the
Australian Football League. Renowned for their grinding
defense, the Magpies won 88 percent of their matches,
outscored opponents by an average of thirty-three points
per game, and went 18–0 in 1929.

The New York Yankees, Major League Baseball (1949–53):
Several other Yankees teams (in the 1920s, late 1930s, and
late 1990s) were significantly more celebrated and star-
studded, but this group is the only one in baseball history
to win five consecutive World Series titles.

Hungary, International men's football (1950–55): Starting
in May 1950, the Hungarian "Golden Team," also known as
the Mighty Magyars, lost only twice in fifty-three matches.
During this span, Hungary outscored its opponents
222–59 with an average of 4.2 goals per game. The team's
1954 Elo rating was the highest ever recorded for sixty
years until Germany topped it in 2014.

The Montreal Canadiens, National Hockey League (1955–60):
The only team in the history of the NHL to claim
five straight Stanley Cups, the Canadiens won or drew
74 percent of their games and exceeded the league scoring
average by more than 400 goals.

The Boston Celtics, National Basketball Association
(1956–69): The Celtics won an unparalleled eleven NBA
championships in thirteen seasons, including one stretch
of eight in a row, dwarfing the achievements of every other
NBA dynasty.

Brazil, International men's football (1958–62): Winners of
two consecutive World Cups, Brazil went undefeated in
three of five seasons and outscored opponents nearly three
to one over fifty-six games, achieving the number-three
all-time Elo rating for an international football team. Five of
its six losses came in minor competitions when it fielded a
B-level squad.

The Pittsburgh Steelers, National Football League (1974–80):
This team made the playoffs six times in a row and won an
unrivaled four Super Bowls in six seasons. It compiled an
80–22–1 record through the 1980 Super Bowl and notched
the second-highest Elo rating in NFL history.

The Soviet Union, International men's ice hockey (1980–84):
After a humiliating upset loss to the United States in the
1980 Winter Olympics, the Red Army team came back
stronger than ever, going 94–4–9 in international
competitions against top opponents over four years. It won
three straight World Championships and a gold medal
at the 1984 Winter Olympics, where it outscored
opponents 58–6.

The New Zealand All Blacks, International rugby union
(1986–90): This All Blacks unit, the first of two in Tier

One, went undefeated in forty-nine straight international rugby union matches over three years, including twenty-three straight international tests—during which they won by an average of twenty-seven points. The All Blacks made a mockery of the field at the 1987 World Cup, scoring 298 points and conceding just fifty-two.

Cuba, International women's volleyball (1991–2000): The Espectaculares Morenas del Caribe won every major women's international volleyball tournament for ten straight years, capturing three Olympic gold medals, four World Cups, and back-to-back World Championships. They went 18–3 in Olympic play and 31–1 at the World Cup, and never lost a match at the World Championships.

Australia, International women's field hockey (1993–2000): The Hockeyroos won two Olympic gold medals, plus four consecutive Champions Trophy competitions, and back-to-back World Cups. They lost only 11 percent of their matches during this span, scoring 785 goals while allowing just 220.

The United States, International women's football (1996–99): The "99ers" dominated at a level unmatched in history, winning the Olympics and the World Cup while posting a record of 84–6–6, compiling a thirty-one-match unbeaten run, outscoring their opponents roughly five to one, and losing only once in a major competition.

The San Antonio Spurs, National Basketball Association (1997–2016): This team's five NBA titles (including three in five seasons) weren't the most in history. But by reaching the playoffs in nineteen straight seasons, posting the NBA's highest-ever long-term win rate (71 percent), and never finishing worse than second in its division, it set an astonishing record for consistency.

Barcelona, Professional football (2008–13): Over these five seasons, Barcelona won a total of fifteen trophies: four Spanish titles, two Champions Leagues (while reaching the semifinals for five consecutive seasons), two FIFA Club World Cup titles, two UEFA Super Cups, two Copa del Rey titles, and three Spanish Supercopas. It won or drew 92 percent of its league matches—one of history's best marks—and outscored opponents by 3.5 goals to one. Its 2011 Elo rating is the highest ever recorded for a club team.

France, International men's handball (2008–15): Les Experts won three of four world handball championships and two European titles and became the first team in the sport to win back-to-back Olympic gold medals. During its peak, from 2008 to 2011, France lost only once in forty-two matches against elite competition and became the first men's team to hold all three of the sport's top titles simultaneously.

The New Zealand All Blacks, International rugby union (2011–15): This second All Blacks unit became the first rugby team to win consecutive World Cups. From 2011 to the end of the 2015 World Cup, it outscored its opponents by an average of nineteen points and amassed a 55–3–2 record that included unbeaten runs of twenty and twenty-two international tests—just shy of the 1986–90 team's record of twenty-three. Its record was 8–1–1 against Australia in the Bledisloe Cup and it won the Rugby Championship (also known as the Tri-Nations) three times out of four.

With my list of sixteen freaks in hand, I turned to the ultimate question of this book: what, if anything, these elite teams had in common, and whether they will reveal any secrets about the DNA of greatness.

TWO

Captain Theory

The Importance of "Glue Guys"

BOSTON, 1957

In the seventh game of the 1957 NBA Finals, with his team trailing the Boston Celtics by a point and roughly forty seconds left to play, Jack Coleman of the St. Louis Hawks received an outlet pass at midcourt. It was the most unlikely kind of basketball gift.

As Coleman turned to make a charge at the Boston basket, his path was miraculously unimpeded. There wasn't a single Celtics player anywhere near him. Nobody in the building could have imagined a scenario in which his efforts wouldn't produce an uncontested and potentially decisive basket.

Over the previous forty-seven minutes and twenty seconds these two teams had engaged in a heaving, tilting, unpredictable basketball game marked by hot spells, cold snaps, and furious comebacks. The tormented crowd at the old Boston Garden—some of whom had camped overnight for tickets—smoked so many cigarettes that the rafters were shrouded in a greasy beige haze.

When Coleman crossed the top of the key, left his feet, and stretched out his arm to roll in a layup, most of the Celtics players stood and watched, saving their breath for what would surely come next: a desperate scramble to redeem themselves.

But just as the ball left Coleman's fingertips, a giant white-shirted blur engulfed him from behind. The blur swiped at the ball as it left Coleman's hand and connected cleanly, slamming it against the backboard and back into play, where a Boston player scooped it up. Somehow, despite overwhelming odds in Coleman's favor, some force of divine providence had intervened to keep the Celtics alive.

No video of this play survives—back then the TV networks didn't see the point in recording live sports—but the radio call does exist, and in it Boston's famously frog-throated announcer, Johnny Most, can't contain himself. "Blocked by Russell! Blocked by Russell!" Most shouts. "He came from nowhere!"

At a shade over six foot nine, Bill Russell, Boston's twenty-three-year-old rookie center, wasn't the tallest of NBA big men. Thin and gangly, he never seemed to have full command of his limbs. He had won a pair of NCAA titles in college and helped the U.S. team win a gold medal at the 1956 Olympics, but the fans in Boston were still getting to know him. They hadn't really known what he was capable of—until then.

More than fifty years later the Coleman Play, as Russell's block came to be known, is still regarded as one of the finest defensive efforts in NBA history, not just because of the gravity of the circumstances—the waning seconds of a Game 7 in the finals—but for the sheer impossibility of the feat. The spot where Coleman caught the ball was roughly forty-six feet from Boston's basket. With a running start, Coleman would have needed only about three seconds to cover the distance. The spot from which Russell began his pursuit (underneath the opposite basket) would have been more than ninety-two feet away. To catch Coleman, by my calculations, Russell had accelerated from a dead stop to reach an average speed of thirty-one feet per second, or twenty-one miles per hour. To get some perspective on this, I looked up the results of the men's hundred-meter final at the previous year's Olympics. The winning time was 10.62 seconds. If Russell had maintained the same average speed for a full one hundred meters, he would have finished in 10.58 seconds, winning the gold medal by a nose. Bob Cousy, the Celtics star and captain at the time, called it "the most incredible physical act I ever saw on a basketball floor."

Inspired by Russell's passion, Boston went on to win 125–123 in double overtime—earning their first-ever NBA title.

Over the next twelve seasons, including that one, the team would draw on this kind of never-say-die energy to win ten more overall NBA titles, including eight in a row. During the streak, the Celtics would play in nine more deciding Game 7s in different stages of the playoffs—and win all of them.

When I set out to identify the best teams in sports history, I knew there would be many difficult judgments to make based on razor-thin margins between finalists. I also knew there would be some no-brainers. The easiest decision of all was to include the NBA's 1956–69 Boston Celtics.

Since they won more championships over a longer period of time than any other team in Tier One, the Celtics struck me as an excellent team to begin with. If there was any one characteristic that all of these outstanding teams shared, the Celtics must have had it in spades.

I began by examining the team's game statistics to see which aspects of basketball it excelled in. Straightaway, I could tell that the Celtics were quantitatively remarkable, but not in the way I'd expected. Boston didn't lead the NBA in the number of points they scored per game, how few points they held their opponents to, or in their average margin of victory. The team's regular-season win rate over those thirteen seasons (.705) and its win rate in the playoffs (.649) were excellent marks but lower than those achieved by other NBA dynasties. According to regular-season Elo ratings compiled by FiveThirtyEight, only one of their eleven championship squads managed to crack the top fifty in NBA history.

Even more curiously, the advanced metrics that statisticians use to measure the contributions of individual players showed that the Celtics never had any individual member whose isolated performance ranked among the best in history. No Celtics player led the NBA in scoring during its string of titles. In seven of its eleven championship seasons, it didn't place a single scorer in the top ten. I quickly set the statistics aside to look for other explanations.

Some of the credit for Boston's success surely belonged to Red Auerbach, the fiery, gregarious, cigar-puffing coach who assembled the team. Auerbach had won 63 percent of his games with two different professional teams before taking over the Celtics and was considered a keen motivator. But Auerbach had never won a title until Boston's streak began in 1957, and his previous Celtics teams had posted a losing record in the playoffs. There was no evidence that Auerbach had suddenly become a tactical genius—the Tier One Celtics ran a basic offense, and he gave the players the freedom to improvise on the court. The biggest knock on Auerbach's influence came in 1966, when he retired from coaching the team to become its general manager. The Celtics went on to win two more titles without him.

Even the team's patriarch, the beloved and forward-thinking owner, Walter Brown, who hired Auerbach and approved his player acquisitions, didn't remain involved during the team's entire thirteen-season masterpiece. He died in 1964.

All of this was confusing. If the Celtics' burst of greatness wasn't a function of statistical dominance, superstar talent, an aggregation of players with unusual ability, or the product of consistent and excellent coaching and management, then what was it?

There is zero chance that the Celtics got lucky. Their freakish run was too long for that. The only explanation that made sense to me was that this team, like the Hungarians of the 1950s, was somehow better than the sum of its parts. As spongy as this might sound, there must have been a rare bond between the players that coaxed superior performances out of people who wouldn't have achieved them somewhere else.

The phrase "team chemistry" has been tossed around so often that it has earned a prominent spot in the Hall of Fame of sports clichés. But for the life of me, I had no idea what the term represented. Was it a function of how long a group of athletes had been playing together, and how well they could anticipate their teammates' next moves? Was it a measure of how well their strengths offset their weaknesses? Or was it a reflection of how much everybody on the team liked one another and how splendidly they got along?

The basic idea behind chemistry is that a team's interpersonal dynamics will have an impact on its performance. On teams with good chemistry, the thinking goes, the members see themselves as a family and enjoy a heightened sense of personal loyalty that pays dividends in competition. The legendary American football coach Vince Lombardi, who led the Green Bay Packers to five NFL titles in the 1960s, was a proponent of this idea. "Individual commitment to a group effort," he once said, "that is what makes a team work, a company work, a society work, a civilization work."

There's surely something to this. Many great teams I've seen firsthand enjoyed a high level of esprit de corps, whether on the field or sitting around playing poker in their underwear. When scientists have examined teams in other contexts, such as business or the military, they've noticed that the more cohesive and positive a group perceives itself to be, the better it will perform in many respects—from meeting sales goals to sharing information to fostering individual acts of battlefield bravery. But where does this cohesiveness come from? And beyond that, is cohesiveness the thing that *causes* a team like the Celtics to become successful, or is it a by-product of success?

Most Tier One teams had a core of players who stayed together through the duration of the streak and became exceedingly good at coordinating their play. Yet this kind of consistency of personnel wasn't limited to teams in Tier One—many teams have had stable rosters but failed to achieve the same elevated results. Moreover, for every team in the top tier of my study that seemed to be tightly knit, with players who came from similar backgrounds and formed lifelong friendships, there was another that had been riven at times by internal feuds and divisions. I didn't see a pattern there.

When it came to the Celtics, there was another problem with the notion that their success was derived through chemistry. Boston's dominance continued for so many years that from the beginning to the end, the roster turned over almost completely. This suggests the team's internal dynamics shifted, too.

There were, however, two Celtics players whose careers overlapped the streak precisely. And one of them was Bill Russell.

Before Russell arrived in 1956, Boston had never won an NBA title. In his rookie year—the one in which he blocked Jack Coleman's layup in Game 7 of the Finals—that changed. Then, twelve years later, after winning championship number eleven, Russell retired from basketball and left his team to cope on its own. The Celtics promptly collapsed, posting their first losing record in twenty years. The timing of these events was so uncanny that I started to entertain a radical idea. I wondered if Russell, himself, had been the catalyst.

Looking over all of the various and conflicting accounts of the Coleman Play, there's no doubt that it was an astonishing physical act. But something else about the moment stood out: it was a supreme expression of *desire*. In the seconds before deciding to give chase, Russell, a twenty-three-year-old playing in the biggest game of his life, had just botched a dunk attempt that would have given his team a three-point lead. From where he stood, there were fans in the fifth row with better odds of stopping Coleman. Russell hadn't flown into action because anyone expected him to but because he could not bear to see his team lose.

The more I studied Russell, the more central his role on the team seemed to be. In 1963, when Bob Cousy retired, Russell had been appointed captain. Three years after that, when Auerbach quit coaching, the Celtics had become such an extension of Russell's personality that he was installed as a player-coach. Russell hadn't just provided the spark that launched his team's explosion of titles, he had been its designated leader.

On a whim, I decided to make a list of the names of the primary player-leaders of these sixteen teams to see if any of their careers also served as bookends for their teams' Tier One performances. Here are the names:

Syd Coventry, Collingwood Magpies
Yogi Berra, New York Yankees*
Ferenc Puskás, Hungary
Maurice Richard, Montreal Canadiens[†]
Bill Russell, Boston Celtics[‡]
Hilderaldo Bellini, Brazil[§]
Jack Lambert, Pittsburgh Steelers[¶]
Valeri Vasiliev, Soviet Union**
Wayne Shelford, New Zealand All Blacks[††]
Mireya Luis, Cuba
Rechelle Hawkes, Australia[‡‡]
Carla Overbeck, United States[§§]
Tim Duncan, San Antonio Spurs[¶¶]

* The Yankees didn't name an official captain during Berra's tenure.
† Richard took over as captain in the second season of the team's five-title streak.
‡ Russell took over in '63 after longtime Celtics captain Bob Cousy retired.
§ Brazil replaced Bellini with Mauro Ramos shortly before the '62 World Cup.
¶ Lambert became the Steelers' defensive captain in '77. Sam Davis was the offensive captain.
** Vasiliev left the Soviet team in '83 and was replaced as captain by Slava Fetisov.
†† Shelford took over from David Kirk after the '87 World Cup.
‡‡ Hawkes became captain in '93, a co-captain in '95, and later part of a captaincy rotation.
§§ Overbeck shared the captaincy with Julie Foudy during part of the team's run.
¶¶ Tim Duncan became the Spurs' captain in '03 after David Robinson retired, and had several co-captains.

Carles Puyol, Barcelona
Jérôme Fernandez, France*
Richie McCaw, New Zealand All Blacks†

The results of this little exercise stopped me cold. The Celtics weren't the only team whose Tier One performance corresponded in some way to the arrival and departure of one particular player. In fact, they *all* did. And with an eerie regularity that person was, or would eventually become, the captain.

Collingwood's run of titles, for instance, began the year Syd Coventry replaced the team's incumbent captain, while the Soviet hockey team's glory years began when Valeri Vasiliev became the designated leader. The captaincies of Rechelle Hawkes of the Australian women's field hockey team and Mireya Luis of the Cuban women's volleyball team overlapped precisely with their teams' Tier One streaks, too. For the Montreal Canadiens, the 1987–90 All Blacks, and the U.S. women's football team of the late 1990s, their grandest stretches of achievement ended the moment their longtime captains departed.

Depending on the team and the sport, the people who wear the armband or have the letter *C* stitched to their uniform are chosen sometimes by teammates, sometimes by coaches. In rare cases, it's governed by seniority. Some American football teams elect different captains for every game, while some teams don't designate them at all. In cricket, the captain traditionally runs the show on the field—choosing the bowlers, setting the batting order, and deciding how fielders are positioned, among other things. In some sports, the captaincy comes with a small increase in pay, but for the most part it's an honor that carries with it a handful of extra responsibilities.

The crucial component of the job is interpersonal. The captain is the figure who holds sway over the dressing room by speaking to teammates as a peer, counseling them on and off the field, motivating them,

---

* Fernandez became France's captain when Olivier Girault retired after the '08 Olympics.
† Kieran Read was briefly captain while McCaw was injured.

challenging them, protecting them, resolving disputes, enforcing standards, inspiring fear when necessary, and above all setting a tone with words and deeds. As Sean Fitzpatrick of the 1986–90 All Blacks once said of his captain, Wayne "Buck" Shelford: "He was a guy you could walk over broken glass for, because he just had that manner about him."

Baseball managers, when asked about the secrets of team cohesion, like to use the word "glue." There's no dictionary entry for this particular usage, but it's meant to describe an intangible quality that fuses a team together. In baseball, where teams compete for as many as eight months a year and can play close to two hundred games between spring training and the postseason, togetherness is critical. It's glue that supposedly prevents teams from splintering into cliques or being torn asunder by egos. It was another usage of the term that came to mind, however. When individual players devote themselves to unifying the team, baseball managers call them "glue guys."

In his 2015 book about leadership, Alex Ferguson, the legendary former manager of England's Manchester United, echoed the idea that one influential player can unify an entire team. Once a match begins, the manager no longer influences the outcome. "On the field, the person responsible for making sure the eleven players acted as a team was the club captain," he wrote. "Even though I imagine some people think this is a ceremonial position, it is far from that." In corporate terms, Ferguson added, a captain chosen to transmit the manager's intentions to the team was equivalent to the manager chosen to run a division. "He is the person responsible for making sure the agenda of the organization is pursued."

Ferguson wasn't the only famous coach who made this point. Duke University's Mike Krzyzewski, who has won more games than any basketball coach in the history of the NCAA's Division I, once wrote that while talent and coaching are essential, the secret to greatness is something else: "The single most important ingredient after you get the talent is internal leadership. It's not the coaches as much as one single person or people on the team who set higher standards than that team would normally set for itself."

There is no question that Bill Russell had lofty standards. From his tireless and urgent play on the court to the fact that he often got so nervous before games that he would vomit in the locker room, he never seemed to let up. It's fair to say he was one of the glue guys baseball managers talk about. But is it also possible that Russell or any other single player can generate the kind of mystical contagion that allows a team to play beyond its natural ability?

All of this pointed to an idea I had never seriously considered: Could it be that the one thing that lifts a team into the top .001 percent of teams in history is the leader of the players?

This concept leaped out at me so early in the process, and was so tantalizingly simple, that it made me uncomfortable. I had only started my research, and I didn't believe that the secret component of the world's greatest sports teams could be so easy to spot. Beyond this, I couldn't understand how one member of a team could lift it so high and keep it there for so long. I thought of something H. L. Mencken once wrote: "There is always a well-known solution to every human problem—neat, plausible, and wrong."

I knew there was no empirical way to measure a captain's influence. In order to hang the success of these Tier One teams on "captain theory," I knew I would have to identify a bundle of traits that these men and women had in common, no matter what sports they played. The theory would hold only if their temperaments, personality quirks, and modi operandi fell into some discernible pattern.

Before I set off on that journey, however, I ran into another, more immediate obstacle to captain theory. The more I learned about the personality of William Felton Russell, the less he seemed to conform to my notions of what great leaders are like.

To be blunt, he didn't seem like captain material.

The trouble with Russell started on the court, where—although he won more NBA championships than anyone, played lockdown defense, pulled down a then-record 21,620 career rebounds, and was elected to the Hall of Fame the first year he was eligible—he didn't score much. With a career average of 15.1 points per game, he never once led the Celtics in that category. In an era when most teams ran their offenses through the center position, this made Russell highly unusual. Rather than bearing more of the responsibility for scoring points, he'd ceded that vital role to his teammates.

Though blessed with rare speed, stamina, and leaping ability, Russell wasn't a can't-miss prospect. He'd been so uncoordinated in high school and had such atrocious fundamentals that the only college program that wanted him was the University of San Francisco, which didn't have its own gym. Even after Russell led the team to fifty-five straight wins and two improbable intercollegiate titles, some NBA scouts remained wary of drafting a center who had trouble dribbling and wasn't a gifted shooter.

What distinguished Russell on the court was his dedication to playing without the ball. In the 1950s, basketball defenders were taught never to leave their feet. Russell not only took to the air to block shots, he went after shots most people considered unblockable. He focused his efforts on anticipating rebounds, clogging the lane, intercepting passes, and setting and evading picks. According to modern defensive metrics, Russell's career mark in "defensive win shares" is the best in NBA history—and by a 23 percent margin.

Russell's defensive mindset didn't stop on the court, however. It permeated the way he interacted with the public. Time and again, Russell drew fire for comments made in brusque and sometimes defiant interviews. "I owe them nothing," he once said of the fans. Russell was so appalled by the racism he experienced at home that he once said, "I play for the Celtics, not Boston." After his retirement, when the Celtics made plans to retire his jersey number, he refused to participate in the ceremony unless the team held it in private with only his teammates in attendance. "I never played for the fans," he explained. "I played for myself and for my team."

At a time when the public liked its athletes buzz-cut and apolitical, Russell was the only player in the league with a goatee, a clear violation of the NBA's no-facial-hair rule, which had been enacted in 1959 because of him. He later graduated to capes, Nehru jackets, love beads, caftans, and sandals, and hung around Greenwich Village coffeehouses listening to protest music. He became a tireless and outspoken advocate for civil rights.

The most glaring example of Russell's oppositional nature came in 1975, when he was tapped for the Hall of Fame. In a terse statement, Russell said he would not attend the ceremony and would not consider himself a member. "For my own personal reasons, which I don't want to discuss, I don't want to be a part of it," he said.

Nobody could think of any reasonable argument for turning down the Hall of Fame. Many people suspected Russell's refusal was an act of protest in support of all the talented black players who had not been enshrined, although he hadn't chosen to say that. Boston's sportswriters didn't care one way or the other. While they acknowledged that he was a special basketball player, they suggested that he was a selfish, arrogant, ungrateful, and petty person.

To recap what I'd learned about Russell: His shooting and ball-handling were substandard; he didn't score many points; he was surly with the fans, bristled at the conventions of the NBA, and didn't care one bit about public relations. "He really wasn't very friendly," said Elvin Hayes, a former opponent. "If you didn't know him you'd probably be just like, 'Man, he's the nastiest guy in the world.'"

None of this suggested that Russell was a leader at all, much less the winningest captain in the history of professional basketball, if not the entirety of sports. But the fact remained that Russell's record was the best, and together with the shooting guard Sam Jones, he was one of only two members of this freak team who remained through its entire run.

I had no idea how to reconcile this.

———

When I first encountered the mystery of Bill Russell, I had somehow walked the planet for more than forty years without giving much thought to a question that seems pretty fundamental to human affairs: If you knew you were heading into the toughest fight of your life, whom would you choose to lead you?

Most of us carry a faded old picture in our heads of what a great captain looks like. It's usually an attractive person who possesses an abundance of strength, skill, wisdom, charisma, diplomacy, and unflappable calm. These people are not supposed to be difficult to spot. In our imaginations they're talkative and articulate, charismatic but firm, tough but gracious, and respectful of authority. We expect leaders, especially in sports, to pursue their goals with gusto but to never wander from the principles of sportsmanship and fair play. We believe, as the Stanford social psychologist Deborah Gruenfeld put it, that power is reserved for the kind of person "who possesses some combination of superior charm and ruthless ambition that the rest of us don't."

The men and women who captained these Tier One teams did not, at a glance, meet this standard. They enjoyed vastly different levels of talent and fame. Some were household names; others were decidedly not. In fact, the more I learned about them, the more their profiles diverged from what I'd been conditioned to expect.

NANTES, FRANCE, 1986

On a clear and chilly afternoon in November, the New Zealand All Blacks arrived in Nantes to play the French national rugby team at the paradoxically named Stade de la Beaujoire, or "stadium of beautiful play." In the slanting autumn sun, its white concrete buttresses looked like the sun-bleached bones of a carcass.

The crowd, which had arrived well before kickoff, was high on a hate bender, waving banners and shouting the words to "La Marseillaise." One week earlier, down in Toulouse, these teams had played the first leg of a scheduled two-match series ahead of the 1987 Rugby

World Cup, in which both teams were favored to make the final. In Toulouse, the French had received a flogging from the Kiwis, who ran wild and dominated the scrums in a 19–7 victory. The French fans had responded by booing their own team off the field.

As the French players spilled into the stadium tunnel before the match, they made no secret of their desire for revenge. Two of them began exchanging head butts while another banged his skull against a concrete wall until his forehead was smeared in blood. Their eyes looked crazed—by some accounts as wide as Ping-Pong balls. "I'm sure they were on some form of juice," New Zealand's Buck Shelford said, "and it wasn't bloody orange juice."

Though he was already twenty-eight years old and a fixture in New Zealand's domestic league, Shelford was unknown to the larger rugby world. Born in the rural province of Rotorua, which is known for its thermal pools and geysers, Shelford was a member of New Zealand's indigenous Maori tribe. With his dark hair, narrow eyes, prominent cheekbones, and strong jaw, he certainly looked the part of a rugby captain. Even in a passive state, his face conveyed strength, purpose, and command—or *mana,* as it's known in Maori.

Though many rugby writers were not fans of Shelford's—they thought he was undersize and a step too slow for the number-eight position—he had fought his way onto the national team the year before. Toulouse had been his All Blacks debut and he'd made the most of the opportunity, tackling with abandon, muscling the French players aside during fearless runs, and even diving over the line in the second half to score the decisive try.

Shelford, and everyone else in the stadium that day, knew the French would be coming for him. At this point in history, the rules and customs of rugby union had not yet been tidied up to suit the tastes of polite audiences. As a result, its matches were as appallingly violent as anything on live television. And when it came to the dark arts of finger breaking, eyeball gouging, and testicle torquing, the French were without peer. "Dirtiest fucking country in the world," Shelford said.

About fifteen minutes into the game, as he lay on the ground after a tackle attempt, Shelford got his first taste of the French plot—in the form of a kick to the face. Shelford felt warm blood filling his mouth and ran his tongue around to survey the damage. He'd lost most of three teeth. He spit out the fragments and shook his head. Nice try, he thought. But he wasn't coming off.

Five minutes later, another French player, Éric Champ, sucker punched Shelford in the side of the head and tried to bait him into a fight. "Every ruck they climbed into they punched and kicked us," Shelford remembered. With halftime approaching, the score was 3–3, but several All Blacks had been injured—the most serious of them hooker Sean Fitzpatrick, who took a raking to the head that left a three-inch gash above his eye. The French, Fitzpatrick told me, "made sure I knew where I was."

Before the break, during a defensive ruck, Shelford grabbed the ball from a French player and ripped it free. Just then he saw a French prop named Jean-Pierre Garuet-Lempirou diving at him, headfirst, in full horizontal flight. The Frenchman rammed Shelford in the middle of the forehead. "He knocked me out cold," Shelford remembered. "It took me two minutes to come around." As Shelford regained consciousness, a teammate, Jock Hobbs, told him he had to stay in the game because there was no one left on the bench to replace him. Everyone else was injured.

Shelford had no intention of quitting.

After halftime, the sight of Shelford returning to the field enraged the French, who decided it was time to double down on their *mauvais actes*. About ten minutes in, the French captain, Daniel Dubroca, fell to the ground with the ball. Shelford reached down, grabbed hold of it, and ripped it away. Dubroca, arguably France's toughest player, saw an opportunity to finish Shelford for good.

"He kicked me right in the nuts," Shelford said.

After rolling around on the turf for a few moments, Shelford sat up to try to get his wind back. Eventually he grabbed a water bottle and, as he put it, "chucked a little down the old knickers" to numb the pain. "Man, did it bloody hurt," he said.

Once again, he returned to the match.

By this point, Shelford had lost three teeth, received a sucker punch to the head, been knocked unconscious, and absorbed a boot to the balls. The French had already scored two penalties, and a few minutes later they broke through with two consecutive tries to make the score 16–3 in their favor. The All Blacks were limping, the crowd was howling, and the referee seemed unable to stanch the spiraling violence. The bleaker the situation became, however, the more vigorously Shelford competed—running, passing, tackling, and rucking as if he thought he could win the match single-handedly. The carnage had driven him to play harder.

In the closing minutes, Shelford took another blow to the head, this time from a Frenchman's forearm. He'd been able to shake off the last one, but not this time. A teammate waved the referee over to make sure Shelford left the match. "I hadn't a clue where I was," he said. "I knew I was concussed. I didn't really know where I was running." This bloody, brutal match, won 16–3 by France, became known as the Battle of Nantes, earning a dubious place in rugby lore. In a next-day recap, the *Sunday Times* described it as a "massacre."

Afterward, the New Zealand dressing room was a quiet, morbid place. The All Blacks didn't lose often, and no one had ever seen them be so physically dominated. Shelford, still woozy from the concussion, stood up from his stool to change out of his kit. As he slipped out of his briefs, or "strides," the pall was broken by a teammate pointing at Shelford's groin. "Holy shit, look at that!"

Shelford hadn't simply been kicked in the balls by the French captain. He'd been raked. At his feet there was a small puddle of blood. His thighs were stained red and caked with bits of fatty tissue. Worst of all, his scrotum had been torn open and one of his testicles had fallen out of the breach. It was dangling between his knees.

The team physician came scurrying over. He told Shelford to pull up his shorts and meet him in one of the surgeries upstairs. To close Shelford's wound, the doctor had to administer sixteen stitches. "They packed it all away and everything still works," Shelford said later. "I didn't realize testicles are so fucking big."

The story would turn Buck Shelford into an overnight folk hero. From that point on, no reasonable list of rugby's toughest players would ever exclude him. Though he wasn't a superior athlete, his uncompromising style of play made him so indispensable to the team, and so inspirational, that the following year he was named captain.

Shelford's extraordinary performance in Nantes seemed like an extreme version of Russell's effort on the Coleman Play. After suffering an injury that would have caused 99.9 percent of the male population to crawl whimpering into an ambulance, Shelford had been so focused on the game that he didn't realize he'd been ripped apart. Both Russell and Shelford clearly had an insurmountable will to win.

Yet Shelford's actions that day, as courageous as they were, did not seem especially necessary. The All Blacks had already done what they needed to do in France. They'd come to play the next-best team in the world at home and had kicked them around in Toulouse. Under these hostile circumstances, splitting the series was a victory. There was no compelling reason to continue playing so hard, especially when it became clear that winning was unlikely. It would have made more sense for Shelford to save the battle for the World Cup. In the grand scheme, what Shelford did wasn't tactical.

The story of Shelford's mauled scrotum is only one example of alarmingly reckless behavior by these Tier One captains. Collingwood's Syd Coventry once returned to action two weeks after suffering a fractured skull, while New Zealand's Richie McCaw played the 2011 Rugby World Cup with a broken, swollen, and distended foot that made every step feel like walking on hot coals. Mireya Luis, the future captain of the Cuban women's volleyball team, once reported to practice four days after giving birth to her daughter, then played in a match at the World Championships fourteen days later. Bill Russell, according to one account, played in (and won) an NBA Finals Game 7 against the Lakers after being stabbed in his left arm the night before while trying to break up a bar fight. At best, this willingness to play through pain suggested that these Tier One captains had seriously warped priorities. At worst, it suggested they might be out of their minds.

A quick review of the biographies of the sixteen captains in Tier One made the picture even more confusing. As I went over my notes, I made a list of all of the reasons these men and women didn't fit the profile of exemplary leaders and why it seemed unlikely that captains were the secret ingredients of great teams. There were eight of them:

1. They lacked superstar talent.

Most of the Tier One captains were not the best players on their teams, or even major stars. They often arrived with skill deficiencies and had been described by coaches as average players. Some had been forced to fight hard just to make it to the elite ranks and were at some point overlooked, benched, or put on waivers. When lined up next to glamorous, charismatic, and supremely talented leadership icons like Michael Jordan, they looked about as formidable as a mariachi band.

2. They weren't fond of the spotlight.

The men and women in Tier One didn't enjoy the trappings of fame and rarely sought attention. When it did find them, it seemed to make them uncomfortable. Off the field, they were often quiet, even introverted—and, in a couple of cases, famously inarticulate. As a group, they hated interviews, spoke in bland monotones, and treated reporters indifferently. They opted out of award ceremonies and media events and often turned down endorsement deals.

3. They didn't "lead" in the traditional sense.

I had always believed that, on a team, the mark of a leader was the ability to take over the game in critical moments. But most Tier One captains played subservient roles on their teams, deferred to star players, and relied heavily on the talent around them to carry the scoring burden. If these captains weren't the kinds of athletes who took the big shot, I could not understand how they led, or how they could possibly qualify as elite leaders.

4. They were not angels.

Time and again, these captains played to the edge of the rules, did unsportsmanlike things, or generally behaved in a way that seemed to threaten their teams' chances of winning. This included bowling over rival players for no apparent reason and berating (in two cases even assaulting) officials, coaches, or team executives. They were tough on opponents, too—tripping them, tossing them to the ground, pinning them to the turf, whaling on them, or calling them unprintable names.

5. They did potentially divisive things.

If you tried to imagine what a team leader would do to sabotage a team, the odds are that these Tier One captains had attempted it. On various occasions they had disregarded the orders of coaches, defied team rules and strategies, and given candid interviews in which they'd spoken out against everyone from fans, teammates, and coaches to the overlords of the sport.

6. They weren't the usual suspects.

The most striking thing about my list of Tier One captains was who *wasn't* on it. Some of the most glaring absences include Jordan, the co-captain of the Tier Two Chicago Bulls, who is widely considered the greatest basketball player in history; Roy Keane, the captain of a Manchester United team that also landed in Tier Two and who from 1998 to 2001 piloted his team through the most impressive three-season stretch in English football history; and Derek Jeter, the wildly popular twelve-year captain who led the New York Yankees to nine playoff appearances and a World Series title from 2003 to 2014.

7. Nobody had ever mentioned this theory.

During my travels as a sportswriter, I'd grilled a hodgepodge of celebrated athletes, coaches, and executives about what made their teams successful. Whether it was Isiah Thomas of the Detroit Pistons, Reggie Jackson of the New York Yankees, the general manager Ron Wolf of the Green Bay Packers, the college football coach Bobby Bowden, or the Brazilian football legend Arthur Antunes Coimbra, better known as Zico, none of them had ever singled out the captain as a team's driving force.

8. The captain isn't the primary leader.

On most teams, the highest position in the pecking order belongs to the coach or manager. After all, the coach usually appoints the captain. There's another powerful stratum of management above the coach, too—a team's owners and front-office executives. Surely their contributions, and their willingness to spend money, played a significant role.

The men and women who led these sixteen Tier One teams were not what I expected. Although their careers neatly bracketed their teams' winning streaks, there was plenty of evidence to suggest that I'd really discovered something else—that the most dominant teams in history had succeeded without traditional leaders. Though I hadn't found any evidence to refute "captain theory," my research had raised sufficient doubts. Before I went any further, I decided to explore some alternative hypotheses.

CHAPTER TWO TAKEAWAYS

- Every winning streak is bounded by two moments of transformation, the one where it begins and the one where it ends. For the most dominant teams in sports history, these moments had an uncanny correlation to one player's arrival or departure—or both. This person not only displayed a fanatical commitment to winning, they also happened to be the captain.

- Most of us have developed a model of what leaders of superior teams ought to be. We believe they should possess some combination of skills and personality traits that are universally considered to be superior. We don't believe they should be difficult to spot in a crowd. We expect their leadership ability to be obvious. The leaders of the sixteen teams in Tier One did not match the profile.

THREE

Talent, Money, and Culture

Alternative Explanations

Most of the theories I'd rounded up over the years about the nature of team greatness, such as "discipline" and "work ethic," had the same fundamental problem. They were so abstruse I couldn't think of any way to quantify them.

Hiding in my notebooks, however, were five frequently cited qualities of superior teams that seemed at once both plausible and researchable. They are: the presence of an otherworldly superstar, a high level of overall talent, deep financial resources, a winning culture maintained by effective management, and, finally, the most widely accepted explanation of all—superior coaching. I set out to kick the tires on each of them.

Theory 1:
It takes a GOAT.

One widely held belief about elite sports teams is that they owe their success to the contributions of a single player whose physical talents, playmaking instincts, and clutch performances belong to a category of one. In sports lingo, athletes like these are often described as the GOAT, the greatest of all time.

The rosters of the Tier One teams gave this theory immediate credibility. They didn't just contain a handful of players who'd set scoring records, won some prestigious MVP award, or been named by their sporting federations as one of the greatest athletes in history. They were overflowing with them. In all, twelve of the sixteen teams in Tier One enjoyed the services of a GOAT candidate. They are: Collingwood's Gordon Coventry (Syd's kid brother); the Yankees' Joe DiMaggio; Hungary's Ferenc Puskás; Maurice Richard of the Montreal Canadiens; Brazil's Pelé; Soviet hockey's Viacheslav Fetisov, Sergei Makarov, and Vladislav Tretiak; Cuba's Regla Torres; Australian field hockey's Alyson Annan; Michelle Akers of the U.S. women's football team; Barcelona's Lionel Messi; French handball's Nikola Karabatić; and Dan Carter of the 2011–15 New Zealand All Blacks.

Evidence of GOAT theory was just as compelling in Tier Two, where team rosters included such legends as Michael Jordan, baseball's Babe Ruth, football's Alfredo Di Stéfano and Johan Cruyff, ice hockey's Wayne Gretzky, rugby league's Ellery Hanley, field hockey's Dhyan Chand, and water polo's Dezső Gyarmati.

These superstars unquestionably made their teams better. What's harder to know is whether the talent of a GOAT by itself is the catalyst that propels a team into Tier One. In a few cases, mostly in European football, a GOAT candidate from a top-tier team also wore a second strip. Di Stéfano, Cruyff, and Messi all played both for their Tier One or Tier Two club teams while competing separately for their national teams. As of 2017, however, none of these superstars had won a World Cup title.

It's also clear that the presence of a GOAT doesn't guarantee success at the team level. Dozens of GOAT candidates have played for teams that achieve elite results. Karch Kiraly, for instance, was named the greatest men's player of the twentieth century by the international volleyball federation—but even though his U.S. team won a pair of Olympic gold medals in 1984 and 1988, its failure to dominate other tournaments kept it out of the top tiers. The same was true of Luciana Aymar, the Argentine field hockey midfielder who received the hockey federation's player of the year award eight times. In four Olympics (2000 to 2012), her teams never won gold.

If there's any one sport where the presence of a GOAT candidate should make the most difference, it's basketball. With just five players per side, basketball teams were the smallest units in my study and the ones where the contributions of individual players should matter the most. Among basketball experts, there is a strong consensus view that superstars play an outsize role. As Dean Smith, Michael Jordan's coach at the University of North Carolina, once said, "Basketball is a team game. But that doesn't mean all five players should have the same amount of shots." If the GOAT effect is the primary force of a freak team, then it stands to reason that its impact would be the most pronounced here.

Given that the 1956–69 Boston Celtics didn't have an otherworldly offensive star, the GOAT theory was already limping a bit. But maybe the Celtics were the exception to the rule—the only elite basketball team that did not have a GOAT on its roster.

I started by compiling a list of the best overall performances by individual players in NBA history based on player efficiency rating, a statistic developed by the sports columnist John Hollinger. PER takes into account both offense and defense. It gives individual players a score based on a tally of the positive contributions they make on the court—not just scoring but also blocking shots and grabbing rebounds—minus the negative things they do, such as missing shots or turning the ball over. After adjusting for the number of minutes played, PER is expressed as a rate.

Here are the players who own the ten best single-season PER performances in NBA history through 2016:

1. Wilt Chamberlain   31.82   1962–63 San Francisco Warriors
2. Wilt Chamberlain   31.74   1961–62 Philadelphia Warriors
3. Michael Jordan   31.71   1987–88 Chicago Bulls

4.	LeBron James	31.67	2008–09 Cleveland Cavaliers
5.	Michael Jordan	31.63	1990–91 Chicago Bulls
6.	Wilt Chamberlain	31.63	1963–64 San Francisco Warriors
7.	LeBron James	31.59	2012–13 Miami Heat
8.	Stephen Curry	31.46	2015–16 Golden State Warriors
9.	Michael Jordan	31.18	1989–90 Chicago Bulls
10.	Michael Jordan	31.14	1988–89 Chicago Bulls

And here are the five players who have the top PERs for their entire careers, according to basketball-reference.com:

1.	Michael Jordan	27.91
2.	LeBron James	27.65
3.	Shaquille O'Neal	26.43
4.	David Robinson	26.18
5.	Wilt Chamberlain	26.13

If the GOAT effect held true in basketball, these lists suggested that Wilt Chamberlain's Warriors teams of the early 1960s ought to have racked up a string of championships. Michael Jordan, the best player in NBA history by career PER, ought to have played on a Tier One team, too, with LeBron James close on his heels.

Here are the seven NBA teams that qualified for the top two tiers:

TIER ONE

1. 1956–69 Boston Celtics
2. 1998–2016 San Antonio Spurs

TIER TWO

3. 1990–98 Chicago Bulls (six titles in eight seasons)
4. 1948–54 Minneapolis Lakers (five in six)
5. 1979–88 Los Angeles Lakers (five in nine)
6. 1983–87 Boston Celtics (two in four finals appearances)
7. 2010–14 Miami Heat (two in four finals appearances)

Looking at these charts side by side, there were a few encouraging signs. LeBron James delivered the 2010–14 Miami Heat into the second tier, while David Robinson of the Spurs (number four in career PER) was present for five of the nineteen seasons that composed that team's Tier One performance. Michael Jordan's Bulls, the winners of six NBA titles in eight seasons, missed out on Tier One by a hair—they failed to match the number of championships won by the Celtics or the incredible consistency of the Spurs.* In any case, the Bulls distinguished themselves as the top of the class in Tier Two.

The rest of the list, however, didn't do GOAT theory any favors. No team that Chamberlain or O'Neal played for managed to crack the top tiers at all, while Golden State's Stephen Curry had only one title to his name as of 2016. Yet it was the absence of a single Celtics player on either of these PER lists that posed the biggest obstacle to GOAT theory. The best finish in career PER for any member of that magnificent Boston team was the point guard Bob Cousy at number seventy-eight. In terms of single-season PER, nobody from the Celtics even cracked the top 250. The most dominant team in basketball history didn't just lack a GOAT—it didn't have a single elite player.

None of this evidence suggested that GOATs were the silver bullet I'd been searching for. In a backward way, however, it did erase one of my earlier concerns about captains.

Astonishingly, only two of the GOAT candidates on the sixteen Tier One teams also captained them. In every other case, the most dominant teams in history had hierarchies in which the leader of the players was not the go-to superstar. So even though these teams had GOATs, they

---

* Some analysts argue that the Bulls, who played at a time when there were twenty-seven to twenty-nine teams in the NBA, faced longer odds of winning a title and would have been as dominant as the Celtics if they, too, had played in an era when there were only eight to fourteen teams. Others contend that during the early days of the NBA, the talent was more concentrated and teams stayed together longer, which made the average team tougher to beat.

hadn't tapped them to lead. This suggested that a team is *more* likely to become elite if it has a captain that leads from the shadows.

Theory 2:
It's a matter of overall talent.

In 2010, four education researchers from two universities in Texas conducted an experiment to measure the impact of individual talent on team performance. The subjects of the experiment were 101 undergraduates enrolled in a large survey class.

Over the course of the semester, the students were given a series of fifteen-question quizzes based on reading assignments. After answering the questions individually, they broke into eighteen teams of five to seven members and were instructed to discuss the questions together and submit their answers as a group. In the group setting, they were allowed to see which answers they had gotten wrong and given extra chances to correct them.

The researchers started by looking at the student teams that had shown the least improvement as a group in relation to their individual scores. These low-performing teams had one trait in common—a wide ability gap. They usually consisted of one high-achieving academic "superstar" surrounded by students with average to low grades. "The greater the superstar status, as compared with the rest of the group, the lower is the achievement of the overall team," the researchers wrote. Most teams, if asked whether they wanted a high-achiever to join them, wouldn't hesitate to say yes. When it came to taking quizzes, however, the presence of a single star actually had a negative effect.

So what kinds of teams fared the best?

The top-performing student groups in the study were the ones with a high number of skilled—though not necessarily star—students, whose abilities fell within a narrow range. In other words, the best teams had "clusters" of above-average performers.

To figure out why this was the case, the researchers listened to recordings of the groups as they deliberated. On teams where there was a large ability gap, they wrote, "the superstar, or highest-performing team member, dominated the discourse." As this person took charge, the other students showed a tendency to back off, even when they believed—correctly—that the high achiever was wrong. Because of this, their group scores suffered.

In sports, I'd seen the same kind of situation occur on teams with one standout player. On these units, the marginal athletes would defer to the star, who insisted on taking a vast majority of the shots, even when a player of lesser skill was wide open.

On the cluster teams, however, the researchers found that discussions about the quiz responses were more democratic. Many members of the group chimed in, and the debates tended to be longer and more thorough, with everyone having their say. More often than not, the researchers wrote, these kinds of groups "were able to come to a consensus on a correct answer choice." In other words, this study showed that for units roughly the size of basketball teams, the collective talent level, and the ability to work democratically, turned out to be far more valuable than the isolated skill of one supreme achiever. "Having a superstar on your team is only beneficial if the rest of the team also scores relatively high," the researchers wrote.

The same principle—the power of a talent cluster—seemed to apply to famous teams across many different disciplines. In business, there were the Nine Old Men who built Walt Disney's animation studio, for example, or the programmers who developed Google's search algorithm. Historians often cite the general brilliance of the framers of the U.S. Constitution. Scientists point to the three-nation Manhattan Project that developed the first nuclear weapon, the Oxford University team that developed penicillin, and the small knot of Soviet engineers who designed the Sputnik satellite. These groups weren't driven by a single visionary but by an extraordinary concentration of brainpower.

The sports world has had its fair share of talent clusters. Some of the most prominent examples are the U.S. basketball "Dream Team" at the 1992 Olympics, which included Michael Jordan, Larry Bird, and Earvin "Magic" Johnson; the 1981–90 San Francisco 49ers of the NFL, which paired Joe Montana, Jerry Rice, and Ronnie Lott with the legendary coach Bill Walsh; and Real Madrid from the late 1950s, whose roster included Alfredo di Stéfano, Ferenc Puskás, Francisco Gento, and Raymond Kopa. These teams all wound up in Tier Two.

To see if "cluster theory" explained the success of the teams in Tier One, I turned to baseball. In this sport, as I noted earlier, teammate interaction plays a limited role while the performance of individual players has a larger impact. Studies have shown that baseball teams that continue to add more talent do not reach a point of diminishing returns. The more stars a baseball team has, the better it should be. If there is a correlation between talent clusters and superior performance, baseball was the one sport where it would absolutely have to exist.

To identify the most abundantly talented teams in baseball history, I turned to wins above replacement, a formula that uses game statistics to measure how much more (or less) each player contributes to their team's victories than a statistically average player would. Here are the top ten teams in baseball history by the combined WAR of their players (in both hitting and pitching) through the 2015 season, as determined by FanGraphs:

1.	1927 New York Yankees	66.3
2.	1969 Baltimore Orioles	65.1
3.	1998 Atlanta Braves	64.6
4.	2001 Seattle Mariners	63.3
5.	1905 New York Giants	61.4
6.	1976 Cincinnati Reds	60.5
7.	1997 Atlanta Braves	60.3
8.	1944 St. Louis Cardinals	59.4
9.	1939 New York Yankees	59.3
9.	1931 New York Yankees	59.3

This list suggested that the Yankees of the late 1920s and early 1930s—whose Murderers' Row of power hitters, including Babe Ruth and Lou Gehrig, swatted 158 home runs in 1927 (more than triple the league average)—were the kind of talent cluster that should have made a run at Tier One. It also predicted great things from the Atlanta Braves of the late 1990s, the only team to appear on the list in two consecutive seasons. Nonetheless, those prolifically talented Yankees, with two championships in three years, didn't make either of the top tiers. The Braves won their division fourteen times in a row from 1991 to 2005, which allowed them to slip into Tier Two, but they managed to win only a single World Series.

Even in baseball, a sport where there's no such thing as too many superstars, the deepest clubs didn't rise to the top.

The most glaring problem with the list, however, was the absence of the 1949–53 Yankees—the only baseball team in Tier One. This team had some excellent players during its streak of five titles, including the Hall of Famers Yogi Berra and Phil Rizzuto. Joe DiMaggio played in the first three seasons of the streak, although he was on the downslope of his career. Mickey Mantle joined the team as a rookie in 1951, but his peak years were still to come.

Statistically, however, these Yankees were anything but a juggernaut. The best individual result for a Yankee player during that five-season span, in terms of single-season WAR, was a number seven finish in 1950 by Rizzuto. While it's true that the Yankees' manager, Casey Stengel, liked to "platoon" his players based on the tendencies of the other teams' starting pitchers—which limited their playing time and held down their statistical totals—it was impossible to argue that this was baseball's most richly talented team. By every metric I looked at, from simple numbers like home runs, batting average, or earned run average to more complex measures, these Yankees underwhelmed. Their combined talent ranking, as measured by WAR, never rose higher than 150 on the all-time list. And in 1953, when the Yankees won ninety-nine games—the most in any season during the streak—its aggregated WAR barely cracked the top ten in *Yankees* history.

To give cluster theory one more chance, I looked at the results of an experiment conducted by the Spanish football power Real Madrid. Starting in 2000, the team's president, Florentino Pérez, enacted what came to be known as the Galáctico policy. Each summer, between seasons, the team would open the vault to sign one of the sport's top stars—a list that grew to include Luís Figo, Zinedine Zidane, Ronaldo, and David Beckham. The result was a cluster of talent the likes of which modern football had never seen.

The immediate effect of the experiment was spectacular: Real Madrid won two Spanish league titles and a Champions League trophy in its first three seasons. But as time progressed, the team's growing collection of superstars struggled to gel, and the team failed to win any trophies in the next three seasons. Despite its abundance of talent, Real Madrid's performance declined. In 2007 the Galáctico policy was scuttled.

I have no doubt that the Texas researchers were onto something. Any elite team needs a passel of skillful players, and it's probably better if their abilities are balanced. Nevertheless, my analysis of baseball in general, the Yankees in particular, and the experience of Real Madrid didn't support the idea that a talent cluster is something teams have to have in order to achieve and sustain freakish success.

Theory 3:
It's the money, stupid.

Every year, depending on what happens in free agency or the transfer markets, fans all over the world set to carping about the unfair profligacy of some professional team, be it the Los Angeles Dodgers or Paris Saint-Germain. The charge that's leveled, time and again, is that this team is using its financial resources to buy a championship.

Spending the most money on players doesn't guarantee titles, of course. The Yankees, for example, outspent the average major-league team from 2002 to 2012 by more than $1.2 billion, but all it earned them was a single World Series win. We just saw what happened when Real Madrid opened its checkbook.

There's no doubt that in professional sports, spendthrifts do enjoy some competitive advantages. In 2014, *The Economist* found that in the English Premier League, a team's payroll was the single most important performance variable. Each season, the final league table closely tracked what the teams shelled out for players. Likewise, several studies of player payrolls in baseball have demonstrated that teams that spend significantly more than the major-league average tend to win more than 50 percent of their games. So whether or not liberal spending guarantees titles, it does produce extra wins.

The strongest evidence in Tier One for "deep pockets theory" was the presence of Barcelona. During its run of titles between 2008 and 2013, this team enjoyed the fruits of a series of record-breaking broadcast, sponsorship, and licensing deals. In 2013 it earned revenue of six hundred million dollars (adjusted for inflation), which was triple its annual income in the decade prior, making it the world's second-richest football club and giving it the wherewithal to retain existing superstars like Lionel Messi while also bringing in new ones. During its five-season run of dominance, Barcelona spent more than four hundred million dollars in player transfer payments alone, in addition to what it paid the players in salaries.

Nobody would argue that money is irrelevant in football. Most fans believe that the best winning formula is to mix high spending with a commitment to develop talent—a model that Barcelona would come to epitomize. But the financial histories of the sixteen Tier One teams made one point clear: Barcelona was an outlier.

In fact, more Tier One teams seemed to have hit their strides during periods of relative poverty. Collingwood, the Aussie rules team, was so cash-poor that other clubs routinely poached its stars, while the San Antonio Spurs rarely ranked in the top half of the NBA in player payroll during their 19-season streak. Even teams that did have more money than their competitors didn't lavish it on talent—the tightfisted executives who ran the 1949–53 Yankees and the 1974–80 Pittsburgh

Steelers were famous for bargaining hard with the players to hold down salaries.

When it came to pocket depth, there was a sharp divide between professional Tier One teams like Barcelona, which must pay high salaries determined by the market, and national teams—like Cuba, Hungary, and Australia—which compete in global events. Because national teams have virtual monopolies on the players from their home countries, there is little competition for their services. If athletes don't like what the national team wants to give them, they either have to opt out entirely or renounce their citizenship.

Several national teams in Tier One operated under shoestring budgets. The members of the women's volleyball team from Cuba were paid so little that during international tournaments rival teams felt sorry for them and took them out clothes shopping. U.S. football officials once locked the members of the women's national team out of practice before the 1996 Olympics after they demanded a contract that would pay them enough to avoid taking second jobs or relying on subsidies from their parents.

There was one national team in Tier One to which player salaries mattered immensely, however—the 2011–15 New Zealand All Blacks. Because the rules forbid players from competing for the national team if they signed with a professional rugby club in another country, the New Zealand Rugby Union, which oversees the All Blacks, had to find a way to keep its top athletes at home by paying them market-competitive salaries. To that end, the NZRU began a campaign to sell sponsorships and broadcast rights that ultimately netted a team record ninety-three million U.S. dollars in revenue in 2015.

This fundraising effort surely helped the All Blacks maintain a competitive team, but in the end it seems unlikely that money alone was the catalyst. The NZRU's revenue was a drop in the bucket compared to the nearly three hundred million dollars England's Rugby Football Union earned in the same year.

When it came to freakish success, lavish spending seemed to have little to do with it.

Theory 4:
It's a question of management.

The fourth theory on my list is the notion that freak teams are prod-ucts of a long tradition of institutional excellence, or a *culture* of win-ning. Here, again, there was a lot of material to work with—eleven of the sixteen teams in Tier One are representatives of one of the world's most admired historical sports dynasties.

The Montreal Canadiens have collected more Stanley Cups than any other NHL team and became the source of enormous cultural pride for French Canadians. In Brazil, the Seleção, as the national foot-ball team is known, has not only won more World Cups than any other national team, it has become the country's secular religion. Barcelona, which ranks third in history in European football championships, has become so deeply intertwined with the political identity of the independent-minded province of Catalonia that the team's slogan—painted on the seats of its stadium—is "Més que un Club" (more than a club). The same mixture of historical success and tribal zealotry can be seen, if to a lesser degree, among fans of the Steelers, Yankees and Celtics—three teams that have all won the most overall champion-ships in their sports.

This kind of institutional gravity manifests itself in hundreds of small ways, from the lifelong dreams children harbor of playing for these dynasties, to the internal dynamics of the team and how the play-ers go about their work. When most people think about culture, they're talking about a team's traditions and habits. As important as it seems, however, culture is a tricky thing to measure. The idea that the ghosts of the past are primarily responsible for a team's ascent to greatness is, after all, basically a vote for the paranormal.

The fans of these iconic teams may have louder voices and greater expectations, and will exert immense pressure when their teams aren't winning, but in the end the fans of lesser teams make a lot of noise, too. In sports, where players have short careers and coaches come and go, a team's cultural resonance and the size of its trophy cabinet don't play positions on the field. In reality, a team's ability to uphold a tradition of excellence comes down to something rather mundane—the quality of its upper management.

Some of the executives who ran the sixteen Tier One teams were revered for their skillful stewardship: Paulo Machado de Carvalho, the business mogul who served as the director of Brazilian football during the team's back-to-back World Cup wins; the Yankees owners Dan Topping and Del Webb and the general manager George Weiss; several generations of Pittsburgh's Rooney family; and Joan Laporta, the brash and controversial architect of Barcelona's 2008–13 dynasty. Others, however, had executives that seemed less than brilliant. The Communist regimes of Hungary and Cuba spied on their players and forbade them from playing abroad, while the overlords of Collingwood and U.S. women's football nearly ended their teams' runs by clashing with the players over wages. It would be a stretch to conclude that these teams were exceptionally well run.

If enlightened management is the key to sustaining a team's culture, and culture is the secret to outsize success, one team in particular would have to be its standard-bearer—the All Blacks. Not only did this team's name appear twice in Tier One, another All Blacks team from 1961 to 1969 also ascended to Tier Two.

The national rugby team of New Zealand is, by any reasonable accounting, the world's preeminent sports dynasty. Since 1903, the All Blacks have won or drawn 80 percent of their international test matches despite New Zealand having a population of 4.4 million in 2013, which makes it roughly the size of Greater Detroit. Its chief rivals—the national teams of England, France, Australia, Argentina, and South Africa—come from nations that have populations up to fifteen times larger.

The New Zealand Rugby Union has handled some aspects of the sport admirably, especially the development of talent. In recent years, as I noted earlier, it has done a fine job of finding revenue to keep pace with rugby machines from larger, richer nations. Not all of its decisions have improved the team's chances of victory, however.

One of the NZRU's most confounding moves came in 1990, when its selectors determined that Buck Shelford, who had never lost a match since he became captain, was no longer fit for the team. The decision to drop him caused such a stir that it led nightly newscasts and sparked the biggest protests in New Zealand history—a total of 150,000 people participated in two hundred separate demonstrations. Sure enough, less than a month later, the team lost to Australia. The All Blacks hadn't been playing especially well, said Shelford's teammate Sean Fitzpatrick, "but it was hardly fair to pin it on Buck."

From there, the NZRU's decisions worsened. A year later, it saw fit to appoint not one but two coaches for the 1991 World Cup—and the team bowed out in the semifinals. During the next four World Cup cycles, the team's minders inexplicably dropped a star player and one-time captain before a semifinal loss and launched (then scrapped) both a newfangled conditioning program and a "rotation" system designed to allow everyone to play. It once forced the players to take an extended break, leaving them ill-prepared and rusty upon their return. Despite being the pre-tournament favorites in four out of five World Cups from 1991 to 2007, New Zealand had to wait another twenty-four years to win its second title.

It would be unfair to expect New Zealand's rugby executives to have never put a foot wrong. And it would be foolish to discount the propulsive influence of New Zealand's native rugby culture, which may well be the ghost in the machine. Still, no matter how motivated a team is by the standards of history, it won't achieve its full potential if management continually throws up obstacles. And in the case of the All Blacks, the team's overlords often did exactly that. It would be impossible to argue that the root of this team's success was the elevated wisdom of the people running it. If management didn't elevate the All Blacks, its winning culture must have had another source.

If anything, the struggles of the NZRU provided another small argument for the importance of captains. After all, the team's two decades of frustration began in 1990, when it decided to drop Shelford, the team's unbeaten leader.

Theory 5:
It's the coach.

Having found reasonable evidence to contradict these first four explanations, there was only one alternative theory left—and it would prove so difficult to rule on that it warrants its own chapter. It's the idea that the single force that has the most decisive impact on a team's performance is its coach or manager.

To test this hypothesis, I decided to start at the top by examining the most widely admired coach in American history.

CHAPTER THREE TAKEAWAYS

- One of the least controversial things you can say about a team is that its success is a function of its talent. To be one of the greatest teams in history, this reasoning suggests, a team should possess one of the greatest individual stars of all time or a group of players whose aggregated skill ranks higher, from top to bottom, than any other. Some of the sixteen teams in Tier One had many stars and superior athletes. But some had neither.

- When an organization achieves astounding results, there is a temptation to look beyond the men and women who did the work. We're inclined to believe that the result must be a reflection of the scaffolding around them—a matter of having enlightened management or more financial resources than anyone else. The most enduring dynasties in sports history, however, didn't always have those advantages.

FOUR

Do Coaches Matter?

The Vince Lombardi Effect

LOS ANGELES, 1967

Head down, chin strap unfastened, his mind in a whirl, Willie Davis chugged into the shadows of the stadium tunnel. The team he played for, the Green Bay Packers, held a narrow 14–10 lead at halftime over the Kansas City Chiefs, but as he walked into the locker room and scanned the faces of his teammates, he could tell he wasn't the only one with a knot in his stomach. "There was a bit of fear," he said.

Len Dawson, Kansas City's intrepid, dart-throwing quarterback, had found enough gaps in Green Bay's vaunted defense to rack up 153 passing yards. Just before the half, Dawson had driven his team fifty yards to set up a field goal in the final seconds, and the Packers could sense the momentum shifting in Kansas City's favor.

On that day—January 15, 1967—the Green Bay Packers were the National Football League's defending champions and the undisputed kings of football. The NFL, to which they belonged, was considered far superior to the upstart American Football League, represented by the Chiefs. This game, which would draw twenty-seven million TV viewers and come to be remembered as the first Super Bowl, marked the first time these rival leagues had allowed their respective champions to meet. Nobody had thought it would be much of a contest—the Packers were fourteen-point favorites—but the Chiefs didn't seem to care. They had controlled the pace and set the tone. With thirty minutes of football left, it was anyone's game to win.

Despite the three championships he'd already won and the accolades he'd received as one of the league's best defensive ends, Willie Davis had always played football as if he were hovering just above the cut line. He'd only made it to the NFL because a Cleveland Browns coach came to see one of his college teammates play—he hadn't been drafted until the fifteenth round. After a lackluster two-year stint in Cleveland, Davis was traded to Green Bay in 1960, a team that had only achieved one winning season in the previous twelve. "At that point in my career," he told me, "I could have been considered a case of chopped liver."

The man who'd saved Davis from football oblivion was Vince Lombardi, who had taken over as Green Bay's head coach one year earlier with little fanfare and some novel theories about talent. The turnaround had come quickly. In Davis's first season, the Packers narrowly lost the NFL Championship Game. They went on to win the next two. After a dip in form in 1964, Lombardi defied the racism of the day by rebuilding the Packers with undervalued black players. In 1965, he took the strategy a step further by making Davis the team's defensive captain, one of the first African Americans to hold that title in the NFL. Immediately after Davis accepted the job, the Packers won another championship. When they met the Chiefs in this 1967 title game, Davis was one of six black starters on defense, four of whom would end up in the Pro Football Hall of Fame.

In Davis, Lombardi had seen a rare combination of size, speed, quickness, and intelligence. But he'd also picked up on something else—the kind of hunger that comes from being counted out. This was a quality Lombardi could feel in his own bones. As a highly regarded offensive coordinator for the New York Giants from 1954 to 1958, he'd seemed destined to be a head coach, but the calls never came. Lombardi suspected his Italian surname was an issue, especially when it came to positions with prominent college programs. The only reason he'd ended up in Green Bay was because nobody else would have him. "Coach Lombardi felt as if he had been denied, he had been looked over, passed over," Davis said. "When he got to Green Bay he was determined that this was his opportunity. This was his chance to show that he simply could not be denied."

Depending on where you live and which sport you fancy, the greatest coach in history might be volleyball's Hirofumi Daimatsu, football's Alex Ferguson, basketball's Phil Jackson, or hockey's Anatoly Tarasov. But there is little question in the minds of most Americans that Vince Lombardi was the greatest football coach who ever lived.

Square-jawed and gap-toothed, with dark half-framed glasses and a buzz cut, Lombardi wasn't slick or elegant. On the sidelines he liked to wear suits with white shirts, a skinny tie, and a brown Borsalino hat. He looked like a fire hydrant dressed for a job interview. During his time in Green Bay, Lombardi dragged his team from the bottom of the NFL to the top, winning five championships in seven seasons. The only reason the Packers didn't make it into Tier One was that three of Lombardi's titles were won in years before the NFL's champion met the champion of the AFL.

What distinguished Lombardi the most from other coaches was his knack for oratory. His speeches were simple, forceful, and urgent—rich with emotional overtones and war analogies. At a time when sportswriters had a monopoly on coverage and a weakness for poetry, they shared his quotes in their columns, building a spectacular catalog of inspirational sayings such as "Winning isn't everything; it's the only thing" and "Perfection is not attainable. But if we chase perfection we can catch excellence" and "It's not whether you get knocked down, it's whether you get up."

As the halftime break came to a close, the Packers sat silently in their cramped locker room inside the Los Angeles Memorial Coliseum, a damp mass of nerves and creeping doubt. All that stood between them, the second half, and the prospect of an unthinkable upset was the traditional halftime address from their coach.

Lombardi stood up, folded his jacket over a chair, and walked slowly to the front of the room. "I want to talk to you men," he began. "I want to tell you something. . . ."

As Lombardi began, his leg brushed against Davis's. That's when Davis noticed something unusual—Lombardi was trembling. "At first, I didn't know what to make of it," Davis said. "I didn't know what was causing his emotions to be so strong." Eventually he figured it out. Lombardi's quavering leg had betrayed him. He was terrified of losing.

As Davis remembers it, the coach kept his remarks brief. "You've played thirty minutes adjusting to Kansas City, and you probably experienced everything that they had to throw at you," Lombardi said. "You survived, okay? Now I want you to play thirty minutes of Green Bay football, and let's see if they can adjust to you."

Lombardi finished his speech with a question: "Are you the world-champion Green Bay Packers? Get out on that field and answer me!"

As the team roared out of the locker room, Davis studied the faces of his teammates to measure the impact of Lombardi's words. "It was just so strange, the way it resonated," he said. "For each one of us, looking at each other as we were going on the field, it was like, 'Remember what Coach said. We've got to go and show 'em what we can do now.'"

On the fourth play from scrimmage in the second half, Dawson, the Chiefs' quarterback, dropped back to pass on third down. Davis, from his end position, got an incredible jump, shed his blocker, and rounded the corner. Dawson, sensing Davis bearing down on him, let the ball go too early, placing it just behind his intended receiver. A Packers defensive back, Willie Wood, intercepted the pass. As Wood began galloping toward the end zone, Davis turned downfield to help clear the way. He saw Dawson running directly in front of him, his eyes locked on the ball carrier. Davis planted him on the turf with the sort of force that defies a hundred ice baths. Wood went on to race fifty yards, setting up a touchdown that put the Packers up 21–10.

It's always dangerous to single out one play as the event that presaged the outcome of an entire game. But there is little doubt that this interception sparked by the pressure Davis put on Dawson, was the decisive blow. Davis, the team's defensive captain, had somehow absorbed the passion rumbling inside his coach and taken it onto the field, where he'd let it loose. Green Bay would score two more touchdowns that day, while not allowing the shell-shocked Chiefs to come anywhere near the end zone. When the final whistle blew, it was Green Bay 35, Kansas City 10.

"I don't know if I had another experience in football like that," Davis said. "Every time that ball snapped, whatever I did had to be better than what I managed to do in the first half. There was something about that speech that made me play better. I think Coach Lombardi—he created all of this. If you looked at our performance in the second half, we raised the bar. We raised that bar because of the conversation he had with us."

The reason I flew out to Los Angeles to sit down with Willie Davis was that I believed he was one of the few people on earth who could help me figure out whether coaches are the primary force behind the world's most exceptional sports teams. As I knew from reading his autobiography, Davis believed that his team owed its success, almost entirely, to Vincent Thomas Lombardi's motivational powers.

Davis, eighty years old, lived on a hillside in the prosperous Los Angeles enclave of Playa del Rey in a bright modern home with a transfixing view of the Pacific Ocean. After American football, Davis got an MBA, owned a chain of radio stations, and sat on the boards of several major companies. He became one of the most business-savvy ex–NFL players of his generation.

Nevertheless, Davis was unfailingly modest and quick to deflect credit. I suspected he might be lifting up Lombardi as a way of down-playing his own contribution. When he finished his story about Lombardi's halftime address, I pressed him on the idea that a few words from a coach could make an entire team play harder. "Really?" I asked. "Lombardi could do that just by talking to the team?"

Davis shot me a glance and smiled. "I tell ya, Coach Lombardi probably could have been a great minister, because he said things with the voice. Sometimes the voice had a chilling effect on you." Davis turned away for a moment and stared out the window at the slow-rolling waves. I could tell from the look in his eyes that his mind had drifted back to those faraway football fields.

Then, after a long silence, he let go from the depths of his lungs. *"Crap, crap, crap! What the hell's going on?"*

The voice was no longer Davis's raspy baritone; it was sharp, forceful, and urgent. I knew immediately what he'd done: He'd conjured the spirit of Vince Lombardi. "He could say something and it would just grab you and do something to you," he said. "It was like he could make you rise to play at a level you didn't even know about."

Given that he coached before the advent of unrestricted player free agency, Lombardi had a level of authority modern coaches can only dream about. He could ride the Packers mercilessly, even after wins, without having to worry about defections. If he'd been a coach in a different era, a time when players had more mobility, it's possible his demands would have scared away the talent. But because his players were captives to the Packers, Lombardi was able to work on them, to fuse their personalities with his.

Davis believed that the quality at the center of Lombardi's character was an overwhelming desperation to prove his value. He used his words, and the blunt force of his personality, to make this sense of longing contagious. "He dwelled so heavily on that," Davis said, "until he had every player feeling absolutely the same way." Even when the Packers were good, they played like a team clamoring for recognition.

There is no question that Lombardi knew exactly what he was doing and that he understood the power of his gift. "It is essential to understand that battles are primarily won in the hearts of men," he once said. "Men respond to leadership in a most remarkable way and once you have won his heart, he will follow you anywhere." Leadership, Lombardi added, "is based on a spiritual quality—the power to inspire, the power to inspire others to follow." On another occasion he said, "Coaches who can outline plays on a blackboard are a dime a dozen. The ones who win get inside their players and motivate."

The depth of Willie Davis's belief in his coach had been so convincing that I flew home fully expecting that this kind of influence, this Lombardi effect, would be a common theme among the coaches of the sixteen teams in Tier One.

I started my study by examining how successful these coaches had been before their teams began their historic runs. If a brilliant coach is the key to winning, I assumed that most of these men had come to their Tier One teams with strong histories of achievement.

The best résumé of the bunch belonged to Jock McHale of the 1927–30 Collingwood Magpies. Before his team began its streak of four consecutive titles, McHale had taken his teams to eight Australian rules football Grand Finals and won two of them. As I worked my way down the list, however, I was surprised to discover that McHale had no peers.

The other coaches in Tier One fell into one of three inferior categories. The first had seven members: Red Auerbach of the Boston Celtics, Brazil's Vicente Feola, Cuban volleyball's Eugenio George Lafita, Chuck Noll of the Pittsburgh Steelers, Soviet hockey's Viktor Tikhonov, Alex "Grizz" Wyllie of the 1980s New Zealand All Blacks, and French handball's Claude Onesta. These men had made favorable impressions before joining Tier One, in some cases by winning a single major title or a majority of their games as a head coach, sometimes at a lower level of their sport. Others had won trophies as assistants. They were solidly middle class.

The second grouping consisted of four members: Casey Stengel of the New York Yankees, Toe Blake of the Montreal Canadiens, Brazil's Aymoré Moreira (who took over in 1962 after Feola fell ill), and Steve Hansen of the more recent All Blacks. The prior résumés of these men were anything but enviable. They had zero significant titles to their names and had either been fired from a major job or had posted an overall losing record.

The most eye-opening category was the third one, which included Hungary's Gusztáv Sebes, Australian field hockey's Ric Charlesworth, Gregg Popovich of the San Antonio Spurs, Tony DiCicco of the U.S. women's football team, and Barcelona's Pep Guardiola. These five coaches had little to no previous coaching experience at all.

Compared to what I'd expected, the distribution of names was essentially upside down. There were more greenhorns and retreads than seasoned winners. Moreover, five of the sixteen teams in Tier One had continued their winning streaks even after their coaches quit, retired, got sick, or were pushed out.

When it came to coaching a Tier One winning streak, having loads of expertise or a steamer trunk full of trophies was not a requirement. It didn't even seem to matter if a team had employed the same coach the whole time.

If having a glorious track record didn't matter, I wondered if the key element might be the one Willie Davis had described in Vince Lombardi—the ability to inspire.

Some of the Tier One coaches were known for their intensity and for challenging players with fire and brimstone. San Antonio's Popovich and New Zealand's Wyllie were two prominent examples. But for every sharp tongue in the group, there was someone like Barcelona's Guardiola, who made a point of keeping a distance from his players and talking to them calmly and only when necessary, and who rarely ventured into the dressing room. Brazil's Feola—a rotund and heavy-lidded fellow—was so detached at times that he appeared to be napping on the bench. These men were never remembered for delivering stirring speeches. Nobody ever pinned their sayings to the corkboard. In fact, some of these Tier One coaches were not seen as inspirational figures but as objects of loathing. Many of Stengel's Yankees considered their manager to be an annoying buffoon, and they sometimes disregarded his instructions entirely. Viktor Tikhonov, the coach of the Soviet Red Army hockey team, was such a cold disciplinarian that his players openly despised him.

While inspiration may be a valuable asset in a coach, it didn't seem to be the common thread, either.

The next aspect of coaching I looked at was tactics—the idea that these Tier One coaches might have devised sophisticated strategies that put their teams a step ahead.

Several Tier One coaches did, in fact, bring significant tactical advancements to their teams. Under Guardiola's watch, for example, Barcelona perfected a hypnotic, possession-oriented style of play known as *juego de posición*, or tiki-taka. The strategy called for the players to develop a sixth sense for where to move the ball, and to whom, depending on where they were on the pitch. The Australian field hockey coach Ric Charlesworth was widely acclaimed for his innovations, too, which included a system of ice-hockey-style shift changes to keep his players fresh.

Once again, however, the pattern wouldn't hold. A nearly equal number of Tier One coaches were not prizewinning strategists. Pittsburgh's Chuck Noll and Boston's Red Auerbach never employed anything beyond a limited repertoire of basic offensive plays and left behind no major innovations to speak of. The French handball coach Claude Onesta delegated tactics to one of his assistants, and Cuba's Eugenio George Lafita allowed the players to run practices and devise their own game strategies. Brazil's Feola was so laid-back in his approach that he often let the veteran players manage the team.

I decided to take a closer look at the tactical approach of one coach in particular, Gusztáv Sebes, whose Hungarian national football team, the Mighty Magyars, had so thoroughly outfoxed the English team during that 6–3 win at Wembley in 1953.

Sebes had developed his football philosophy by working with a long line of innovative managers, including Hungary's Béla Guttmann, who later became an influential manager in Brazil. Drawing on these ideas, Sebes organized the Hungarians to play a fluid style of football that was a precursor of the 4-2-4 formation Brazil perfected during its Tier One dynasty. The ideas weren't entirely new, but to teams like England, which had used the same old methods for decades, they were a monumental leap forward.

To most European football fans, the two most important ingredients for lasting greatness are a team's tactical approach and the quality of its manager. Other factors, like financial resources, the overall quality of the players, the presence of a GOAT, the captain, and the overall club culture, rank farther down the list. And among the great strategic minds in football history, Sebes enjoys a prominent position.

Sebes was famous for his tactical talks, in which he would detain the team for as many as four hours as he scribbled plays on the blackboard. In his 2008 book, *Inverting the Pyramid: The History of Football Tactics,* Jonathan Wilson described Sebes as an "inspirational and meticulous" manager with a sharp eye for detail. As Wilson noted, however, football is not played on a blackboard. No matter how brilliant a team's strategy is in theory, its success on the field requires the players to execute it. And sometimes the players will have their own ideas.

Ferenc Puskás, the short, thickset captain of the Hungarian team, was an irrepressible character. He was tough and relentless on the pitch, had a reflexive disrespect for authority, and didn't knuckle under to anyone. Early in his career, he often clashed with coaches, referees, and football authorities. In a 1997 oral history, Rogan Taylor and Klara Jamrich wrote that as a sixteen-year-old, when Puskás made his professional debut, the other players found his demeanor shocking. "His voice was often the loudest on the park, issuing a stream of instructions and criticisms directed sometimes at players many years his senior." On the national team, he was so outspoken and independent-minded that some in Hungary came to believe that he had just as much control of the national team as Sebes did.

While he acknowledged that he and Puskás discussed team matters off the field, Sebes said his captain never doubted his judgment or told him what to do. On the pitch, Puskás said he never tried to orchestrate the team's play, in large part because the players knew one another so well that it wasn't necessary. "But I screamed a bit if there were passes going astray," he said. Puskás also expressed deep affection for Sebes, whom he described as one of the most genuine and honest people he'd ever known and "the real heart and head of that golden team."

Yet when it came to following Sebes's instructions, Puskás made it clear that he had a mind of his own. "He was a street footballer from small childhood," said Les Murray, a Hungarian-born football journalist. "He had not much time for coaching or coaches. He once told me that every time Sebes would go through this ritual of drawing all sorts of squares and diagrams on the blackboard in the dressing room before a game, he would lead the team out, and in the tunnel he would tell them to forget all that nonsense. 'We'll just play the way we normally play,' and they would always win."

If Sebes was perturbed by his captain's behavior, he never expressed it publicly—in fact, he was full of praise. "Puskás had a brilliant sense of tactical requirements and the ability, in a matter of seconds, to realize what was necessary to surmount a problem. . . . He was never a selfish player, despite his own abilities, and didn't hesitate to lay off the ball to a better-placed colleague. He was the real leader of the team on the pitch, encouraging and driving others on."

In 1956, when Puskás fled Hungary, Sebes and many of his former teammates continued on—but the spell was broken. "The national team was never the same again," Nándor Hidegkuti said. "I often played his position afterward, but I couldn't make up for his absence. He was not only a great player and captain but also a 'playing coach.' He saw everything, exerted great discipline over the whole team, and could analyze footballing situations on the run. A few brief instructions on the field from him and all our problems were solved."

None of this information should discount the fact that Gusztáv Sebes laid the framework for the Hungarian dynasty—that's certainly true. It does not suggest, however, that the primary source of this team's brilliance was Sebes and his blackboard. If anything, it makes a stronger argument that Hungary's best asset was a captain who had the confidence to follow his manager's prescriptions when they suited the team and to ignore them when they didn't.

In the end, I couldn't find any evidence that a coach's tactics were the unifying principle.

Unable to find anything that Tier One coaches had in common, or any strong evidence that they were the elixir I'd been looking for, I began to consider a question that seemed like sports blasphemy: Do coaches matter at all?

Ferenc Puskás once said that in big matches, "it's not the coach who really carries the burden, it's the players. The coach can try to set the mood, talk through the game, encourage and explain, but in the end it's the players who have to solve the real problems on the pitch."

This dim assessment was something I'd heard before. During his days with the Boston Celtics, in a rare lighthearted interview, Bill Russell once took a jab at his coach. "Red can say he made you, but he can't put that ball in the hoop." In his 2009 Hall of Fame induction speech, Michael Jordan made a similar point about winning teams. "The organization has something to do with it, don't get me wrong," he said. "But don't try to put the organization above the players."

Even some prominent coaches had expressed similar views. Alex Ferguson, the legendary coach of Manchester United, who won thirteen Premier League titles, five FA Cups, and two UEFA Champions League trophies in twenty-six seasons with the team—and who is held in the same esteem in the rest of the world as Lombardi is in the United

States—believed that coaches only do so much. "As hard as I worked on my own leadership skills, and as much as I tried to influence every aspect of United's success on the field," Ferguson wrote, "at kickoff on match day things moved beyond my control."

Though the overall body of scientific research is thin, several academics and seasoned statisticians have tried to measure the relative importance of coaches at the elite levels of sports. These studies support three basic conclusions:

1. Coaches don't win many games.

In Major League Baseball, where every bunt, steal, sacrifice, pitching change, and player substitution is subject to the manager's approval, there is a widely held belief that these small decisions add up to a decisive whole. But a study conducted by the statistician Neil Paine found that for 95 percent of major-league managers, in-game decisions were worth no more or less than a two-game difference in the team's record over a 162-game season. His study also suggested the players had far more impact. In fact, the performances of a handful of top stars had more influence on the season's final standings than the decisions of all of the league's managers combined.

2. Coaches don't have a big impact on player performance.

In a 2009 study published in the *International Journal of Sport Finance,* a team of researchers from four universities used thirty years of data from the NBA to look at how individual players performed both before and after coming into contact with a new coach. While fourteen of the sixty-two coaches they studied did seem to get slightly more out of their players, the other 77 percent had impacts that ranged from neutral to negative. "Our most surprising finding," the authors wrote, "was that most of the coaches in our data set did not have a statistically significant impact on player performance relative to a generic coach." Even for the highest-performing coaches in the study, including Phil Jackson and San Antonio's Popovich, the differences were negligible.

3. Changing coaches is not a cure-all.

In 2011 the Dutch economist Bas ter Weel studied what had happened when teams in his country's top professional football league, the Eredivisie, fired their managers during a slump. He discovered that distressed teams that changed managers, and distressed teams that stayed the course, achieved almost precisely the same results. In other words, sacking the coach was no more effective than simply riding it out. A similar investigation of National Hockey League teams conducted in 2006 also found that the effect of changing coaches was almost neutral—but that over the short term, most teams that made swaps performed worse than teams that decided not to.

The notion that a coach is not a team's driving force, or that coaches might spend most of their time futzing in the margins and might even be interchangeable, is a difficult idea for most of us to comprehend. The majority of the billion or so humans who played team sports as children, as I did, formed their views at a time when they didn't question whether their coaches mattered. We were wide-eyed kids. They were unimpeachable authority figures. Our athletic careers fizzled out before we ever had a chance to update our views.

History hasn't given us many reasons to change our minds. Time and again, celebrated coaches have hopped between teams and enjoyed similar success—Phil Jackson, Bill Parcells, Don Shula, Herbert Chapman, José Mourinho, Fabio Capello, and Pep Guardiola, among many others. The prevailing view in modern sports is that the mobility of talent and the increasing narcissism of star athletes have made coaches more indispensable than ever.

When it comes to a legend from the past like Vince Lombardi, who was a master motivator, an oratorical savant, a keen psychologist, and a gifted tactician, we instinctively believe that he was the team's most important figure. And really—why shouldn't we? If a historically elite team had a historically elite coach, how many more steps of analysis are necessary?

I decided to circle back to the only coach in Tier One who seemed to have Lombardiesque qualities—Collingwood's Jock McHale. Known in Australian rules football as the Prince of Coaches, McHale began his career in 1912, and had been nearly as succesful after his Machine team's golden era as he'd been before it. He went on to coach Collingwood to five more Grand Final appearances, adding another pair of titles. He retired after thirty-seven seasons with a 66 percent win rate.

McHale, like Lombardi, was considered a master motivator with some unusual, even radical, ideas about how to make sure a team played as one. The first was a disdain for individual heroes. "I had no time for a side built up around three or four star players," he once said. "Give me a fit bunch of players with a good general level of ability." McHale enforced this ideology, just as Lombardi did, by exercising a level of control that would be impossible today. He insisted that every member of the team, no matter how talented, be paid the same wage. He also demanded that his own pay be kept low—so low, in fact, he worked at a Melbourne brewery to make ends meet. On two occasions during the Great Depression, when Collingwood cut the players' salaries, McHale insisted on taking the same percentage hit. Other teams in the league would have paid him handsomely to defect, but his loyalty to Collingwood ran too deep.

McHale was innovative as well, widely credited with inventing a position known as the ruck rover and for teaching his players to work at a faster tempo and improvise. "I did not set out with any specific intention of building a football machine," he once said. "I never liked the term, because it suggested the side was a combination which worked to a rigid plan and could not think. And if there is one quality we demand at Collingwood, it is the quick-thinking player with a dash of imagination."

His combination of brilliance and steadfast commitment to the team engendered enormous respect from the players and made McHale a legend in Australia. Just as the NFL's Super Bowl trophy was named after Lombardi, McHale's name was affixed to the medal given to the winning coach of the Grand Final.

McHale was clearly a special, Lombardi-level coach. In this case, it's tempting to skip directly from correlation to causation and conclude that the credit belongs entirely to him. But there is one important caveat. His greatest stretch, the four seasons between 1927 and 1930, began when McHale decided to replace the team's incumbent captain with a fellow named Syd Coventry.

In his twelve-year playing career at Collingwood, Coventry was the epitome of McHale's ethos. As a ruckman, he rarely scored, focusing instead on unglamorous tasks like clearing the ball with long kicks out of his team's end, doling out hard hits on opponents, and making tactical adjustments on the fly. At five foot ten and 190 pounds, he was small by the standards of Aussie rules football. With a weak smile and a receding hairline, he did not look the part of the team's chief protector. Only his muscular arms and long battered nose betrayed the kind of work he did on the field.

One of the hallmarks of his play, according to a history of the team, "was the ability to lift the Magpies when they were in trouble." During one match against rival Carlton, for instance, Coventry ran full speed into a pack of opposing players and "needlessly" bowled them over, earning a caution from the referee. Later, when a teammate asked Coventry why he'd done something that could have gotten him booked, the captain said he'd done it to "revitalize the side."

McHale had created the "all for one" atmosphere in the club, but Coventry was the one who enforced it. On two occasions, when Collingwood cut the players' wages and his teammates were on the verge of walking out in protest, it was Coventry who talked them out of it. Without him, this team would never have made it to Tier One.

The truth about coaches is that they do matter. It would be foolish to suggest otherwise. As the studies show, some of them do move the needle, even if their impact isn't as dramatic as you might think. Surely there are intangible qualities to organizing a team that statistics can't measure.

But this book is not about teams that win more games than they lose. It's about how teams achieve lasting, freakish greatness. The coaches of history's most triumphant sports teams were not gods. They weren't necessarily big names. Most of them had not seen extraordinary success before and would not find it again. Their personalities and philosophies fell at points all over the spectrum.

In reality, professional athletes are different from our adolescent selves. By the time they make it to the elite ranks, they have developed their own wellsprings of motivation and have spent thousands of hours practicing. They know when their footwork needs tightening or their conditioning has fallen off, and they have a firm grasp on tactics. To bring a team to the top, coaching only goes so far. A team's fate depends on what the players do.

Because Vince Lombardi looms so large in our minds, we have been fitted with blinders. We've failed to notice that the Packers didn't become *the Packers* until Willie Davis showed up. We've forgotten that Davis shared his coach's desperation to win and that it was Davis, in the second half of that 1967 Super Bowl, who converted this mutual urgency into action. The same principle applied to Hungary, Collingwood, and many other Tier One teams, whose coaches—including Auerbach, Blake, Guardiola, Onesta, Popovich, and Stengel—all enjoyed close and sometimes contentious relationships with their captains.

Viewed through this lens, many of the finest teams from Tier Two also seem like products of a charmed partnership. The long winning streak of the New England Patriots corresponds precisely to the fruitful association between the coach, Bill Belichick, and his quarterback and offensive captain, Tom Brady. The same could be said for Phil Jackson and Michael Jordan of the Chicago Bulls, Joe Montana and Bill Walsh of the San Francisco 49ers, and Alex Ferguson and the midfielder Roy Keane of England's Manchester United.

We've also missed another telling fact. Many of the coaches and managers from teams in Tier One, including Blake, Guardiola, McHale, and Wyllie, and also from Tier Two—football's Franz Beckenbauer and Johann Cruyff in particular—had been highly decorated captains before becoming managers. This suggests the lessons these men learned on the field about the power of captaincy might have informed the way they constructed the units they coached.

The public has a tendency to view coaches as singular forces. In reality, my study showed that even the most revered ones came packaged as part of a twin set. The only way to become a Tier One coach is to identify the perfect person to lead the players.

With this, I had eliminated the last of my five alternative explanations. In doing so, I'd only bolstered the theory I started with—that the person who is most responsible for the genesis of an elite team is the captain.

CHAPTER FOUR TAKEAWAYS

- One of the first lessons we learn as children is to respect authority. We imbue our parents, and our teachers, with special powers. We believe it's up to them to mold us. Sports fans project the same idea onto coaches. The conventional wisdom is that the coach, rather than the athletes who compete, is the primary force behind a team's success. On an elite team, therefore, the coach must be a special kind of genius. On the sixteen teams in Tier One, this was simply not the case.

- That said, there are coaches who seem to possess some dollop of magic. They have shown the ability to reframe the game with tactical innovations, to build cultures that are more powerful than any individual, or to move people to do spectacular things through their words, if not the force of their will. In sports, however, these coaches only achieved their greatest success when they had a player serving as their proxy on the field. The other half of this partnership was the captain.

PART II

THE CAPTAINS

The Seven Methods of
Elite Leaders

In the fall of 2010, Bill Russell hadn't laced up a pair of sneakers for forty-one years. He had worked as an NBA coach, a TV broadcaster, an author, and a motivational speaker. A famously reluctant celebrity, he'd let down his guard a bit—agreeing to cut ribbons, sign autographs, and hand out trophies—the sorts of things he would have once disparaged. He'd become basketball's éminence grise.

To me, however, Russell was still frozen in the 1960s—the central figure in an unsolved mystery. Even as I built a case for the primacy of captains, I did not understand how someone who actively defied the conventions of his sport and projected so much contempt in public could have been a superior leader.

From the outset of my research, one thing I noticed about Russell and the other Tier One captains was that when their careers ended, people always said some version of the same thing: There would never be anyone else like them. Since they did not conform to our notional models of leadership, their achievements were viewed as laboratory accidents that could never be repeated. If that were true, I wondered, what could I possibly learn by studying them?

That fall, Russell gave an interview to the *New York Times*. The occasion was the happy news that President Barack Obama had tapped him to receive the Presidential Medal of Freedom, the highest civilian honor bestowed by the U.S. government, in recognition for both his athletic achievements and his lifelong support for human rights. In a throwaway line, the article addressed one of the most baffling incidents from Russell's past—his refusal to participate in his 1975 Hall of Fame induction ceremony. The Hall of Fame, Russell explained, is an institution that honors individuals. Russell had declined, he said, because he believed his basketball career should be remembered as a symbol of *team* play.

So far as I could tell, this was not something Russell had ever said before. It wasn't something I'd heard from any elite athlete—especially in America. Here in the birthplace of Hollywood, the land of the rugged individualist, a place where people still sleep on freezing pavement to buy Michael Jordan's shoes, most superstars go out of their way to stand out.

All at once, the puzzle pieces of Russell's confounding personality started fitting together. He didn't score many points because his team didn't need him to. He didn't care about statistics or personal accolades and didn't mind letting teammates take the credit. "It was never about contracts or money," he once said. "I never paid attention to MVP awards or how many endorsements I had lined up. Only how many titles we won." Russell devoted himself instead to defense, and to doing whatever grunt work fell through the cracks.

It occurred to me that Russell's radically defensive, team-oriented approach to basketball and his prickly, credit-deflecting posture off the court were two sides of the same coin. His resistance to basketball awards was a rejection of the universal instinct to separate individuals from the collective. His brand of leadership had nothing to do with the outside world or how he was perceived. It was entirely focused on the internal dynamics of his team. So long as the Celtics won titles, he didn't mind if nobody noticed his contributions.

Russell's teammates didn't think he was complicated and aloof; to them he was more like an action hero: simple, consistent, pure of heart. "Russell was the winningest person I've ever been around," his teammate Tom Heinsohn said. "He had helped us out so many times, and we believed in him so much, there was a communion of spirit and a belief in each other."

Bill Russell wasn't a defective person, as some suspected him to be. I realized that his style of captaincy was just so unusual that nobody recognized it. The public never connected his atypical leadership to the atypical success of the Celtics. These were viewed as separate, unrelated things.

It's true that these Tier One captains, in the contexts of their various sports, *looked* like one-offs. They were certainly nothing like the flawless leaders of our imaginations. As I compiled their biographies, however, I noticed something else: how closely they resembled one another. To a spooky degree, their behaviors and beliefs, and the way they approached their work, lined up. The impulsive, reckless, and putatively self-defeating behavior they exhibited was, in fact, calculated to fortify the team. Their strange and seemingly disqualifying personal traits were not damaging but actually made their teammates more effective on the field. These men and women were not aberrations after all. They were members of a forgotten tribe.

In all, there were seven things they shared in common.

THE SEVEN TRAITS OF ELITE CAPTAINS

1. Extreme doggedness and focus in competition.
2. Aggressive play that tests the limits of the rules.
3. A willingness to do thankless jobs in the shadows.
4. A low-key, practical, and democratic communication style.
5. Motivates others with passionate nonverbal displays.
6. Strong convictions and the courage to stand apart.
7. Ironclad emotional control.

In Part II of *The Captain Class,* I will explore each of these seven leadership characteristics by looking at specific examples of how these men and women approached competition; how they challenged, inspired, and communicated with their teammates; and how they exercised control over their own emotions. Along the way, I'll examine some of the scientific research that helps to explain why these traits might have produced first-tier results.

FIVE

They Just Keep Coming

Doggedness and Its Ancillary Benefits

BARCELONA, 2000

Minutes before kickoff, the riot police in their menacing black helmets took positions at all four corners of the pitch, batons at the ready. Standing behind the touchline in his white jersey, Luís Figo reached for the leather band on his neck that held a horn-shaped cornicello—an amulet worn to ward off the curse of the evil eye. As he jogged onto the pitch before kickoff, he bowed his head and gave it a kiss.

It was a damp chilly night in late October and a hundred thousand people had packed Barcelona's Camp Nou, Europe's largest stadium, to see Figo play. It is safe to say that the vast majority of them were eyeing him with maximum evil. As he came into view, the fans let go a terrifying full-throated racket, blowing whistles, screaming, *"Whore!"* and waving bedsheet banners on which they had scrawled words like "traitor," "liar," and "Judas."

As Figo joined his teammates, he playfully stuck his fingers in his ears, then, with a weary half smile, waved both palms high above his head, hoping this small acknowledgment would be enough. It wasn't.

As the noise intensified, a hail of objects flew over the heads of the riot cops—coins, bottles, phones, even a bicycle chain. The corners of Figo's mouth fell. Every time he glanced at the stands, fans flipped him the middle finger. Figo had not understood the gravity of what he had done. He started to look worried.

Three months earlier, in the summer of 2000, Figo, a tall, dark-haired, and impossibly handsome winger who was considered one of the world's best players, had made a wrenching decision. Barcelona had hit a rough patch and decided to change managers. After five seasons playing at Camp Nou, Figo had developed a wandering eye. He told his agent to start testing the transfer market.

The era of the mercenary international football superstar, or Galáctico, had not yet begun. Players of Figo's caliber were supposed to declare their allegiance to one elite team and stay put; they were not supposed to bounce around. Though Barcelona would profit wildly from the explosive growth of the football business in the coming years, its proud fans still viewed the game as a tribal rite. A player's ties to the club were ties for life. Though Figo was born in Portugal and had started his career in Lisbon, he had come to be seen as a compatriot. The fans believed that Barcelona had captured his soul.

When Figo announced he was leaving, it had been a sobering blow. But the details of his move made it unthinkably worse. Figo hadn't left to seek his fortune in England or Italy. He'd struck a sixty-million-dollar transfer deal to join Real Madrid.

In 1939, when the reign of the fascist Spanish dictator Francisco Franco began, the fans of Barcelona, in the independent-minded and politically radical region of Catalonia, had come to view Real Madrid as the morally bankrupt club of the ruling Madrileños, while theirs was the righteous team of the resistance. This political divide was a prism that distorted everything in Spain into a pretext for sectarian warfare. People who were born into one of these two spheres of influence never traded sides. The hatred could be astonishing to outsiders, and the frequent meetings between these two football clubs, part of an ongoing series known as El Clásico, were as hotly contested as any rivalry in sports. A handful of players had competed for both teams, but none had been superstars, let alone a future winner of the coveted Ballon d'Or. Figo was both. This match on this misty October night marked his first trip to Barcelona in the enemy uniform.

Since there was no precedent for this, nobody knew what to expect. For a week before the match, the Spanish press had stoked the fire. *Sport* published a poster in which Figo's face was superimposed on a banknote with the word *"pesetero"* (money-grubber) scrawled above it. Not only was the stadium packed, but ten million Spaniards, roughly a quarter of the population, watched on television. It wasn't inconceivable that Barcelona's fans, should they lose, would set the stadium on fire.

Even under normal circumstances, Figo was a difficult opponent to plan against. Tall, strong, and exceptionally fast, with impeccable instincts for the ball, his attacks on goal were almost unstoppable. Barcelona's new manager, Lorenzo Serra Ferrer, knew that Figo would get his chances, but a goal, no matter the outcome, would be a humiliation.

In the days before the match, Ferrer had decided to assign a "man marker" to Figo—a rare tactical move in football. This player would be asked to fasten himself to Figo—blocking him, tackling him, and trying to steal the ball at every opportunity, even if it meant playing out of position. But Ferrer had a problem: He didn't think any of the team's regular defenders could do the job under this sort of pressure. For days, Ferrer and his coaching staff deliberated. The press speculated that he would choose the Dutch right back Michael Reiziger, who was the team's fastest and most seasoned right-side defender. But on the morning of the match, when Ferrer announced his decision, it wasn't Reiziger. He'd chosen an untested twenty-three-year-old named Carles Puyol.

Barcelona fans didn't know much about Puyol. It was just his second season with the senior club and he wasn't an established defender, let alone a star. His most identifiable feature wasn't his play but his hair—a thick mane that touched his shoulders and flopped around on the field. The combination of his curly locks, pronounced brow, and bulbous facial features made Puyol stand out among his handsome, neatly trimmed teammates. He looked like a member of a prehistoric hunting party.

One year earlier, with Puyol's path to the starting lineup blocked, Barcelona's then-manager, Louis van Gaal, had cut a deal to sell him to lowly Málaga. The only reason Puyol didn't go was that he'd refused to leave. The club had let him stay, but still wasn't sure what to do with him. After playing mostly on the left side of the defense, he'd been slotted in at center back, mainly because nobody thought he had the speed to play wide. Even so, he was short for that position and not particularly clever with the ball. To shut down Figo, this country boy from the Catalan mountains would have to switch to the right side of the defense, where he'd be forced to do everything backward.

Whether or not Puyol had a future at Barcelona, Ferrer knew that he had quick reflexes. The season before, he had faced Figo in training and, while overmatched, hadn't been completely embarrassed. And there was one advantage Puyol had in spades—he cared desperately. Puyol grew up in a tiny town called La Pobla de Segur idolizing Barcelona's sports teams and used to burst into tears when the football team lost. Perhaps more than anyone on the club, Puyol had taken Figo's betrayal personally. At the very least, the job of defending Barcelona's honor would fall to a patriot.

As the players took the field, the atmosphere at Camp Nou had never been so tense. Puyol, his teammates, and everyone else in the stadium knew that this was one of those moments when a future is either made or broken.

From the opening whistle, Carles Puyol chased Luís Figo forward and back, from the right wing to the left, all but tethering himself to the tall Portuguese. "I followed him everywhere," Puyol said. "Where he went, I went."

From the first Real Madrid attack of the match, Puyol began testing the limits of the referee's tolerance. He'd plant a hand on Figo's shoulder for a split second or slip one under his arm to throw off his balance. Each time, Figo angrily smacked his hand away—prompting Puyol to argue for a foul. In one early encounter, after Figo received the ball, Puyol came up behind him, grabbed his side, and spun him a hundred and eighty degrees, killing his momentum. The referee let it go. At twenty-six minutes, Barcelona scored, going up 1–0. Ferrer's "Puyol plan" was starting to work.

In the final ten minutes of the first half, Figo received the ball in Barcelona's end, but Puyol knocked it away with a perfect tackle. Then, when Puyol realized Figo might be able to recover the ball, he sprung back to his feet and belly flopped onto the turf, directly in front of Figo's spikes, to block his path. After Puyol caught up to another ball aimed for Figo and headed it away, Figo flashed a look of disgust.

Just before the fortieth minute, the battle reached a decisive moment. After a Barcelona corner kick, Real Madrid's defense cleared the ball to a void on the left wing near midfield, where Figo was lying in wait. Sensing that his opportunity had arrived, Figo took off after the ball in a full sprint, several steps ahead of Puyol. Given Figo's speed, there was no question he would arrive at the ball first and try to charge upfield toward Barcelona's lightly defended goal. It was the sort of play he'd converted a hundred times.

Puyol, breathing heavily, long strands of sweaty hair matted to his face, knew that he would never catch Figo in the open field. Given Figo's head start, he would not be able to make a clean tackle, either. His only hope was to wait until Figo paused to collect the ball at his feet and, in that fraction of a second, take him down. At best, Puyol would probably earn a yellow card—a caution that would allow him to continue playing. At worst, if he raked Figo, or tackled him too violently, he might be given a red card and ejected. As Figo reached the ball, Puyol left his feet. The fans held their breath.

Figo's plan was to tap the ball forward and then launch himself into the air to hurdle Puyol's tackle. But Puyol's aim was dead-on. He caught Figo's right boot squarely, sending his leg shooting out sideways. Figo catapulted over Puyol's sliding body, landed on the turf on his left shoulder, and slid helplessly over the dead-ball line, his momentum carrying him to the barrier. Garbage pelted the pitch as the fans roared in delight. Figo stood up dejectedly, scoured by the catcalls from the stands, letting the noise wash over him.

Puyol didn't stop to gloat over his handiwork. He popped up and waved his teammates over for the throw-in, his face blank and unemotional. As the referee reached for his black book and his cards, Barcelona's fate, and possibly Puyol's, hung in the balance. Yellow meant salvation, red doom. It was yellow.

A minute later, Real Madrid won a free kick at Barcelona's end and designated Figo to take it. Figo unleashed a screamer, but as it reached the wall of Barcelona players, one of them leaped up and blocked it with his head. Puyol. In less time than it takes to warm up a bowl of oatmeal, the hirsute caveman from Pobla de Segur had become a household name.

In the second half, Figo's frustration spilled over. At sixty-five minutes, Puyol got between Figo and the ball and backed into Figo until he toppled over. After righting himself, Figo lashed out, delivering a forearm to the back of Puyol's head. This earned Figo a yellow card and prompted some of the night's most thunderous applause. Barcelona scored its second goal at seventy-nine minutes, and just then the sky opened. Given the wet conditions, the match was effectively over. Minutes before the whistle, Figo, soaked and downcast, chased a ball into the corner. The fans rose up as one, screaming, pointing, and pelting the pitch with debris. As two water balloons landed near his feet, Figo stopped and backed away. The defeat was complete.

The final score would read Barcelona 2, Real Madrid 0. But the true meaning of the outcome could not be captured on a scoreboard. Judas had been neutralized.

Speaking to reporters after the match, Ferrer said that Puyol had played "at an outstanding level." One Barcelona newspaper called Puyol "implacable and impeccable" while *Marca* gave him credit for being "the eternal shadow of Figo, turning him into a bit-part player."

In a postmatch interview, Puyol further endeared himself to the fans by playing down his role. He'd been given a job and had done it; there was no reason to award him a gold star. "I had only one purpose and that was to stop him," Puyol said.

Looking back, Puyol acknowledged that the day he marked Figo was the day he became known in Barcelona. But that wasn't what mattered to him. "We won," he said, "which is most important."

On that glorious night in 2000, Barcelona's fans had no idea what was ahead. They could not have imagined what this team was about to accomplish, or what Carles Puyol was about to become.

One of the highest compliments coaches can pay athletes is to describe them as relentless, to say that they just keep coming. Not every star has this quality. Some have a tendency to take games off; others shrink in critical situations. Among the Tier One captains, however, this trait was displayed over and over.

Bill Russell's Coleman Play, Buck Shelford's performance at Nantes, and Puyol's destruction of Luís Figo are prominent examples, but there are many others. After leaving the ice during a 1952 playoff game with a concussion and a bloody gash on his forehead, for instance, Maurice Richard of the Montreal Canadiens returned in the third period, his leaking wound wrapped in bandages, to skate past three Boston defenders and score the game-winning goal.

Other Tier One captains were famous for their preparation and conditioning. During one stretch of her career, Carla Overbeck, the U.S. women's football team's fittest athlete, played 3,547 consecutive minutes in sixty-three straight matches without leaving the field, while Cuba's Mireya Luis spent so much time practicing her leaping that her kneecap cracked open, forming an angle of separation doctors measured at thirty degrees. Immediately after the Pittsburgh Steelers selected Jack Lambert in the NFL draft, he began showing up at the team's practice facility to study film—something his coaches had never seen a rookie do. Lambert developed such an intricate knowledge of the defense that his coaches installed him at middle linebacker, where he would have to call the defensive plays and contend with much larger interior linemen. By the end of the season, said fellow linebacker Jack Ham, "I forgot the fact that he was a rookie."

If any Tier One team leader best embodies the virtue of doggedness, it is Lawrence Peter Berra, the catcher for the New York Yankees.

In 1941, the teenage Berra—better known as Yogi—had attended a crowded tryout for Branch Rickey, the general manager of the St. Louis Cardinals. Afterward, another local kid, Joe Garagiola, was offered a contract with a five-hundred-dollar signing bonus, while Berra was offered half as much, with no bonus. "I don't think you'll ever be a big-league ballplayer," Rickey told him.

It might have ended there, but Berra kept practicing—every day, sunup to sundown—in the sandlots near his home. And several months later, when the Yankees offered him a contract, he held out for the same five-hundred-dollar bonus Garagiola had received.

When Berra arrived in the major leagues in 1946, his future was still far from certain. Though just five foot seven, Berra was so thick and barrel-chested that he weighed almost 190 pounds and wore a size-seventeen shirt collar. He had jug ears, prominent facial features, and a heavy brow. He appeared woefully out of place on the Yankees, a team that had become the most glamorous brand in American sports thanks to the exploits of Babe Ruth and a roster of matinée idols including Lou Gehrig, Tommy Henrich, Charlie Keller, and Joe DiMaggio. In the stands, the papers, and even his own dugout, he was greeted by eye rolls, crude jokes, and monkey gestures. The sportswriter Jimmy Cannon once likened him to a "bull penguin." Eventually the Yankees' front office—concerned that Berra might be hazed out of baseball—told the players to leave him alone.

Berra could certainly handle a bat. In his first trip to the plate for the Yankees, he hit a home run, and collected eight hits over seven games. But even though he had a proficient swing, his batting style added to his clownish image. Most Yankee hitters tried to be disciplined—to wait for a pitch in their power zone—but Berra batted like he was late for the train. When he fell behind in the count, he would swing at almost any pitch so long as it was a broom's length from the strike zone. Teammates laughed as he sometimes left his feet to hit a ball or swung at a pitch that bounced in the dirt.

Though people mocked his swing-at-everything approach, Berra hit .280 in his first full season in New York, posting a near-elite .464 slugging percentage and striking out only twelve times. Over his entire career, in fact, Berra struck out in only 4.9 percent of his plate appearances, about half the typical rate of his era, and 79 percent less often than the average major leaguer in 2015. In fact, Berra would become one of only ten players in baseball history to hit thirty or more home runs in a season with fewer than thirty strikeouts.

There was one practical threat to Berra's future with the team, however: He was not a very good catcher. During his first season, Berra's decision-making and technique behind the plate were so sloppy that he was benched. "As a catcher," one reporter wrote, "Berra is a hindrance to the pitchers."

In his second season, he played in only about half the team's games, often in the outfield. The Yankees pitchers preferred to work with his alternate and, when Berra did play, wouldn't allow him to call pitches. Although the Yankees made it to the World Series in 1947, the Brooklyn Dodgers humiliated Berra by running at every opportunity, stealing five bases on him in just three games and forcing the Yankees to move him to the outfield.

During spring training in 1949, the Yankees' manager, Casey Stengel, decided to send Berra to school. He brought in Bill Dickey—a legendary former catcher and Hall of Famer—to teach Berra how to play the position. The two spent hours together as Dickey tweaked everything from Berra's positioning and signal calling to his throwing mechanics. As Dickey pounded him relentlessly with balls from close range, Berra worked until he was caked in dirt and sweat.

At the same time, three of the Yankees' veteran pitchers—Eddie Lopat, Vic Raschi, and Allie Reynolds—decided that if they wanted to win, they, too, would have to help make Berra a better catcher. The pitchers, who had become close friends off the field, even gave this mentorship a nickname: the Project. Lopat, Raschi, and Reynolds shared with Berra everything they'd learned in their long careers in the game. Berra was so committed to learning that he and his wife, Carmen, moved to the New Jersey neighborhood where the pitchers lived so the conversations could continue over dinner.

Berra's improvement was so dramatic that by 1950, he wasn't just considered a passable catcher but an outstanding one—quick, agile, and adept at blocking balls. In that season he threw out 56 percent of attempted base stealers (the league average was 49 percent), and by 1958 he would play eighty-eight games without making an error. Berra also became one of the most durable catchers, leading the American League eight times in games caught and manning the plate in both games of a doubleheader 117 times (a feat some modern catchers never attempt once). In 1962, when the Yankees played a marathon game against the Detroit Tigers, Berra—who was thirty-seven at the time—stayed behind the plate for all twenty-two innings.

From his shaky beginnings, Berra went on to win fourteen league titles with the Yankees in nineteen seasons and ten World Series titles overall, the most for any player. He set a record for home runs by a catcher and won three MVP awards. He was elected to the Hall of Fame in 1972.

It should come as no surprise that Berra, or any athlete who makes it to the highest levels of sports, was unusually determined. But the brand of perseverance Berra, Shelford, Puyol, and the other Tier One captains showed is peculiar, even among the elite.

The main point of difference is that their natural ability seemed to bear no relation to the size of their accomplishments. Something enabled them to set aside their limitations and tune out the skepticism from their critics. But what was it? What allows some people to press on until they achieve mastery?

Over the past four decades, the psychologist Carol Dweck has become one of the world's preeminent experts on the subject of how people, especially children, cope with challenge and difficulty. She has devoted her work to studying the mindsets with which people approach challenges and how those mindsets can be improved.

In one of her earliest studies, conducted at the University of Illinois in the 1970s, Dweck and her research team put sixty kids, all about ten years old, through a test. First they were given eight relatively easy pattern-recognition problems. As they worked, Dweck asked them to talk about what they were thinking and feeling. After they finished, Dweck gave them four "failure" problems that she knew were too difficult for children their age. As she monitored their strategies, she again asked them to share their thoughts as they worked.

While solving the easy problems, most of the children spoke positively about the test and their performances. They were uniformly happy and confident. But when faced with the harder "failure" problems, most of the children's moods turned dark. They said they didn't like the test, or felt bored or anxious. When asked why they thought they weren't doing well, they didn't attribute their struggles to the difficulty of the problems—they blamed their own lack of ability. Faced with adversity, their problem-solving skills deteriorated, too. They simply stopped trying.

A smaller group of kids had a different reaction, however. Faced with the failure problems, they kept working. They didn't think they were dumb; they believed they just hadn't found the right strategy yet. A few reacted in a shockingly positive way. One boy pulled up his chair, rubbed his hands together, and said, "I love a challenge." These persistent kids, as a group, hadn't been any better at solving the easy problems. In fact, their strategies suggested that they were, on average, slightly less skillful. But when the going got tough, they didn't get down on themselves. They viewed the unsolved problems as puzzles to be mastered through effort.

The results were stark: Eighty percent of these "mastery-oriented" children maintained the same level of problem-solving ability on the tough questions as they had on the easy ones. And a smaller portion, about 25 percent, actually improved their strategy levels. These children weren't any smarter, but they outperformed the children who felt helpless. Dweck went on to show that the two types of children had different goals. The helpless kids were preoccupied with their performance. They wanted to look smart even if it meant avoiding the difficult problems. The mastery-oriented children were motivated by the desire to learn. They saw failure as a chance to improve their skills.

In 2011, a group of five researchers at Michigan State University tested Dweck's conclusions by monitoring the brain activity of college students as they realized they'd made an error on a problem. Just as Dweck's research suggested, the electrical activity in the brains of the helpless, fixed-mindset students essentially shut down when faced with failure. They avoided looking for newer, better strategies. The brains of the mastery-oriented students, however, crackled with activity as they considered new approaches.

What Dweck ultimately discovered is that these children had different ideas about the nature of ability. The helpless kids viewed their skills as fixed from birth. They believed they were either smart enough to do something, or they weren't, and it was up to others to render a verdict. The mastery kids had a more malleable sense of their intelligence: They believed it could be grown through effort. "They don't necessarily think everyone's the same or anyone can be Einstein," Dweck said, "but they believe everyone can get smarter if they work at it."

While common sense suggests that a person's natural ability should inspire self-confidence, Dweck's research showed that in most cases, ability has very little to do with it. A person's reaction to failure is everything.

When applied to sports, Dweck's research offers a possible explanation for how these Tier One captains—though not the most talented athletes—managed to overcome their weaknesses to exceed the accomplishments of those with greater gifts. I suspect they were not only "mastery-oriented" people, they were likely members of that rarefied

25 percent whose skills and strategies improved in the face of difficulty. Because they viewed their abilities as malleable, and because they were more motivated by learning and improving than by appearing to be capable, they never lost faith. While some athletes might have reacted to a proposed transfer to Málaga, a blown tryout in St. Louis, or a poor performance in the World Series by concluding that they weren't good enough, these captains only grew more determined.

Dweck's research did leave one question unanswered, however. It's one thing for individuals with a "mastery" mindset to achieve outstanding individual results. But when it comes to the leader of a team, this attribute will only make a difference if it rubs off on the other players. The next question, then, is this: Can a captain's doggedness make an entire team play better?

Over the years, Buck Shelford has grown weary of telling the Story. In interviews, he waves off the delicately phrased questions about his hideous injuries at Nantes. "That was a pretty tough game. I had a few injuries in that game," he once said. "It's a man's sport. You've got to be tough to play the sport. If you're not tough, you go and play something else."

What's often overlooked about the Battle of Nantes is what happened immediately afterward. At the 1987 World Cup, six months after losing to France, New Zealand outscored Italy, Fiji, and Argentina in the tournament's group stage by a hard-to-fathom margin of 156 points. It held Scotland to three points in the quarterfinals, then bludgeoned Wales 49–6 to reach the final, where it met up once again with its old adversaries, the French. This time, New Zealand sent them home, 22–9.

After the World Cup, Shelford's coaches named him captain. And from that moment until he was controversially dropped from the team in 1990, the All Blacks never tasted defeat. Not once. It's as if the mastery mindset Shelford displayed at Nantes had flipped a switch that made the whole team unbeatable. But how could this be?

On the field, Shelford's focus never weakened. When he wasn't exhorting teammates in the dressing room to play harder, he was driving them to the point of collapse on the field. During a 1989 test match against France, New Zealand's Murray Pierce got a nasty cut on his cheek that clearly required stitches. As he walked toward the bench, the broadcast audio picked up Shelford's voice calling from behind, ordering Pierce back to the field. "No medical attention for these men," the commentator said. "You'll take the pain when you're with the All Blacks." Asked after the match about Pierce and other injured teammates, Shelford said, "I think they'll survive through the night."

On another occasion, after his team beat Wales by fifty points, Shelford told a reporter, "I think we could pick it up a little bit." When the reporter reminded him that the team had scored ten tries, Shelford shrugged. "Yeah, that's a good tally," he said. "But you never know, it could've been thirteen or fourteen."

The same unceasing drive was something displayed by Russell, Puyol, Berra, Richard, and every other captain in Tier One. Early struggles culminated in a defining moment, a breakthrough that left no doubt about their desire to win at any cost. And in each case, after they had established this fact, their teams began to turn the corner. The pattern was so consistent that it suggested their doggedness might, in fact, have been contagious.

One of the first scientists to explore the dynamics of group effort was a French agricultural engineer named Maximilien Ringelmann. In 1913, Ringelmann conducted an experiment in which he asked his students to pull on a rope, both individually and in groups, while he measured the force they exerted. The conventional view was that people in a group would have more power collectively than they did alone—in other words, adding people to the pulling group would have a multiplying effect on the force.

But the results showed something surprising. While the force applied did grow with every new person added, the average force applied by each person fell. Rather than amplifying the power of individuals, the act of pulling as a team caused each person to pull less hard than they had when pulling alone. Later researchers coined a name for this phenomenon. They called it social loafing.

Since then, the experiment was rediscovered and psychologists set out to replicate it. In 1979, a group of scientists at Ohio State University asked their test subjects to shout as loud as they could and recorded the decibel levels they produced. Next the subjects were put in groups and asked to repeat the shouting. The results mirrored Ringelmann's: Each person's group shouts were up to 20 percent less loud than their individual ones. Time and again, researchers tried some variation of Ringelmann's rope test and got the same results. It was a fact of human nature. The less identifiable one person's effort is, the less effort they put in.

To add a twist to the Ohio State experiment, researchers at Fordham University decided to look at whether social loafing could be overcome. They wanted to see whether one person giving a maximum effort could incite others to improve their performances. The scientists grouped their shouters in pairs and, before they began shouting, told them that their partner was a high-effort performer. In these situations, something interesting happened. The pairs screamed just as hard together as they had alone. The knowledge that a teammate was giving it their all was enough to prompt people to give more themselves.

This experiment demonstrated that high effort, or just the perception of high effort, is transferrable. In other words, the Ringelmann effect can be counteracted. The antidote is the knowledge that someone else in the group is leaving nothing in reserve.

The Fordham study seemed to confirm my suspicions about Tier One captains: Their displays of tenacity could have positively influenced the way their teams performed.

Carles Puyol slipped through the front door of a modest hotel in downtown Barcelona on a sunny February morning in 2015. There was no publicist or entourage in tow—just a man in designer denim carrying his phone and a set of car keys. Puyol, about to turn thirty-seven, had recently retired from football. He told me he'd cut back from the seven or eight daily cups of coffee he used to drink in his playing years, but his bouncing legs suggested otherwise. "Let's go, let's go," he said, motioning to my recorder.

Puyol's tiny hometown in the Catalan mountains hadn't had a youth football program, so he'd played an indoor version of the game called *fútbol sala*. The older boys would only let him play if he agreed to be the goalkeeper—a job he performed by hurling his body onto the floor with such abandon that he developed back problems. It wasn't until age fifteen that he joined a real football team. Puyol's parents had not seen a champion in their son. They urged him to focus on his studies, not football. But after two years of organized play, he'd impressed his coaches enough that they called Barcelona to see if the junior team would give him a tryout at the relatively advanced age of seventeen. Four years later he would make his debut with the senior club.

Puyol's career took off after the Figo game—as not just a player but a leader. He quickly became a fixture in the center of Barcelona's defense and, just four years later, was elected captain. Puyol also earned a spot on the Spanish national team in 2000 and later became that team's vice captain. At the same time Barcelona was dominating club football, the Spanish team, stocked with Barcelona players, dominated the world—winning two European titles and the 2010 World Cup, earning it a place in Tier Two.

Through it all, Puyol's play continued to be the picture of slobbering effort. While his teammates played a beautiful, rhythmic, and finely calibrated brand of football that hypnotized opponents, Puyol flung himself around the pitch, cleaning up their messes with grunting effort. He would use his body to block screamers—once breaking his cheekbone and forcing him to wear a prosthetic mask on the field. Puyol also became famous for his conditioning—he was the last to leave training, and when he did he would make his way to Pilates or yoga. He played more minutes over three seasons early in his career than anyone but the goalkeeper.

During matches, Puyol's relentlessness was often demonstrated by his intimate relationship with the medical staple gun. During a match in April 2012, in the middle of a tight race for the league title, the manager of the opposing team alerted the referee to Puyol's forehead, which had been cut in a collision with another player.

Puyol dashed over to the trainers with an expression of cartoonish urgency. Unless Barcelona wanted to substitute Puyol (which it didn't), the only option was to staple the wound right there on the sidelines. Puyol was fine with that. His only concern was that the process went quickly. As the trainer examined the cut, Puyol impatiently grabbed at the staple gun as if he wanted to employ it himself. When the trainer snapped the staple in place, Puyol didn't flinch. He ran to the touchline, manically waving his hands at the referee. Minutes later, with Puyol back in place, Barcelona's Lionel Messi scored the winning goal. In an interview, Puyol described the incident as "nothing."

As I showed him a video of the stapling event, Puyol said he hoped he'd apologized to the doctors. "I'm a disaster for them because I rush them," he said. But because he played defense on a team that wasn't very defensive, he hated to miss even a few seconds. "If the other team scored a goal, I would have felt horrible."

Asked why he'd had so many serious injuries in his career, Puyol blamed his playing style and general absence of fear. Even after rehabilitating himself, he added, "I would play the same way as before, with the same intensity. I have always felt I had to give everything. That's how I've always been. It's my way of respecting football and respecting my teammates."

When asked about Puyol, teammates always tell a variation of the same story. During some blowout match against a lousy team, while they were going through the motions, Puyol was running around as if it were the Champions League final. In one version, he sprinted to collect the ball for a throw-in during the waning minutes of an 8–0 win. In another he screamed at a teammate to focus despite a four-goal lead with three minutes to play. In one famous incident during a match against lowly Rayo Vallecano, Puyol ran over to break up a celebration dance by two teammates. Never mind that Barcelona had just scored its fifth unanswered goal. He thought it was disrespectful and didn't want to give the other team any extra motivation. The longer he played, and the more Barcelona won, the more acutely Puyol felt the need to keep the team focused, to keep pulling hard on the rope. "Winning is difficult," he said, "but to win again is much more difficult—because egos appear. Most people who win once have already achieved what they wanted and don't have any more ambition."

In the first four seasons of Puyol's captaincy, Barcelona became the world's most dominant team, winning two Spanish titles and a Champions League trophy. But its pinnacle came during a five-season span, from 2008 to 2013, in which it won or drew 92 percent of its league matches, adding four La Liga championships, two Champions League titles, and a host of other trophies while recording the highest-ever club-team Elo rating. Speaking at Puyol's retirement ceremony, the team president, Josep Maria Bartomeu, called Puyol the best captain in Barcelona's history.

It struck me that Puyol's palpable focus and determination on the pitch might have had the same effect on his teammates that the high-effort shouters had in that Fordham laboratory. As our interview wound down, I asked him whether he thought his effort was contagious. "I think that when you see a teammate go to the maximum and give everything—I don't mean myself, but anyone—what you cannot do is to just stand there and let another team's player pass right by you," he said. "If everybody is giving one hundred percent and you are only giving eighty percent, it shows. So I think it makes everyone go to one hundred percent."

Carles Puyol's uncommon determination to persevere, combined with a willingness to give everything all of the time, was a hallmark of Tier One captains, also typified by Russell, Shelford, and Berra. But it was not the only thing about the way they competed that stood out. At times, as we'll see in the next chapter, their desire to play to the limit sometimes spun out of control.

CHAPTER FIVE TAKEAWAYS

- One of the most confounding laws of human nature is that when faced with a task, people will work harder alone than they will when joined in the effort—a phenomenon known as social loafing. There is, however, an antidote. It's the presence of one person who leaves no doubt that they are giving it everything they've got.

- The captains of the greatest teams in sports history had an unflagging commitment to playing at their maximum capability. Although they were rarely superior athletes, they demonstrated an extreme level of doggedness in competition, and in their conditioning and preparation. They also put pressure on their teammates to continue competing even when victory was all but assured.

SIX

Intelligent Fouls

Playing to the Edge of the Rules

ATLANTA, 1996

Early one July morning, before anyone else was up, Mireya Luis put on her sweats, crept out of her dormitory room at the Olympic Village in Atlanta, and made her way to the phone banks to do something her teammates could never know about.

Nine hundred miles away, in a modest farmhouse on the outskirts of the Cuban city of Camagüey, an old woman named Catalina picked up the receiver. "Hello?"

At first there was silence on the line.

Then came sniffles, then heaving sobs.

Mireya was the youngest of Catalina's nine children. Tall and slim with wide-set almond-shaped eyes and a broad smile with a gap between her front teeth, she had always drawn people in with her natural warmth. Yet underneath she was tenacious. When Mireya was a child, Catalina watched her spend hours practicing her leaps in the yard by trying to pluck fruit from the mango trees. Catalina had reluctantly allowed her daughter to leave home to join the national volleyball team in Havana at sixteen and backed her decision to stay, even when her coaches told her she was too small to be an attacker. Now, at twenty-nine, her daughter, sobbing on the other end of the line, was a national celebrity. The team she captained had won a World Championship, an Olympic gold medal in Barcelona in 1992, and three consecutive World Cups.

The Cubans were not the tallest, most athletic, or most technically skilled volleyball team. But they did have one giant advantage—the way they hit the ball. In training, the Cubans would raise the nets by eight inches to match the height of the men's game. They strengthened their legs by leaping one hundred times onto a tall box while holding weights. "They hit harder than some men's teams," noted Mike Hebert, a retired American volleyball coach who saw them practice. "Every attempt appeared to have the spiker's reputation riding on it."

Luis, at five foot nine, was several inches shorter than a typical attacker and not considered the team's all-around best player. Her raw athleticism, however, made her the unquestioned star of the show. A teammate, Marlenis Costa, said Luis once jumped so high that her toes brushed the bottom of the net. "She got scared because she thought her feet might get tangled on the way down," Costa remembered. "Her leaping ability was supernatural."

To opponents, Cuba's swagger was both off-putting and profoundly intimidating. In prematch warm-ups, the players would pound the ball at full speed, forcing their opponents on the other side of the net to duck for cover. "We are respected," their coach, Eugenio George Lafita, once said, "but not always well liked." Inside Cuba, they were adored. Since the players were exclusively dark-skinned, their success had become a point of pride for all Afro-Cubans, and even more so for women. Smiling, close-knit, and self-possessed, they became known as Las Espectaculares Morenas del Caribe, "the Spectacular Black Girls of the Caribbean."

On the July morning in Atlanta when Luis called her mother, however, her team was feeling homesick and demoralized. The Cubans had spent many grueling months in Japan training against teams in that country's top-notch professional league, and the Castro regime had decided not to allow them to play professionally abroad after the Olympics, as some Cuban male athletes had been allowed to do.

In Atlanta, ever since they discovered that the Olympic beauty salon had hairdressers who specialized in black women's hair, they had put more effort and enthusiasm into getting daily treatments than preparing for matches. The Cubans had sleepwalked through a pair of lopsided losses to Russia and Brazil during group play and had barely squeaked into the tournament's knockout round. Luis worried that the day had finally come when the players had lost their will. She understood what was at stake and that it was her job, as captain, to do something.

Yet Luis had been keeping a secret from her teammates. Her knee, which had been surgically repaired several years earlier, was badly swollen. She wasn't sure how effective she could be on the court. She had even considered retiring after the Games.

After Luis finished pouring her pent-up emotions into the receiver, there was no response. For a second, she thought her mother might be confused about who was calling.

"Mommy, it's me. . . ."

"Me who?" Catalina replied coolly.

Mireya wondered if something was wrong. "Mom," she said. "Is everything okay?"

"The people of Cuba are doing very badly!"

"Yes, I know, but . . ."

"Listen here," Catalina said. "I didn't give birth to a daughter so she could go and cry in front of her adversary. And don't go to the hairdresser anymore, because I saw you changed your hair. You went to Atlanta to play volleyball, not to get your hair groomed!" Catalina gave her daughter some tactical advice for the next match, and then she hung up.

Luis dabbed at her eyes and tried to calm herself. She didn't want her teammates to see her upset. Her mother's message couldn't have been clearer. She hadn't raised a quitter. Luis was part of something larger than she was and had a responsibility to control her emotions. There was no choice but to find a way to pull her team through this.

In their next match the Cubans found their groove, brushing aside an inferior U.S. team to advance to the semifinals—but they knew better than to celebrate. Their semifinal opponent, Brazil, led by the tenacious veteran Ana Moser and the fiery attacker Marcia Fu Cunha, was the only team they genuinely feared.

The Brazilians were taller and stronger than the Cubans—and nearly their equals in confidence. The teams were so similar in temperament, in fact, that they had once been friends, sneaking out to nightclubs to party during international tournaments. Two years earlier, before the 1994 World Championships in São Paolo, the Brazilians made it clear they were tired of second place. They were quoted in the papers guaranteeing they would win. When the Cubans arrived, the Brazilian players were so frosty that the Cubans suspected their coach had forbidden them from socializing. Despite the snub, and the raucous Brazilian crowd that packed an outdoor football stadium for the final, the Cubans humiliated their old friends in straight sets. After the match, Brazil's players wouldn't even make eye contact.

In their group stage match in Atlanta, the Brazilians, thirsty for revenge, had taken full advantage of the distracted Cubans, returning the favor by wiping them off the court in straight sets. Luis knew that Brazil, which had dropped only a single set in the tournament thus far, might beat them even if they were playing their best. To win, Cuba would have to find some way to encourage the Brazilians to beat themselves. It was time for extreme measures. "In Atlanta we were past strategies," Luis told me. "It was fundamental. We were out for victory at any cost."

The Cuban team had always thrived on animosity. The more hostile the crowd, the better they played. Luis did not believe the Brazilians possessed the same mental toughness. "We knew we could get to them," she said. "They're very passionate about their volleyball, with a strong character—but at the same time, they are very weak. No, wait. . . . Not weak. Sensitive."

The day before the semifinal, Luis held a players-only meeting to reveal her plan. She wanted her teammates to offend the Brazilians during the match—to shower them with insults.

Volleyball teams, which play face-to-face, have long used psychological tricks to gain an advantage over their opponents—glares, shouts, smirks, the occasional pointed finger. Luis believed it was time to take this strategy to a new level.

Her teammates were confused. "What do you mean by 'insult' them?" they asked.

"Let's say whatever we want," she said.

"Like what?" they asked.

"The worst things one woman can say to another."

Shouting expletives at your opponent wasn't explicitly barred by volleyball's code of conduct—but it certainly violated the spirit of sportsmanship. It was the sort of thing that could incite the referee to eject players from the match. But faced with the most dire situation her team had ever faced, Luis decided that the higher ideals of sport would have to wait. She had made a coldly rational, premeditated decision to test the boundaries of the rules.

There are two activities in polite society in which it's okay to do harmful things to other people in the pursuit of victory. The first is war. The second is sports. Part of the deal, however, is that there are some lines not to be crossed.

In war, the use of chemical weapons, the targeting of civilians, and the treatment of prisoners are dictated by international conventions and subject to prosecution by war crimes tribunals. In sports, athlete conduct is codified by the rules and enforced by referees and governing bodies that place a heavy emphasis on sportsmanship. The guiding principle is that it's not whether a team plays hard to win but that it plays with honor.

The beginnings of this code can be traced back to England, where the preferred athletic pastimes of the upper classes demanded close attention to decorum. This kind of thinking can still be seen during cricket matches at Lord's and in the mannerly rules and traditions of Wimbledon, where players are still required to wear white. Sport was supposed to be the province of upright ladies and gentlemen. You wouldn't try to psych out your opponents by calling them names.

These Victorian ideals have faded over time as sports fans develop stronger stomachs for the occasional demonstration of unkind play—but this permissiveness doesn't apply to everyone. Team captains the world over continue to be stripped of their duties for offenses that have nothing to do with the performances of their teams and might be shrugged off if committed by another player. If a captain skips practice, gets arrested, criticizes management, goes after a heckler, or squabbles over their contract, they're often judged by a different standard.

During his six-year captaincy of England's national football team, for example, David Beckham absorbed withering criticism for everything from his "ridiculous" haircut to a lack of "combative will" to the fact that he once cried on the sidelines during a World Cup quarter-final loss. In 2006, Beckham became so dispirited that he resigned the role. His successor, John Terry, was questioned not for his toughness but for his moral fitness. He was twice stripped of the armband—once amid allegations that he had an affair with a teammate's ex-girlfriend (while he was married), and a second time for allegedly making racist taunts to an opponent. English officials, defending their decision to demote Terry before his taunting case had been heard, cited "the higher profile nature of the England captaincy, on and off the pitch."

The one captain I've met who epitomized what people expect a modern leader to be is Derek Jeter of the New York Yankees.

When the team named him to the role in 2003, the decision was met with a chorus of hosannas. Handsome, calm, serious, and stoical, Jeter played hard every day and won renown for his clutch hitting. He was a homegrown Yankee and a perennial All-Star shortstop who had already helped the team win four World Series titles and five American League pennants. More important, Jeter was a refreshing alternative to the headlines of the day, which were dominated by the antics of boorish, overpaid athletes who took performance-enhancing drugs, misbehaved off the field, or projected a callous disregard for anyone but themselves.

Jeter showed up, signed autographs, put his head down, and competed. If there was any magma smoldering inside him, he never allowed it to surface. He didn't start brawls on the field—or even participate in them once they'd begun. He wasn't a doper or a cheat. He came from a solid family, stayed out of trouble, and performed good works for charity. He pulled off the rare feat of serving as a positive role model for kids while still projecting the crackling celebrity of a leading man.

But what puzzled me about Jeter's tenure is how few trophies he collected. In the twelve seasons he held the role, the Yankees won the World Series only once. The team was a perennial contender, but compared to the Yankees dynasties of the past it proved unable to finish.

To Jeter's adoring public, which even included fans of other teams, the lack of trophies didn't matter. His star power helped turn the Yankees into a thriving business—during his captaincy, the team opened a new $1.5 billion stadium and saw its annual ticket revenue grow beyond four hundred million dollars in 2010—more than twice what the team had been worth the day he made his debut. The near-universal praise for Jeter's leadership had everything to do with his image and his behavior. Jeter was considered a great captain because he never indulged any dark impulses and hewed to the highest principles of sportsmanship.

Derek Jeter was good for baseball. He was certainly good for business. Nevertheless, as I quickly discovered, his personality, his approach to competition, and his team's performance on the field couldn't have been more different from the captains in Tier One.

Mireya Luis was by no means the only elite captain who had a propensity to do controversial things.

In 2015, the New Zealand All Blacks arrived in England for the Rugby World Cup as the world's number-one-ranked team and the tournament's prohibitive favorite. In the early minutes of their opening match against Argentina, however, they seemed as if they might buckle under the pressure. Rusty and rhythmless, the All Blacks fumbled balls and dropped passes while Argentina's scrappy, swarming defense neutralized their attack.

Late in the first half, after the referee awarded a penalty against New Zealand, the Argentines took quick advantage—snatching the ball from a pile of All Blacks near the halfway line and passing it to their captain, Juan Martín Fernández Lobbe. As Lobbe turned downfield, it was clear that the All Blacks did not have the personnel in place to prevent Argentina from making a run for their try line.

At the crucial moment, however, just as Lobbe made his break into the open field, he stumbled, giving the All Blacks just enough time to regroup. The replay official, watching on television, noticed that Lobbe hadn't botched his footwork. As he passed a pile of players lying on the ground, New Zealand's captain, the flanker Richie McCaw, had straightened his leg and slyly extended his toes a few inches, tripping Lobbe. McCaw was penalized and sent to the "sin bin" for ten minutes. The crowd booed him relentlessly.

In the second half, New Zealand mounted a comeback, erasing a 16–12 Argentine lead with two tries in the last twenty-five minutes to win the match by ten points. Yet the only thing anyone wanted to talk about afterward was McCaw's unsportsmanlike behavior. "It was one of those things, as soon as it happens you wish you hadn't done it," McCaw told reporters. "I knew straightaway it was a reflex thing that . . . wasn't the right thing to do and I suffered because of it."

McCaw's explanation did little to quell the outrage. Fans from other countries had long believed that the All Blacks, and in particular McCaw, were cheats who never missed an opportunity to play offside, launch an elbow at an opponent's face, hold down a tackled player a second too long, or—as in this case—stick out a foot. English reporters denounced McCaw's actions as "sneaky" and "snidy," while an Australian paper Photoshopped a picture of his head onto the body of a grub. He didn't fare much better at home, as one New Zealand columnist called his actions "cynical" and an "indiscretion" of the sort that had "fueled his reputation as a man who has pushed the rules to the absolute limits." Another roasted him for violating "the Kiwi sense of fair play" by not immediately owning up to the foul but rather waiting to be caught—and for failing to apologize to Lobbe.

McCaw's play was a clear example of a player breaking the rules in an effort to gain an advantage. There was nothing sportsmanlike, or intelligent, about it. What irked people more than this, however, was that it seemed to be part of a pattern. For McCaw, testing the limits of the rules was a strategy. Throughout his career, he'd made a point of seeking out the referees before matches to talk to them about how tightly or loosely they planned to call the match and what specific things they would be looking for. Then, armed with that knowledge, he would play right up to the borders of the referee's tolerance. One Irish paper said McCaw had made an "art form" of reading the referees.

By aggressively testing the rules in the Argentina match, and expressing contrition only for the way his actions had affected his team, Richie McCaw had violated those universally held notions of fair play. To the public, the fact that he was the team's captain only made it worse.

McCaw's pattern of behavior and code of competitive morality hadn't won him global admiration. The things that were said about him in the wake of the tripping affair had never been said of Derek Jeter. Yet there was no questioning his team's results. Coming into the 2015 season, his tenth as captain, McCaw had led the All Blacks to 95 wins in 116 matches. He would become the first and only captain to lift the World Cup trophy twice in a row.

One of the things I noticed about the Tier One captains was how often they had pushed the frontiers of the rules in pressure situations, sometimes with ugly results. What I had not understood is that these flare-ups were not always impulsive acts performed in the heat of battle. In some cases, they were premeditated.

The Omni Coliseum was nowhere near capacity for the women's volleyball semifinal, but it didn't sound empty. Brazilian fans—hundreds of them, all clad in canary and united by their fervent desire to see Cuba beaten—had jammed the lower bowl to wave flags and dance in the footwells. One guy slipped through security with a trumpet. Others had smuggled in snare drums and congas. During the player introductions they greeted the Cubans, Mireya Luis in particular, with a hailstorm of boos and whistles. Nobody had any idea what Luis had decided to do.

The Cuban players, wearing white tops and powder-blue bottoms, had taken out the braids and hair extensions they'd worn in earlier matches. It was back to business now. They loitered around their bench, avoiding conversation, trying to stay loose—but the tension was stamped on their faces. After the anthems, as the two teams gathered at the net for the pregame greeting, there were pinched looks, angry glares, averted eyes, and cold handshakes.

The Brazilians came out firing in the first set, winning a side-out on a booming spike from Ana Moser, who then marched unsmilingly to the backcourt to pound a perfect serve. "An ace for Brazil!" shouted the Brazilian TV commentator. The fans went berserk. The Cubans seemed disorganized, bumping into one another on defense and sometimes having no choice but to lob the ball harmlessly over the net. With Brazil ahead 10–3, Luis leaned over and shouted the first insult across the net. *Bitches.*

The Brazilian players reacted calmly. They relayed the remark to the referee, a man named Petrus Carolus Scheffer. He took no action. After Luis spiked the ball to win a point at 12–4 and yelled another obscenity, Scheffer waved her over and held up a yellow card. Luis had been officially warned. The crowd pointed and hissed. Luis hit a serve long. The insults were having no effect. Brazil closed out the set 15–5.

In the second set, the Cubans found their rhythm, and with the score 8–6 in their favor, Cuba's Magaly Carvajal muffed a block, then took up her captain's cause and shouted a few choice words at the Brazilians. She, too, received a yellow card.

After Cuba won the second set 15–8, Carvajal continued the verbal barrage, aiming much of it at Brazil's star, Marcia Fu Cunha. But Brazil, capitalizing on its superior size, prevailed 15–10 in the third, leaving them one set from victory.

Luis called the players together at the end of the break, without the coaches present. If things continued like this, she told them, they would lose. She and Carvajal had been prodding and insulting the Brazilians; now it was time for everyone else to join in.

The two teams battled to a 7–7 draw, bringing the crowd to its feet. After this, the Cubans started letting loose. They crowded the net after points, wild-eyed, shouting at the Brazilians until the veins in their necks bulged. Prostitutes. Dogs. Ugly cows. "We called them lesbians!" Luis recalled. During close encounters at the net, Carvajal said, "we even spat at them." Brazil's most volatile player, Fu Cunha, bore the brunt of it. When the Cubans called her a "son of a bitch," Fu Cunha screamed back at them, "You are the son of a bitch!"

The Brazilians again complained to the referee, this time more indignantly. Cuba's coach, Eugenio George Lafita, who knew nothing about Luis's plan, cupped his hands around his mouth and screamed at his team: "Focus on your game!"

With the score tied at 13, Brazil, now just two points from victory, began responding to the insults the way Luis had hoped. They hit reckless shots, launched their bodies at irretrievable balls, and mourned every mistake by slapping their palms on the court. Fu Cunha was nearly out of control, flailing her arms to exhort her teammates. A Brazilian block attempt sailed out-of-bounds, giving Cuba a set point. Then Carvajal blocked a Brazilian spike to close out the frame. The match would go to a fifth and deciding set.

To this point, the statistics told the story of a virtual toss-up. Cuba had eighty-five attacks and seventeen blocks to Brazil's seventy-five and sixteen, with Brazil holding a six-point edge in service winners. But the scene on the benches told a different story. The emotion of the fourth set, and the insults from Cuba, had taken a toll on Brazil's players. Fu Cunha spent most of the break staring off into the middle distance.

On the Cuban bench, despite the pain in her knee, Luis bounced around like a rabbit, all energy and high fives. Lafita had given up trying to control his team. He sat at the end of the bench, his fingers interlaced over his stomach.

Brazil held tough in the fifth set, even as the Cubans pounded them with insults. With the score tied at 2, Brazil's Fernanda Venturini signaled a play to her teammates, prompting one of the Cubans to yell, "Fernanda, take this play and shove it up your ass!"

At this point, the strategy entered its most dangerous phase. Scheffer, the referee, summoned the two captains to his chair and asked Luis why her team was insulting the Brazilians. "I told him, 'Don't worry, it won't happen again.'" Then she walked back to her teammates and made a gesture that appeared to say "Cool it." But rather than hedging her bet, Luis decided to double down. Once safely out of earshot, she told them, "Girls, we have to keep insulting them!"

As the Cubans found their old swagger, the body language of the Brazilians sagged. Between points they rubbed their foreheads and nervously smoothed their hair. The Brazilian fans, sensing their team's precarious state, began calling the Cubans the same kinds of names, "motherfuckers and cunts, horrible things," Luis remembered. "But my team was calm."

Luis had played a relatively small role thus far, nursing her injured knee. But with the score 12–10 in Cuba's favor, she leaped so high on a spike attempt that she hit the ball straight down over the hands of the Brazilian blockers. When she landed on the court, she reared back and let out a primal scream of joy as her teammates mobbed her. The Cubans could taste blood. Brazil began a desperate wave of substitutions to shore up their blocking, but they had no answer. Soon it was 14–12—match point, Cuba.

After a short rally, the ball came to the Cubans, and Marlenis Costa set it high up in the air toward Luis's side of the court. As Luis watched the ball climb, she began calibrating her footwork. Step, bounce, stutter step, bounce. When the ball began descending she coiled to the floor before vaulting into the air. At the summit of her leap, the heads of Brazil's blockers came roughly to her navel. Then came the ferocious hammer of her right hand.

Plap!

The ball cleared the fingertips of the Brazilian blockers by a foot and roared straight at Fu Cunha, who didn't have a chance. The ball walloped her in the chest and fell to the floor. *"Termino,"* the dejected Brazilian commentator said, emphasizing each syllable. *"Ter-mi-no."*

The match was over. The Cuban strategy had worked. They had survived their toughest test without an ejection, but the adrenaline unleashed by their verbal assault was still flowing. Luis, nose to nose with three Brazilians and full of fire, began screaming and pumping her fists at the net. The Brazilians were outraged. Ana Moser walked to Luis and jabbed her finger through the webbing. *"Respeito!"* she shouted. ("Respect!")

Both teams gathered behind their captains. The Cubans shouted more insults. Fu Cunha ducked under the net and charged toward the Cubans, but Carvajal held out an arm and caught her by the neck, wrenching her head violently backward. Lafita, who could see that the hostility was boiling over, shoved Carvajal away from the melee. "Back off!" he yelled. "Back off!"

As the two teams converged at the tunnel to the dressing rooms, they started shouting and shoving again. Security guards descended. Fu Cunha threw a towel at the Cubans, and they threw it back. Once inside the tunnel, Brazil's Ana Paula Connelly bumped Cuba's Raisa O'Farrill. O'Farrill grabbed Connelly by the hair and yanked her down. That was the spark. Punches flew. "All the Brazilians came out, and then the Cubans, and I was standing in the middle," Luis said. "I was lucky not to get hit." The players threw water bottles and traded punches until the Atlanta police arrived. There were twelve cops, Luis said, "and they were huge. But no one can handle women when they're quarreling."

Once order had been restored, the police told the Cubans not to leave their dressing room, as the Brazilians were considering pressing charges. After consulting with volleyball officials, Brazil decided to drop the matter, but the federation slapped the Cubans with an official censure for their behavior. The Cubans would not be allowed to leave the arena until three A.M., when the last angry Brazilian fans had dispersed.

The match would be remembered as one of the greatest shootouts in volleyball history but also one of the sport's biggest embarrassments. Its legacy is confusing. What Luis had done wasn't some impulsive act like McCaw's extended foot—it had been a calculated offense that violated every definition of fair play. It had also worked. The slurs had woken up the Cubans while discombobulating the Brazilians to the point that they contributed to their own defeat. "They got what they wanted," Brazil's Virna Dias later said.

Though the Cubans went on to beat China in the gold medal game and continued their historic winning streak until Luis retired four years later, there was one lingering question I couldn't answer. How are we supposed to view Luis's "leadership" during this match? Was it the mark of a true champion or a brute?

The list of elite leaders who have done ugly and unkind things to other people in order to push their units forward is, of course, not restricted to sports. Examples can be found in every other competitive realm, including—and in particular—business.

Upon returning to Apple as its CEO in 1997 after many years in exile, Steve Jobs transformed the company from a relatively small, money-losing computer maker obsessed with rival Microsoft to an unrivaled creative juggernaut that created a series of culture-altering products. By 2012, Apple was the most valuable company, by total market capitalization, in U.S. history.

Along the way, however, Jobs earned a reputation as a cruel task-master who routinely brought employees to tears by savaging their work. In his 2011 biography of Jobs, Walter Isaacson cited an incident in which Jobs raged at his engineers when he learned that the new iMac had a CD tray rather than a slot. Jobs once called the employees of a chipmaker "fucking dickless assholes" for failing to deliver a ship-ment on time. In the summer of 2008, when a new Apple product called MobileMe debuted to withering criticism, Jobs summoned the product team to the company auditorium. "Can anyone tell me what MobileMe is supposed to do?" he asked. After listening to team mem-bers give their responses, he said, "Then why the fuck doesn't it do that?"

Jobs fired the MobileMe team leader on the spot.

Berating people over their shoddy work and making them cry is undoubtedly at the outside limit of what's acceptable in the workplace, the stuff lawsuits are made of. While Jobs didn't break any laws, per se, he clearly disregarded the prevailing rules of interpersonal relations. And he didn't seem to care.

Much has been made of Jobs's character flaws. These incidents are the proof his critics cite when they dismiss him as a jerk and a bully and suggest that Apple's freakish success was somehow tainted and unrepeatable. What isn't often noted, however, is that in many cases people responded to these admonishments. While the process was ugly, the result was glorious. In this sense, Jobs wasn't too different from the captains in Tier One. His leadership method presented the same moral quandary.

In 1961, Arnold Buss, a psychologist at the University of Pitts-burgh, published one of the first comprehensive books about human aggression. He concluded, based in part on laboratory experiments, that people exhibit two distinct flavors of aggression: The first is a "hostile" one driven by anger or frustration and motivated by the re-ward of seeing someone hurt or punished; the second is an "instrumental" one that isn't motivated by a desire to injure but by the determination to achieve a worthwhile goal.

Buss believed that these instrumental acts—which were task-specific, didn't blatantly violate the rules, and were not intended to do harm—might not really be aggressive at all. They might be better described as assertive. "You have to distinguish between assertiveness and aggression," Buss said. "There is a low correlation between them."

In the decades since, developmental psychologists have flirted with the idea that "instrumental" aggression might not always be a pestilence, and that aggressive people can be exceptionally clever at navigating social dilemmas. In a 2007 book, *Aggression and Adaptation: The Bright Side to Bad Behavior,* a team of American psychologists noted that nearly all of the most highly ambitious, powerful, and successful people in business display at least some level of hostility and aggressive self-expression. The authors didn't go so far as to argue that these behaviors constitute "moral goodness," but they didn't dismiss them as the mark of evil, either. "Aggressive behavior offers avenues for personal growth, goal attainment and positive peer regard," they wrote.

When these notions are applied to Steve Jobs, Mireya Luis, Richie McCaw, and the other Tier One sports captains who sometimes stepped over the line, the controversial decisions they made take on a different cast. They didn't test the boundaries of the rules in order to hurt people, although injuries to bodies or feelings were possible. Their goal was to win. There was no question that the captains who made a habit of testing the boundaries of the rules would never be revered by the public the way Derek Jeter was. But this theory suggested that calling their behavior thuggish was an oversimplification. These were aggressive acts that pushed the limits of what's acceptable, but they were also instrumental.

This idea, that aggression is a skill, is something many elite captains instinctively endorsed. Didier Deschamps, the former captain of the French club football team Olympique de Marseille and the French national team, both of which earned places in Tier Two, put it best. On the occasions when he felt compelled to commit a foul, there was always aggression behind the action, "but I was never animated by the desire to hurt someone." These acts, he said, were calculated for the greater good. "We call them 'intelligent' or 'useful' fouls, but they remain fouls, and I took yellow cards so that we didn't face worse consequences." The key, Deschamps said, is to maintain self-control and to know when it's okay to foul and when you are "too far up the referee's nose" to get away with it. "It's something you feel. It's a feeling. It's a form of intelligence."

In 1986, Brenda Jo Bredemeier and David Shields of UC Berkeley interviewed forty athletes about their attitudes toward aggression. They discovered that their subjects had given this question a lot of thought. The athletes felt that sports released them from the responsibility of making moral decisions—in competitions, they could play hard and try to win without having to worry about other people. "When you're on the field," one participant said, "the game is football and behavior is governed by rules. Before and after, behavior is governed by morals." The athletes also noted that the rules were somewhat flexible and that they could adjust their play accordingly. "You should play by the rules," one participant said. "I don't always—but I'm not flagrant."

The athletes in the study disagreed on what kinds of aggressive acts were legitimate, but they all shared the same basic belief: Trying to hurt opponents for the sake of inflicting pain wasn't right, but roughing them up for the purpose of rattling and distracting them was. If these athletes were asked to discuss the actions taken by Mireya Luis or Richie McCaw, they would surely take a far less negative view than the public.

Bredemeier and Shields concluded that the moral meaning of an aggressive act in sports depends on many variables, one of which is the "frame" in which it occurs. While competing, they wrote, athletes exist in a "game frame" where they engage in "game reasoning" that allows them to adopt a code of behavior different from the one that applies in the outside world. They called this phenomenon bracketed morality. This suggests that when athletes take the field they enter a parallel universe—one with different boundaries in which doing what's broadly considered to be moral isn't always the correct move. In other words, once somebody enters the game frame, they judge their own behavior differently, even if the outside world does not.

On a rainy day in Havana in 2015, Mireya Luis watched a video of the final point against Brazil in that 1996 Olympic semifinal, and her net-boxing antics that followed it, with a combination of amusement and mortification. "That was the moment of maximum strength, of concentration, of energy; everything was at a peak," she explained, holding her hand high above the table to demonstrate. I asked her if she had meant those moves to be provocative, to humiliate the Brazilians. "No," she said. "It was a celebration—a release, so to speak."

To most people, the brawl might have seemed like a natural extension of the match—but Luis saw it differently. Once the game was over, the only thing aggression could do was jeopardize Cuba's chances of winning the final. As the fight broke out, she stood between her teammates and the Brazilians, pleading with them to stop. "To me it was very important that no one got injured," she said.

After they won the final, the Cubans were lustily booed at the medal ceremony. Lafita was removed from his position as coach for the next two seasons—likely a result of his inability to control the team—but the Cubans continued their dominance for four more years.

I asked Luis how she felt, in retrospect, about the abuse her team had heaped on the Brazilians and the public scorn it brought them. "I've always been very respectful of teams and players," she said. "When you're competing, as long as you don't hurt . . . well, we were hurting them verbally, but I guess it depends on the stakes, the circumstances, the moment." Aggression, she said, "is part of the game, too. And how you do it is important. I don't think we did this in a cruel way. It wasn't meant . . . I don't know how to tell you. It wasn't nice, but it was a show that derived from the pursuit of a medal."

As a captain, Luis was always aware of what sort of emotion she was projecting. Even in the tensest situations, and even when she wasn't feeling happy, she would try to exude a breezy self-confidence. "I always tried to transmit joy, or energy, with my smile," she said. "It motivated my team." To Luis, aggression was another deliberate act, one of many faces a leader must put on—an example of something scientists describe as "surface acting."

Once the Brazil match had ended, the acting needed to stop. "That's what it means to be a professional," she said. "You can't turn your professional behavior into an external weapon. You're only supposed to use it during the game. It's no good for anything else. Because once you leave the court, people have to see you as a regular human being. I've always wanted to see myself as a strong, aggressive volleyball player when the circumstances called for it." People who are aggressive all the time, she said, "are just rude."

But those moments with Brazil were quite rude, I reminded her.

"Yes," she answered. "But they're moments."

The captains of the world's sixteen greatest sports teams were not angels. They sometimes did nasty things to win, especially when the stakes were highest. They didn't believe that being sportsmanlike all the time was a prerequisite for being great.

The people in the stands, or the journalists who cover companies like Apple, see things differently than the participants. They live in the "normal" world, where conventional principles of decency preside. The people inside the struggle, however, live between a different set of brackets. In the game frame, there are prescribed penalties for misbehavior. You get a yellow card. You get ten minutes in the sin bin. You get expelled from the match. You get suspended. If it serves a purpose, and you manage to get away with it, then it is, as Deschamps put it, an intelligent foul. While these actions may have the potential to be hurtful, hurting people isn't the point.

In sports and many other competitive pursuits, we're taught from an early age that there is no difference between how you compete and who you are. Some leaders, like Derek Jeter, lived by this credo and won universal praise for doing so. But the Tier One captains considered this a false choice. They believed that what mattered was another distinction—the difference between leaders who worry about how they're perceived and leaders who drag their teams through challenges by any means necessary.

The world puts a lot of pressure on athletes, especially captains, to be champions and paragons of virtue. But these two things do not always correlate. It's sometimes one or the other. The most decorated captains in history understood this.

CHAPTER SIX TAKEAWAYS

- The most universal tradition in sports is the code of sportsmanship. In every country and culture, there is a form of judgment that supersedes the one displayed on the scoreboard. We believe that there is a right way to win and a wrong way, and that a person's character is revealed in moments when their morals are tested. On sports teams, the one player who is held to this standard more than any other is the captain. On the sixteen greatest teams in history, however, the captains were not immune to pushing the rules to the breaking point. In fact, they often did so intentionally.

- When it comes to behaving aggressively, there is a persistent view that a person who does so must be suffering from some kind of psychological or spiritual deficiency. What people fail to understand is that all aggression is not the same. There is a "hostile" variety that is intended to do harm and an "instrumental" form that is employed in pursuit of a worthwhile goal. While the captains in Tier One often did ugly things, they did so while operating within the fuzzy confines of the rules of sports. The difference between a captain who upholds the principles of sportsmanship at all times and a captain who bends it to its edges is that the latter captain is more concerned with winning than with how the public perceives them.

SEVEN

Carrying Water

The Hidden Art of Leading
from the Back

In the predawn gloom of a September morning in 1996, outside printing plants across Italy, truck drivers lit cigarettes and fired their engines. In their cargo bays sat roughly 401,000 copies of *La Gazzetta dello Sport,* the hot-pink broadsheet that serves as Italy's football bible. On this particular morning, the drivers traced their routes with a bit more urgency. *La Gazzetta* had a scoop.

In two days, Italy's best team, Juventus, would be hosting Manchester United for a match in the early stages of the UEFA Champions League, the annual tournament between Europe's leading professional clubs. In advance of the match, *La Gazzetta* had sent a reporter to England to profile United's captain, Eric Cantona, a haughty, volatile Frenchman known as King Eric.

Cantona was famous for his brutal candor. He was not afraid to criticize opponents or even teammates and had once used an interview to describe his manager as a "bag of shit." The editors must have figured Cantona would say something newsworthy before the big match. He had not disappointed.

After offering his thoughts on various Juventus players, Cantona came around to the topic of Didier Deschamps. Cantona knew Deschamps well. The two men were members of the French national team. Unlike Cantona, Deschamps was not a flashy player or a glamorous celebrity. He was a defensive midfielder who almost never scored. Early in his career, Deschamps had been considered such an expendable player that his club team, Olympique de Marseille, had loaned him out to another team.

One year earlier, in 1995, Cantona had been suspended from football for eight months after karate-kicking a heckler during a match in England, and Deschamps had been chosen to replace him as France's captain. Cantona hadn't appreciated being pushed out. He didn't have much use for Deschamps, either. Players like Deschamps, Cantona told the reporter, can be found "on every street corner." Deschamps was a "limited" footballer, he continued, whose entire job was to feed the ball to better players. The best thing one might say about him, Cantona added, is that he was a *porteur d'eau*. A water carrier.

Cantona's remarks leaped from *La Gazzetta*'s pages that morning and beat a path across Europe, prompting such headlines as "Deschumps!" in London's *Mirror* and "You're a Dud Deschamps" in the Scottish *Daily Record*.

The match, played at Turin's Stadio delle Alpi, wasn't especially memorable. Juventus took an early lead from a penalty, then fell back into a defensive posture as Cantona and his United teammates hammered fruitlessly at their goal. The final score was 1–0. But for the assembled media, the match was only a prelude to the main event—the postgame interviews. Deschamps knew there would be a phalanx of tape recorders trained at him and that whatever he said would be replayed all over the world.

Deschamps was unassuming but proud. Unlike Cantona, he'd already earned a pair of European club titles, one with Juve and another as captain of Marseille. Before he retired in 2001, he would become one of only three captains in my study to lead two different teams into Tier Two. How he would respond was anybody's guess.

Deschamps started by telling the reporters he had approached

Cantona after the match and asked him what he'd meant by his comments. All Cantona had said in return was "Forget it." Known for his piercing glare, Deschamps displayed it then. This was the moment when he was supposed to fire back.

Deschamps didn't follow the script. Rather than batting down Cantona's insult, he calmly accepted it. "I don't mind being called a water carrier," he said.

In the seventh century B.C., Chionis of Sparta swept the sprinting events at the Olympics. The Greeks decided to honor him by carving his name on a stone memorial at Olympia. Two hundred years later, when Astylos of Croton surpassed the feat, the poet Simonides of Ceos immortalized him in an epigram. The wrestler Milo of Croton, who won titles in six consecutive Games, showed up in the writings of Aristotle and Cicero.

Since then, civilizations have fallen all over themselves to lionize star athletes. An account from Mongolia around A.D. 1240 cites a match involving a Mongolian wrestling champion, the undefeated Buri Bokh, organized and attended by Genghis Khan himself. By the Late Middle Ages in Europe, jousting knights charged one another with lances bearing ribbons given as favors by the ladies of the court who swooned at their valor.

One of England's first celebrity athletes was James Figg, a practitioner of fisticuffs, or bare-knuckle boxing, who by some estimates won a headache-inducing 269 fights—one of which was the subject of an ode published in 1726 in the *Spectator*. The American boxing champion Jack Dempsey once called Figg the father of modern boxing. By the nineteenth century, boxing matches in England were attracting more than twenty thousand spectators while jockeys, golfers, and tennis players, alongside the stars of team sports like rowing, rugby, and football, earned their own devoted followings and were given individual awards for being deemed the "most valuable" or "best and fairest."

The progenitor of the modern cult of celebrity athletes was baseball's Babe Ruth. Six foot two and barrel-chested, Ruth was the gregarious son of a Baltimore pub owner who had a folksy air and a mischievous streak. Coming along during the 1920s when radio, newspapers, newsreels, and motion pictures spawned an explosion of mass media, Ruth was bombarded with attention—but he didn't seem to mind. In addition to smashing home run records with his long-limbed uppercut, he played himself in a handful of movies, hosted a radio show, performed in vaudeville acts, and appeared in advertisements for gasoline, chewing tobacco, cigarettes, breakfast cereal, and underwear. In 1930, "the Babe" made eighty thousand dollars, which was more than President Herbert Hoover. "Why not?" Ruth famously said. "I had a better year than he did."

In the middle of the century, television raised the stakes. For the first time, the entire world was able to watch Brazil's Pelé play football in real time. His astonishing talent, and his smiling, carefree aura, made him one of the first global celebrities—recognized and mobbed in every city he visited. Once, when a reporter asked Pelé how his fame compared to Jesus's, Pelé replied, "There are parts of the world where Jesus Christ is not so well known." In the mid-1980s, thanks to his otherworldly feats on the court and a groundbreaking advertising campaign by Nike, Michael Jordan demonstrated that an athlete's fame could be more financially lucrative than his athletic ability.

Although these GOAT candidates like Ruth, Pelé, and Jordan played on teams, each with their own complicated dynamics, the fans didn't see them as pieces of a larger whole. They believed that the size of their talent was so immense, and their contributions so vital, that whether they were captains or not, their leadership was assumed.

On most teams, the players don't bother to challenge this perception publicly. After all, it's the stars people pay to see. But in a few cases, when pressed on the subject, some of the more blunt captains in the top tiers of my study hinted that behind the scenes, the hierarchy of the team was vastly different than the public might imagine.

In the dressing room, former Manchester United captain Roy

Keane once wrote, "the gap between what we do—and feel—and other people's reality is alarming. The media hero is not necessarily the Man in here. . . . Ditto the crowd pleaser. We live in a make-believe world created by the media, which is largely though not entirely, fiction. The fictional hero is often an arsehole."

Alex Ferguson, Keane's manager at United, also believed that a player's raw athletic ability and their fitness for leadership are distinct and separate things. "Yes, there are elements of symbolism to the role, because the captain is the man who always gets to lift the trophy," Ferguson said. "But I only ever wanted a leader, rather than someone who might look good on top of a cake."

There's no question that an athlete can play both roles at once. Ferenc Puskás, Yogi Berra, and Maurice Richard all compiled glamorous offensive numbers worthy of GOAT consideration while leading their teams into Tier One. Puskás holds the all-time international scoring record with eighty-three goals in eighty-four matches.

The majority of captains in the top tiers of my study, however—like Didier Deschamps—were not considered sensations. Syd Coventry, Valeri Vasiliev, Buck Shelford, Carla Overbeck, and Carles Puyol, among others, were hardly fixtures on MVP lists.

Beyond this, most of the Tier One captains had zero interest in the trappings of fame. They didn't pursue the captaincy for the prestige it conveyed—if they pursued it at all. In 2004, when Carles Puyol's teammates unanimously elected him captain, his was the only dissenting vote. "I thought it was more ethical to vote for others," he told me. In 2011, after Barcelona won the Champions League final (the team hadn't lost a match he'd played in that season), he handed the captain's armband to a teammate, Éric Abidal, who had recently returned from treatment for liver cancer. It was Abidal who lifted the trophy. "It was a gesture of comradeship not very often seen," Barcelona's David Villa said. "It is one of the most important moments a captain has—and he gave that to Abidal."

All of my research showed that contrary to the public view, it is possible for a water carrier who prefers toiling in the service of others to become a strong captain. In fact, superior leadership is just as likely (if not more so) to come from the team's rear quarters than to emanate from its frontline superstar. Carrying water, especially on defense, is clearly vital to a team's success, even if it's not something that inspires people to compose epic poems or chisel their names in stone.

Still, as I noted earlier, great leaders are—by definition—supposed to reveal themselves in moments of maximum pressure, when the game is on the line. In these instances, it's the leader who is supposed to step in to make the dazzling clutch play. If most Tier One captains did not do this, I wondered, then how, exactly, did they lead?

Buried inside an obscure 1997 clinical psychology textbook called *Aversive Interpersonal Behaviors,* there is a chapter titled "Blowhards, Snobs, and Narcissists: Interpersonal Reactions to Excessive Egotism." The authors were a Wake Forest University professor and a handful of his undergraduate students. The paper concluded that self-centered people who project arrogance through their speech and body language tend to be viewed less favorably by others and can weaken a group's cohesion.

The most significant thing about this paper was the identity of one of its student co-authors, a twenty-one-year-old named Timothy Duncan. Duncan wasn't just another psychology major at Wake Forest. He was the star of the basketball team.

Growing up on St. Croix in the U.S. Virgin Islands, Tim Duncan dreamed of becoming a champion swimmer. Hurricane Hugo destroyed the local pool in 1989, taking his pathway to the Olympics with it. Not long after that, his mother died of breast cancer, a day before his fourteenth birthday. Duncan didn't take up basketball until he was a high school freshman, and although he'd shot up to six foot eleven by his senior year, he was so skinny and raw that most recruiters weren't sure he'd ever be able to hold his own in the paint against major college competition. Wake Forest was the only major program to offer him a scholarship. Duncan matured so quickly, however, and worked so hard to hone his game, that the same year that research paper was published the San Antonio Spurs picked him number one overall in the NBA Draft.

From the moment he arrived in San Antonio, Duncan seemed determined to abide by the conclusions of his undergraduate thesis. He never asked for special privileges, never skipped practices, never bristled at being dressed down after poor performances. On the court, he didn't hang on the rim after dunks or stare down opponents. Gregg Popovich, the Spurs' coach, once said Duncan didn't have any "MTV" in him. When a twenty-two-year-old Duncan showed up to receive the NBA's Rookie of the Year award in 1998, he wore mesh shorts and a ratty T-shirt and barely cracked a smile. He seemed to have no interest in being singled out or telling his story to the world. "You guys just write what you want to write," Duncan once told reporters. "Stop trying to analyze me."

On the night of June 25, 1999, Duncan won his first NBA title in the fifth game of a series against the New York Knicks. Once the Spurs had collected their trophy, I followed the rest of the media into their jubilant locker room.

At this point in his career, Tim Duncan had never seen so many cameras. If he'd been Babe Ruth or Pelé, he would have taken this moment to soak in the adulation. But after Duncan got his hands on the trophy, I watched him carry it calmly across the room and open the bathroom door. He pulled his teammate and closest friend on the team, David Robinson, inside with him, and slammed it shut. Whatever emotions needed to pour out of Duncan in that moment, they were none of the public's business.

On the court, Duncan might have had the scoring ability to challenge Michael Jordan, who was putting up twenty-nine points per game at the time, but rather than focusing on taking every shot, Duncan often passed the ball to open teammates. He set picks for the guards, played aggressive defense, battled in the low post, and guarded the rim. His twenty-one-points-per-game average in his first season ranked thirteenth in the NBA, but he finished third in rebounding.

His teammates, in honor of his selfless, no-thrills all-around game, affectionately dubbed him the Big Fundamental.

Over the next few years, basketball writers watched Duncan become a force. They sought time with him to write profiles, but as he continued to ignore them or offer them nothing but affectless responses, the word "boring" appeared in articles—at first affectionately, and then with a critical edge. One columnist even called him "the most boring superstar in the history of sports." In a 2012 survey that asked teenagers to name their favorite NBA player, Duncan didn't receive a single vote.

Duncan's selfless approach to basketball did earn him one prominent fan, however. Bill Russell, the other basketball captain in Tier One, raved that Duncan was the league's most efficient player, the one who wasted the least motion—and emotion—on the court. Russell especially admired the way Duncan played without the ball. "He sets picks to make the offense operate," Russell said, "not necessarily to get himself a shot."

Duncan's coach, Gregg Popovich, said, "His style of play is such a fundamental style that it's not flamboyant or awkward or different from the norm. The norm is what's rare now: You have everybody doing everything every which way. He does things the way we were coached when we were little kids—his footwork, his body movement, everything that he does. It's not sexy. But it's efficient."

In an era when the economics of the NBA made it difficult for teams to maintain steady rosters, most players of Duncan's elite caliber believed it was their job to focus on scoring while their rotating cast of "support" players took care of the rest. Duncan took a different view. He helped the Spurs survive the roster churn by demonstrating a rare level of flexibility. He switched positions throughout his career, pivoting between center and power forward depending on the composition of the team. Sometimes his offensive metrics were off the charts, other times his defense predominated.

Off the court, Duncan did something else that was unheard-of—he agreed to be paid less than his market value so the team would have more space under the NBA's salary cap to sign better players. In 2015, Duncan's two-year, $10.4 million deal was shockingly far below what he could have demanded on the open market, but it allowed the Spurs to acquire the power forward LaMarcus Aldridge, who outearned Duncan by more than four to one.

The best way to look at one's teammates, Duncan said, is that "you're helping them as much as they're helping you."

When Duncan retired in 2016, his teams had won five NBA championships and had made the playoffs in all nineteen of his seasons. Individually, he managed to set the most impressive mark of all— winning more games with one team than any player in NBA history. There would be no fawning goodbye tour, however. Duncan kept his retirement plans private during the season, then announced his decision with a 146-word letter to the fans, which ended: "Thank you to the city of San Antonio for the love and the support over these years. Thank you to the fans all over the world. Much Love Always, Tim."

It's as if Duncan had used his Wake Forest thesis as a blueprint for how to be an effective teammate in a league where "narcissists" and "blowhards" were the lords of the realm.

The public never fully got Duncan, but his teammates did. His leadership turned out to be something of a graduate seminar on the value of carrying water. Duncan was the rare captain who had the talent to take over games and put up some of the NBA's gaudiest statistics. But his approach to leadership compelled him to suppress his skills, and even his salary, in order to focus on fixing whatever happened to be broken. He wasn't concerned with his public image, only that his team won.

One of the great paradoxes of management is that the people who pursue leadership positions most ardently are often the wrong people for the job. They're motivated by the prestige the role conveys rather than a desire to promote the goals and values of the organization.

Researchers who have studied superstar CEOs have noticed that as these people raise themselves up, they often lower others. They have a tendency to make their subordinates feel incompetent and under-authorized, which creates a vicious cycle. The employees increasingly withdraw, and as they do, the star CEO becomes pessimistic about their ability and begins to "overfunction," causing their charges to withdraw even more. Tim Duncan's style of leadership took the opposite course. By lowering himself, he was able to coax the maximum performance out of the players around him.

The late J. Richard Hackman, a professor of social and organizational psychology at Harvard, spent much of his academic career out in the field, where he logged hundreds of hours embedded with many different kinds of teams as they worked—basketball teams, surgical teams, airplane cockpit crews, musical ensembles, and even elite U.S. intelligence-gathering units inside the CIA. A six-foot-six former high school basketball player, Hackman believed the most valuable insights came from teams that performed together under intense pressure in environments that didn't allow them do-overs.

One of Hackman's central beliefs was that people were far too quick to assume that the success or failure of a team was directly attributable to the person running it. "We mistakenly assume that the best leaders are those who stand on whatever podium they can command and, through their personal efforts in real time, extract greatness from their teams." In reality, only 10 percent of a team's performance depended on what the leader did once the performance was under way. But when it came to that 10 percent, Hackman found no evidence that a leader's charisma, or even their specific methods, made any difference. It didn't even matter if the leader performed all of the key leadership functions on the team—all that mattered was that these jobs got done. When good leaders saw these conditions eroding, they would tinker with new strategies to get things back on track. Leaders, Hackman believed, were more effective when they worked like jazz musicians, freely improvising with the flow of things, and less like orchestra players, who follow a written score under the direction of a conductor.

Duncan was eminently flexible. He carried water on the court and put the team's goals above all. Hackman called this style of leadership the functional approach. "From a functional perspective," he wrote, "effective team leaders are those who do, or who arrange to get done, whatever is critical for the team to accomplish its purpose."

Tim Duncan's leadership style fell into line with those of other elite captains, but his example did leave one question unanswered.

The Tier One captains had varying levels of talent. Some were superstars in their own right—most were not. Duncan's basketball skills put him at the high end of the scale. When his team found itself in a precarious situation, his teammates knew that if he wanted to, he had the ability to swoop in to save the day—to take the big shot. Most of the other captains didn't have that power. They had unspectacular skills or played rear-facing positions.

Richie McCaw of the New Zealand All Blacks, for instance, played flanker—the most physically demanding position in rugby, which required him to spend most matches engaged in close, brutal contact. He spent so much time tackling, grappling, and trying to strip the ball from opposing players that he rarely scored and often left the field looking like he'd lost a boxing match.

Even for a defender, Carla Overbeck of the U.S. women's national football team posted anemic offensive totals—in her entire international career, she scored only seven goals. The moment she won possession of the ball, she would instantly begin looking for a teammate to pass it to. Even if she saw a chance to run at the goal, she would scuttle the impulse. "No. I'm not going to do it," she told me. "I'm going to trap the ball and give it away."

So what about these kinds of players? How did they lead?

Carla Overbeck's 1996–99 U.S. women's football team was one of the most remarkable collections of talent in sports history. Behind its telegenic goal-scoring heroines Mia Hamm, Julie Foudy, and Brandi Chastain, the team amassed an 84–6–6 record in international games over those four years, giving it a 94 percent win-or-draw rate that compared favorably to history's best men's teams. Yet if you asked a hundred people who the captain of this team was, odds are none of them would name Carla Overbeck. It's unlikely they would even remember her name—in large part because that's the way she wanted it.

After the U.S. won the World Cup, Overbeck's teammates happily indulged in a weeks-long victory tour marked by dozens of pep rallies and television appearances—but she wasn't interested in this part of the show. She flew home to Raleigh, North Carolina, to see her family instead. Asked what she'd been doing on the day her teammates appeared at a raucous rally in midtown Manhattan, she said she'd done three loads of laundry. "It just wasn't my personality," Overbeck said. "I've never cared about getting my name in the paper. As long as my team wins, I'm happy. I don't care about all the TV shows. I was glad I wasn't the one they were asking for."

At five foot seven, Overbeck isn't especially tall or muscular. Growing up in the Dallas suburbs, she was such a twig—with skinny legs and arms—that her dad used to call her Termite. On the field, she wore her long brown hair in a tight ponytail, and though she was famous among teammates for her salty language, her face was so cold and stony that she rarely betrayed emotion. While many of her teammates were single, she got married at twenty-four and had a son in the middle of the team's Tier One winning run.

Overbeck did not have the kind of talent Tim Duncan did. She was a defender whose skills, according to one former coach, were "average at best." She did not project the kind of confidence, or game-changing ability, leaders are supposed to display. But Overbeck's humility had an upside for the team. By getting rid of the ball as soon as she had the opportunity, she increased the amount of time it was at the feet of superior athletes—and because she rarely left the pitch, this selfless instinct helped the team generate more scoring chances. The same functional mentality touched everything she did, even off the field. When the U.S. team arrived at a hotel after some grueling international flight, Overbeck would carry everyone's bags to their hotel rooms. "I'm the captain," she explained, "but I'm no better than anybody else. I'm certainly not a better soccer player."

In training, also out of public veiw, Overbeck pushed herself, and her teammates, relentlessly. After some brutal conditioning drill, "they'd be dying, and I'd be like, 'F-ing Norway is doing shit like this.' I'm sure they hated me." Once, during a drill in which the players ran interval sprints until they dropped off from exhaustion, Overbeck outlasted everyone—and then continued running for two more minutes. The next morning, after Overbeck visited the team doctor, her teammates were amazed to learn that she'd done this with a broken toe.

The Fordham study of shouters (see Chapter Five) showed that hard work is contagious and that one player's exertion can elevate the performances of others. But Overbeck's brand of doggedness had another component. Her work ethic in training, combined with her bag-schlepping humility on and off the field, allowed her to amass a form of currency she could spend however she saw fit. She didn't use it to dominate play on the field. She used it to ride her teammates when they needed to be woken up, knowing that it wouldn't create resentment. Anson Dorrance, who coached the team from 1986 to 1994, said he believed Overbeck carried the team's luggage so that when she got on the field, "she could say anything she wanted."

"She had a genuineness about her," her teammate Briana Scurry said. "You knew she was on your side, even if she was laying into you. Carla was the heartbeat of that team and the engine. Everything about the essence of the team—that was Carla."

A water carrier can improve a team by focusing on shoring up weaknesses and enforcing high standards—this much we've seen. But there was still one missing piece of the puzzle. If the chief responsibility of a team leader is to direct the other players on the field, then by all rights these captains must have found ways to influence, if not control, the team's tactics.

For some Tier One captains, this "quarterbacking" function was plain to see. Jack Lambert called the Pittsburgh Steelers' defensive plays, for instance, and Ferenc Puskás functioned as Hungary's in-game manager. Yogi Berra, the Yankees catcher, was responsible for calling pitches and setting the defense. "She always acted as a guide," Marlenis Costa, a teammate, said of Cuba's Mireya Luis. "She wouldn't get mad, but if you did something wrong she would immediately correct it. She would correct any of the mistakes the players made because she had great vision for volleyball."

Nevertheless, many of the water carrier captains in the top tiers of my study played subordinate roles on the field. When crucial plays developed, they were often far away, tending the home fires. No matter how inspiring they were, or how hard they played, I did not understand how support players could dictate the course of events.

Didier Deschamps, the original water carrier, was a prime example of this problem. Despite playing from the back and rarely scoring, he managed to captain Marseille to four straight French championships and a 1993 Champions League title—and to lead the French national team to victory in both the 1998 World Cup and 2000 European Championship. When he sat down for an interview in Paris in 2015, Deschamps began by describing his role on the field precisely the same way Overbeck had. At five foot seven, he knew he wasn't the most physically intimidating midfielder, or the best athlete, so he wasn't concerned about his own performance. He felt free to devote himself to serving others. On the French national team, his primary focus was putting the ball at the feet of the spectacularly gifted goal-scoring midfielder Zinedine Zidane. "For every ten balls that I played, I gave nine to him," Deschamps said. Though he wasn't familiar with the writings of Harvard's Richard Hackman, Deschamps's approach to leadership was as functional as it gets. On a team, he said, "you can't only have architects. You also need bricklayers."

As he talked about his time playing with Zidane, Deschamps made an interesting point—the relationship, he said, went both ways. Yes, he served Zidane by making sure he got the ball, but Zidane relied on him to make those passes.

Zidane, he said, "also needed me."

The idea that a player who serves the team can also create dependency was something I had never considered. Deschamps, as his team's primary midfield setup man, was able to dictate the action ahead of him by deciding which players got the ball. His superstar teammates not only looked to him for passes, they coveted his approval. To Deschamps, carrying water wasn't just a servile act, it was a form of leadership—the sort of command that most of us, up in the stands, don't appreciate or even notice. "I knew I couldn't make a difference with a single move," Deschamps said. "But over the long run, through hundreds of small acts of service and management, I was able to balance things out and to become indispensable."

In other words, while the television cameras tend to focus on the players at the front, the hard work of leadership is often conducted from the rear.

Brazil declared its independence from Portugal in 1822, but it has never been a nation in the way most of us understand the term. It's more of a far-flung collection of provinces, city-states, classes, ethnicities, political viewpoints, religions, and microcultures loosely bound together by a flag. Yet from the moment the first club teams began forming in the late 1800s, there has been one thing every Brazilian could rally behind—*futebol*. "The national football team is the symbol of national identity," Brazil's former coach Carlos Alberto Parreira once told BBC Sport, "the only time the nation gets together."

As the national football team began competing against other countries in the World Cup, *futebol* delivered another gift to Brazil—the notion of Brazilian exceptionalism. It wasn't simply that Brazil won so many matches. The country's unique blend of cultural influences, from footvolley (beach volleyball played with the feet) to the two-four rhythm of the samba, seemed to create the perfect conditions for developing football impresarios: men of all backgrounds who manipulated the ball with unrivaled creativity.

One Brazilian in particular—Edson Arantes do Nascimento, better known as Pelé—was the greatest prodigy football has ever seen. From his debut in 1956 until he quit playing for good in 1977, he won three World Cups, collected more than twenty titles with the club team Santos, and scored more than 1,270 career goals in 1,363 matches. In 1969, when Pelé netted goal number one thousand, Brazilian newspapers split their front pages, giving the milestone equal weight with the *Apollo 12* moon landing.

I had naturally assumed that Pelé was the captain of those World Cup teams. I was surprised to learn that he wasn't.

In 1958, when Pelé was only a teenager, Brazil's captain was Hilderaldo Luiz Bellini, a powerful central defender with movie-star looks who was nicknamed the Ox for his sturdy, immovable presence on the pitch. Bellini was the centerpiece of the innovative "flat-back four" defense Brazil debuted at the 1958 tournament. His job was to hold the middle of the field and mark the other team's best striker—a role that required him to stand his ground while the world's biggest, fastest players plowed into him like a tackling dummy. He often left the pitch with his legs bloodied from the studs of a colliding attacker. On separate occasions, he suffered a broken knee and cheekbone.

While Brazil's brightest lights were the cerebral, creative, and quick-footed scorers like Pelé, it was Bellini who carried the water. In his entire ten-year career with the national team, he never scored a goal.

Before the final of the 1958 World Cup in Sweden, Brazilians were consumed by fear. In the 1950 tournament, their team had blown through the field, only to lose the final at home to Uruguay in heartbreaking fashion. In 1954, they lost to Hungary in the quarterfinals. Although Brazil was heavily favored in 1958, the ghosts of these two defeats weighed on the fans, and even more so on the players. The conventional wisdom was that they lacked toughness. They could build a lead, sure, but could they hold it?

Four minutes into the final, Sweden—playing at home in

Stockholm—scored the first goal after barely allowing Brazil to put a foot on the ball. At that moment, fifty million stupefied Brazilians exchanged knowing looks. Here we go again.

As the Swedes celebrated, the Brazilian captain, Bellini, walked resolutely into the net and scooped up the ball. He knew that his young team was shaken and that the thought of another disaster might consume them—sapping their energy. He walked over to the midfielder Didi, who was responsible for setting up the restart and, as he handed him the ball, gave him one stern instruction: "Hold the team."

Didi took his captain's advice. He tucked the ball under his arm and walked slowly and confidently upfield, telling his teammates to calm down and that it was time to take the fight to "these gringos." Brazil then came alive, scoring four unanswered goals in a 5–2 drubbing and earning its first-ever World Cup trophy. In the end their superior talent had carried the day. But it was Bellini who had provided the backbone.

Four years later, as it trained for the 1962 World Cup, Brazil's team had settled into its position as the world's premier football power. The anxiety of the past had dissipated. Behind the scenes, however, the plot was thickening. The team's technical director, Paulo Machado de Carvalho, had begun to consider a potentially explosive question—whether Hilderaldo Bellini was still the team's best center back.

Just days before Brazil's opening match against Mexico, the door to Carvalho's office swung open. In walked Bellini's backup, a career substitute named Mauro Ramos de Oliveira, known simply as "Mauro." An elegant technical player renowned for being cool over the ball, Mauro wasn't as physical or forceful as Bellini. On this day, however, he had decided to assert himself. He told his boss that he believed he should start in Bellini's place. Oliveira had seen the improvement in Mauro's play and was impressed by his confidence. To the shock of the fans and the press, he not only agreed to make the switch, he also made Mauro the team's new captain.

When reporters learned of the last-minute swap, they flocked to

Bellini to hear his response, expecting—at a minimum—a few cutting words. But Bellini made a statement that consisted of two short sentences. "It's fair," he said. "Now it's Mauro's turn."

As it turned out, Bellini's understated reaction was appropriate. The switch didn't cause protests inside the team or throw its fragile chemistry off-kilter. Mauro came off the bench to lead the Seleção to a second consecutive World Cup title and a place in Tier One, as if he'd been the captain all along. Eight years later in 1970, when Brazil won yet another World Cup, Mauro and Bellini were both long gone. The captain of that team was another member of the rear guard, a right-side defender named Carlos Alberto Torres.

It wasn't surprising to me that Brazil, even with its abundance of talent, still relied on the work of water carriers—this followed the overall Tier One pattern. What I couldn't fathom is how this team had managed to win three World Cups within twelve years without ever using the same captain twice. And in all three cases, when the team selected a new leader, it had never given the job to the best football player in history.

At seventy-four years old, Pelé cut a wan, frail figure; his eyelids were heavy, his shoulders stooped. As he took questions from reporters at an appearance in Manhattan in the spring of 2015, he was asked why he thought Brazil had been able to find so many capable captains during his playing days. Pelé sank into his chair and let a pause unfold. "It's difficult to say why," he said. "I do not know the reason.

"I was invited to be captain," he continued, "but I always said no." His rationale, Pelé explained, was a tactical one. "Listen, if Santos or Brazil's national team has a captain other than me, then we have two players on the field that have the respect of the officials—Pelé and the captain. If I became captain, we would lose one."

Pelé's answer made sense, but it did not explain the second, more confounding mystery of Brazil—the fact that during one of the greatest stretches of dominance in football history, it seemed to grow capable leaders like Copaifera trees. To get to the bottom of this, I bought a ticket to Rio de Janeiro, and on a sunny October morning in 2016, outside a bright, modern condominium in the neighborhood of Barra da Tijuca, Carlos Alberto Torres opened the gate.

Still full of energy at seventy-one, Torres was the last living captain of that golden era—a man who had played with Pelé, lifted the 1970 World Cup trophy, traveled the world, and gone on to become one of Brazil's most respected football commentators. I'd come to ask him how Brazil, of all places, became the land of captains.

Torres began by telling me that during his international career, he had played with many captains from other countries—and had always envied them. Their teams were homogeneous, he said. Their players thought alike and were often well educated. Leading this kind of team seemed like an easy job. "Brazil is another culture," he said. "In Brazil, there is no uniform way of thinking, and there is less formal education. There are some very poor kids who only go to school for a couple of years before they start playing—and the captain has to know that. We need a leader who is a guide for many, many things. So being captain in Brazil tests the deepest nature of your personality. You have to try to understand people, to know their backgrounds. If you understand them better, you can help them more." Torres clasped his hands together. "We need leaders to hold the players, do you understand? If you force a leadership upon them that's not natural, they won't respect the leader."

According to Torres, the complexity of leading the Seleção was mitigated by one thing. The other players who could have been captains, or were captains of their club teams, knew how difficult it was to fuse Brazilian players into an effective whole—and did not hesitate to offer their support. "The other leaders would help you," he said.

I asked Torres about the other enduring mystery of Brazilian football—why, during Pelé's long and glorious career, the team never pressured him to take the armband. And, more broadly, why the team never gave the job to one of its many superstars.

"It's not always the case that the best player is the best captain,"

Torres said. "A player like Pelé is under so much pressure—there is so much on his shoulders with the fans and the press. It's almost better for him to prepare in the best possible way to play a good game, rather than worrying about the functions of a captain. A captain has to be worried all the time, to be focused on solving problems, talking to the coach, seeking the best way for the team to play, and being an intermediary between the team officials and the players. You have to move the best player away from the group so that he can prepare."

What Torres was saying, in other words, was that in Brazil, the burdens of stardom and the burdens of captaincy were both so heavy that they were incompatible. No one could possibly do both. What he didn't say, however, and what was even more unusual, was that everyone on these Brazilian teams, including Pelé, had somehow instinctively known this.

When I started this project, if you had asked me to name one team in sports history that best exemplifies the power of the water carrier, the national football team from Brazil was the last one I would have chosen. But as I flew home from Rio, it occurred to me that the Seleção hadn't been a freak team because it enjoyed the services of the world's best player. It earned a spot in Tier One because it had installed a perfect set of checks and balances.

The reason these teams were so dominant is that the stars knew they could never be effective captains, and the captains, like Bellini, Mauro, and Torres, knew they could never be stars. In Brazil, the only role available to a leader was to carry water.

CHAPTER SEVEN TAKEAWAYS

- The desire to identify special people, pluck them out of a crowd, and shower them with adulation is as old as time. In celebrities, we see the greater possibilities within ourselves. For teams, this instinct can be problematic. We have a hard time separating the influence of the group from the personality of its star. In many cases, we don't. We assume that the team is the star and the star is the team. On the sixteen teams in Tier One, however, the captains were rarely stars, nor did they act like it. They shunned attention. They gravitated to functional roles. They carried water.

- When it comes to a competition, most people believe that the leader of a team is the person who does something spectacular when the chips are down. The leader is the one who takes the buzzer-beating shot. A team member who performs acts of humility off the field, or who assists others in making these decisive plays, is, by definition, a supporting player. The captains in this book suggest we've got the picture backward. The great captains lowered themselves in relation to the group whenever possible in order to earn the moral authority to drive them forward in tough moments. The person at the back, feeding the ball to others, may look like a servant—but that person is actually creating dependency. The easiest way to lead, it turns out, is to serve.

EIGHT

Boxing Ears and Wiping Noses

Practical Communication

On June 4, 1940, Winston Churchill strode to the despatch box at the House of Commons in London to make his second address to Parliament as Prime Minister. The war with Germany was only nine months old but armored divisions of the Wehrmacht had reached the coast of the English Channel. America had not yet entered the war and there were considerable doubts that the French would continue the fight. Half the population expected Britain to fold as well.

After laying out the state of play, Churchill closed his remarks with an appeal to the nation to gird itself for what was to come. "We shall go on to the end," he said. "We shall fight in France, we shall fight on the seas and oceans, we shall fight with growing confidence and growing strength in the air, we shall defend our Island, whatever the cost may be, we shall fight on the beaches, we shall fight on the landing grounds, we shall fight in the fields and in the streets, we shall fight in the hills; we shall never surrender."

Twenty-three years later and 3,600 miles away, on the centennial anniversary of the Emancipation Proclamation, Martin Luther

King, Jr., appeared in Washington, D.C., on the steps of the Lincoln Memorial. On a sweltering August afternoon, he delivered another speech nobody will ever forget. "We have also come to this hallowed spot to remind America of the fierce urgency of Now," he said. "This is no time to engage in the luxury of cooling off or to take the tranquilizing drug of gradualism. Now is the time to make real the promises of democracy."

These immortal addresses, both preserved on tape, had immediate and practical effects on the people who heard them. They also left another legacy: the fervent belief that the right words delivered in a stirring tone will create a chemical reaction inside our bodies that lifts us to a heightened state.

In Hollywood, the big speech became the preferred motivational plot device—not only for fictional political and military leaders but sports figures, astronauts, even poetry teachers. To prepare a group to meet some prodigious challenge, a leader is supposed to draw its members together and talk to them.

But it was here, in this regard, that the captains of the sixteen teams in Tier One deviated the furthest from our image of what makes an eminent leader. These men and women were not silver-tongued orators or fiery motivators. They didn't like giving speeches.

In fact, they made a point of avoiding them.

When I asked Jérôme Fernandez, the captain of the French national handball team, whether he ever gave inspirational talks, he said he'd tried it only once—and it had been a miserable failure. Carles Puyol told me he couldn't remember ever formally addressing his Barcelona teammates. "It's not something I liked," he said. Hungary's Ferenc Puskás was a relative extrovert by Captain Class standards, but even he abstained from pep talks—he believed his teammates were professionals and should be able to motivate themselves. "Puskás didn't waste words," his coach, Gusztáv Sebes, once said. Yogi Berra quit school after the eighth grade without seeming to have mastered basic sentence structure. "He could hardly talk," the sportswriter

Maury Allen said. "Some people said he was dumb as dishwater." The idea of Berra standing on a chair and delivering the Gettysburg Address before a game was preposterous.

Samples of these Tier One captains interacting with their teammates off the field, or even talking about their communication philosophies, were frustratingly hard to find. They usually opted out of promotional appearances and ceremonies and approached interviews like colonoscopies. They hated talking about themselves and rarely elaborated on the business of leadership. When they did agree to speak to the press, they often did so with rote joylessness or even hostility. Once, when the Pittsburgh sportswriter Jim O'Brien arrived to interview Jack Lambert, the Steelers' captain greeted him at his door holding a shotgun. "He had been cleaning it," O'Brien remembers, "but he held it just to throw me off guard or to make me nervous."

One might assume that these men and women were simply the strong, silent type. According to teammates, however, this was not the case. The captains they saw in the dressing room and on the field were different from the ones that appeared in front of the microphones. With their teammates, they weren't aloof. They didn't bristle at questions and offer clipped responses. In fact, they could be downright chatty.

As much as Carla Overbeck hated the public eye, her cloak of reserve dropped the moment a match began. "I was very vocal," she told me. If a teammate made a tackle, she said she would be the first to praise her, "but if they weren't working hard, I would let them know that, too. If I got on someone for not working hard, as soon as they would shred somebody I would be all over them, telling them how great they were." Didier Deschamps said that within the confines of his team, he was rarely quiet. "I talked during the warm-up, I talked in the locker room, I talked on the field, I talked at halftime. And I kept talking afterward. You have to talk. That's how you can correct something." Even Berra was famous for his constant banter at the plate, which was directed both at teammates and opposing hitters. Boston's Ted Williams would get so annoyed with Berra's chatter he'd turn and yell, "Yogi, shut the fuck up."

Carles Puyol may have been a flaccid and earnest interview subject, but on the pitch he came alive. "It's impossible for me to lose my concentration for even a second," Gerard Piqué, a fellow defender, said of playing with Puyol, "because I always have the same song playing behind me, 'Geri, Geri, Geri.'" When Puyol started chanting his name, Piqué would sometimes turn around to ask him what was the matter—to which Puyol would say, "Nothing, just stay awake."

"It's true that I've been very heavy at times with teammates, but never with bad intentions," Puyol said. "It's just my way of trying to help them be attentive."

Having a captain who was publicly reserved but privately voluble helped to create an inclusive dynamic. Most Tier One teams had open, talkative cultures in which grievances were aired, strategies discussed, and criticisms leveled without delay. These groups encouraged everybody to speak up. When Bill Russell took over as the player-coach of the Celtics in 1966, for instance, he didn't become an autocrat. He held open meetings with the team in which everyone was allowed to speak and decisions were made by consensus. During Jack Lambert's captaincy of the Steelers, the team had a long-standing tradition of gathering in the sauna after games—away from the coaches and the press—to both decompress and have unvarnished conversations about how they had played. It was a no-bullshit zone where candor reigned, accountability was demanded, and no one was above criticism. It was also the place where Lambert felt most at home. "It was Jack Lambert's haven," his former teammate Gerry Mullins said. "He'd be the first one in and the last one to leave."

This kind of "oneness" was an area where coaches seemed to play an important role—not necessarily in creating it but in protecting it. Though he was young enough to have played with some of the members of his team, Barcelona's manager Pep Guardiola not only stayed out of the dressing room to make sure the players felt they could talk freely among themselves, he shifted Barcelona's training sessions from mornings to afternoons so the players would eat dinner together afterward. When the star striker Zlatan Ibrahimović came to Barcelona, he said that Guardiola pulled him aside and told him, "Here at Barça, we keep our feet on the ground." The message, Ibrahimović said, was that he was not supposed to behave like "anybody special."

Viktor Tikhonov, the taskmaster coach of the Soviet Red Army hockey team in the 1980s, was not beloved by his players. But by requiring them to train and compete under intense pressure, apart from their families, for as many as eleven months a year, he forced them to bond so tightly that their identities were no longer distinct. Vladimir Krutov, a winger from these years, was once asked what the Soviet players were like as individuals—what reading habits, hobbies, and interests they had. Krutov thought the question was silly. "All the same," he said. "We were all practically the same."

One of the most convivial teams in Tier One was the 1949–53 New York Yankees. On this team, veterans didn't haze the rookies the way Yogi Berra had been hazed—they took them under their wings. They eliminated cliques by hosting team barbecues to which everyone was invited. It was this team's collection of veteran pitchers who, in 1949, took it upon themselves to help turn Berra into a formidable catcher.

As Berra grew into his role as the team's leader, he carried this culture forward—not by being an eloquent speechmaker but by figuring out how to communicate with each of his teammates in subtle ways. Berra developed a reputation as a "pitcher whisperer." He talked to his charges for hours to learn how they liked to approach hitters, but he also studied their temperaments and learned to adjust to their moods. If a pitcher insisted on shaking off his calls, Berra wouldn't hold a grudge. If they needed help, he would dive right in.

After Berra worked with the talkative junk-baller Eddie Lopat for several years, the two men could essentially read each other's minds—and they stopped using pitch signals completely. As the hard-throwing Vic Raschi aged and started to lose velocity, Berra tutored him on how to beat hitters by varying his pitches and changing speeds.

Berra did some of his finest work when his pitchers were struggling. Sometimes he'd tell them to take it easy, or crack jokes to cut the tension. Other times he lit a fire. "Yogi made you bear down," said the pitcher Whitey Ford. By the time Ford played his first full season with the Yankees in 1953, Berra had developed such a peerless reputation for reading hitters that Ford would simply throw whatever pitches Berra called for. "I rarely had to shake him off," Ford said, "and usually when I did, it turned out Berra was right after all." When the twenty-four-year-old Ford got tied up in knots and started to struggle, Berra would call time, walk slowly to the mound, and say something like, "Okay, Slick. The main feature at the movies starts at six. It's four now, and I want to be on time. Let's get this thing over with."

Throughout Berra's eighteen-year career with the Yankees, the team cycled through dozens of pitchers, few of whom ever posted numbers that rank them among the statistical elite. In 1952 alone, Berra worked with fifteen different pitchers who threw at least fifteen innings. Time and again, pitchers of all stripes arrived in New York with untapped potential and reached the summits of their careers under his tutelage. "Berra proved not only to be a good listener," the author Sol Gittleman wrote, "but what every catcher must be: the subtle psychologist and manipulator of his pitchers."

Nobody in Hollywood would have believed it, given his mumbling speech and his famous penchant for malapropisms, like "It ain't over till it's over." But Yogi Berra was the upholder of a culture in which talking was the secret sauce. Truth be told, he was one of the most talented communicators baseball has ever seen.

One of the oldest puzzles of human interaction is why some groups of people, but not all of them, learn to operate on the same wavelength— to think, and act, as one. Scientists who study group dynamics have found some evidence that over time, when a group of individuals become accustomed to performing a task together, they can develop something called shared cognition. Their collective knowledge and experience help them to form a reciprocal mental model that allows them to anticipate one another's responses and coordinate their work more effectively.

In a 2000 study, a team of researchers at Penn State University observed fifty-six teams of undergraduates as they played a combat simulation videogame that required them to interact in order to defeat a virtual enemy. The rare and gifted teams, the ones that were able to develop this kind of shared cognition, demonstrated a remarkable ability to solve problems—not just in routine situations but in complex circumstances they had never seen before. Other researchers have shown that when a team begins to master "unconscious" communication, its overall performance improves significantly—even if the skill level of each individual member stays the same. In other words, it is possible for a team's members to become so familiar with one another that they can predict, unconsciously, how the other members of the group will respond to just about any event.

What these scholars observed in their laboratories suggests that a sports team might perform better on the field if its members merge themselves into some sort of telepathic whole in which everyone knows what everyone else will do next. What they didn't explain, however, is what role communication plays in all of this—and more than that, how the members of effective teams talk to one another.

Over seven years, starting in 2005, a group of researchers from the Human Dynamics Laboratory at the Massachusetts Institute of Technology studied teams from twenty-one organizations, ranging from banks to hospitals to call centers, to see how they communicated and how those communication patterns influenced their performance.

Rather than simply filming these teams at work or giving them surveys as researchers had often done, the MIT team, led by Alex "Sandy" Pentland, deployed some heavy scientific armaments. Each team member was given a wireless multimedia recorder, worn like a name tag, that took digital images and recorded audio, generating more than a hundred data points per minute. As team members interacted during the workday, the badges recorded the identities of everyone they talked to, the tone of voice they used, whether the speakers faced each other, how much they gestured, and how much time they spent talking, listening, and interrupting. By aggregating this "sociometric" badge data from entire teams, they built detailed graphical maps of their communication patterns.

Right away, the MIT study confirmed what we all suspect: that communication matters. Whether a team was packed with talented, intelligent, and highly motivated individuals, or whether it had achieved solid results in the past, its communication style on any given day was still the best indicator of its performance. In fact, Pentland's researchers could predict how a team felt about its work just by glancing at its badge data.

So how did the best teams communicate?

When it came to team productivity, the MIT researchers found that a key factor was the level of "energy and engagement" the members displayed in social settings outside formal meetings. In other words, teams that talked intently among themselves in the break room were more likely to achieve superior results at work. How much time every member of the group spent talking also proved to be crucial. On the best teams, speaking time was doled out equitably—no single person ever hogged the floor, while nobody shrank from the conversation, either. In an ideal situation, Pentland wrote, "everyone on the team talks and listens in roughly equal measure, keeping contributions short and sweet."

The researchers were also able to isolate the data signatures of the "natural leaders" of these productive units, whom the scientists called charismatic connectors. "Badge data show that these people circulate actively, engaging people in short, high-energy conversations," Pentland wrote. "They are democratic with their time—communicating with everyone equally and making sure all team members get a chance to contribute. They're not necessarily extroverts, although they feel comfortable approaching other people. They listen as much as or more than they talk and are usually very engaged with whomever they're listening to. We call it 'energized but focused listening.'"

After reading the bit about charismatic connectors, I remembered an incident that took place at halftime of the 1998 World Cup final between France and Brazil. It involved one of the most accomplished captains from Tier Two, Didier Deschamps.

France had a surprising 2–0 lead, and as the players burst into the dressing room at halftime they radiated a kind of raw, frenetic tension the public rarely sees. One of the first players through the door was the star midfielder Zinedine Zidane, who had scored both goals. Zidane made a beeline for his locker, took off his shirt, lay down on the floor, and put his hands over his eyes—clearly in a state of exhausted torment. Close behind him was Deschamps. Though he did not make a formal speech, Deschamps ran a circuit of the room talking in a rapid staccato to no one in particular. "We have to keep playing," he said. "We don't sit back."

After a few moments, Deschamps made his way over to Zidane, who was still lying on the floor. He crouched over, clamped his hands on either side of Zidane's face, and stared directly into his eyes while imploring him to tighten up his defense.

In the second half, France shut out the Brazilians again while notching another goal in the closing seconds, clinching a 3–0 victory that delivered the French team its first World Cup title. Two years later, the same team, also led by Deschamps, won the 2000 European Championship, cementing its place in Tier Two.

When it came to that emotionally charged scene with Zidane in the dressing room, Deschamps said it was the same sort of approach he always took with teammates. In addition to the words he used, he felt it was also important to touch people while talking to them and to synchronize his words with his body language. "You have to match up what you want to say with your facial expression," he said. "The players know when I'm happy or not. They can hear it and they can also see it."

Deschamps seemed to have arrived at another truth about communication that the MIT study had hinted at: When it comes to being a successful communicator, words are an important part of the equation—but there's a lot more to it.

In the early 1990s, a pair of Harvard psychologists, Nalini Ambady and Robert Rosenthal, set out to test the power of body language. They began by filming thirteen university-level teaching fellows as they delivered lectures to their students. They cut these tapes down to several ten-second "thin slices" for each teacher and muted the audio.

Next they recruited a panel of "judges," who did not know the teachers and had not taken their classes, and handed them a seemingly impossible task: Using only thirty seconds of silent film, the judges would be asked to rate these teachers by fifteen traits including honesty, likability, supportiveness, confidence, competence, and dominance. When the results were in, the researchers compared these ratings to the ratings these teachers had received from students who'd actually taken their courses, to see how differently the two groups perceived them. To their surprise, the ratings given by both students and judges were nearly identical. The "wordless" judges were so good at evaluating the teaching fellows, in fact, that when Ambady and Rosenthal cut the silent tapes down from a total of thirty seconds to just six, there was no significant difference—the ratings given by a new group of judges were only 7 percent less accurate. This experiment suggested that when it came to the impressions these teachers made on people, body language was by far the most significant factor. Their words *barely mattered*.

The results, the authors wrote, "suggest, first, that our consensual intuitive judgments might be unexpectedly accurate and, second, that we communicate—unwittingly—a great deal of information about ourselves."

In his 1995 book, *Emotional Intelligence*, the psychologist Daniel Goleman outlined a theory based on an idea that scientists had been kicking around since the 1960s. Goleman believed that a person's ability to recognize, regulate, conjure, and project emotions is a distinct form of brainpower—one that can't be revealed by a standard IQ test. People who have high emotional fluency understand how to use "emotional information" to change their thinking and behavior, which can help them perform better in settings where they have to interact with others. Goleman also believed that emotional intelligence was closely correlated to the skills required to be an effective leader, and that it can be more significant in this regard than IQ or even a person's technical expertise.

These findings about the power of body language, and the concept of emotional intelligence, helped to round out a fuller portrait of how these Tier One captains got their messages across without delivering speeches. I wondered if the communication style of great captains wasn't solely a matter of how much they talked but also of the emotional energy they put behind their words through body language, facial expressions, gestures, and touch.

To test this idea, I bought a ticket to a basketball game.

The first thing that came to mind while watching the San Antonio Spurs play basketball was that the arena ought to sell playbills rather than programs. From a floor seat in row two, just behind the Spurs' bench during a 2016 game against the New Orleans Pelicans, I noticed that the Spurs players kept up a never-ending dialogue: "Come on, do the work . . . get to the middle . . . step back, step back . . . can't stop moving . . . pace, pace . . . not too much, Patty . . . red, red, red . . . look behind, beeeehiiind!"

During their unrivaled nineteen-season streak of consistency, the Spurs won five NBA titles by playing grinding defense, running disciplined plays with picks and screens, and excelling in the low post. The Spurs were never the stars of the NBA's offensive or defensive statistical tables. But they were outliers in one category: communication. Like other Tier One teams, the Spurs spent a lot of time talking among themselves, mostly as a means of tightening their choreography. The sportswriter Bill Simmons once said the Spurs reminded him of "five buddies maintaining a running dialogue at a blackjack table as they try to figure out ways to bust the dealer."

I'd come to watch this game, in this close-up seat, to observe this talkative ethos for myself. But the larger goal was to figure out what role, if any, "boring" Tim Duncan played in it. It was hard for me to believe that Duncan, someone with the public personality of a vacuum cleaner, could have been this team's "charismatic connector."

Duncan did not consider himself a vocal leader. He rarely raised his voice. "I think over the years I've been more comfortable with the guys and been a little bit more vocal," he said. "I'll go over and pat 'em on the back and pull people along and things like that. But for the most part I'm always a guy that wants to put the pressure on himself." Compared to most of the captains in Tier One, Duncan seemed to have a profound lack of affect. No matter what the situation, his subdued body language and blank facial expression never changed (the satirical newspaper the *Onion* once poked fun at Duncan for this in an article with the headline "Tim Duncan Hams It Up for Crowd by Arching Left Eyebrow Slightly"). If the Harvard psychologists Ambady and Rosenthal had shown people thirty-second tapes of Duncan giving a lecture, they might have fallen asleep.

Even Duncan's tone of voice was colorless. In interviews, win or lose, he spoke in a monotone that made him seem aloof, even rude. One former teammate, Malik Rose, said the key to understanding Duncan was to listen to what he was saying, rather than how he said it—though it wasn't always easy.

In the game's opening minutes, Duncan played like a basketball robot. He wasted no energy, took the minimum number of steps to get into position, and made careful, subtle, fundamentally solid moves in the low post. He spent some time directing traffic on defense—pointing a teammate to a spot on the floor and giving him a little shove in the right direction—but there were few hints of emotion. After converting a rare dunk in the third quarter, Duncan didn't even pump his fist. And later, in the game's final three minutes, when the Spurs scored ten unanswered points to beat the Pelicans by eight, he didn't crack a smile. As Michael Finley, a former teammate, once said: "If you didn't know anything about basketball and just walked into the gym and you just watched his demeanor, you wouldn't know he was the leader of this team."

There was one thing about Duncan that caught my attention,

however—his eyes. They were not piercing. They didn't make people feel like he was scrutinizing the depths of their souls. But he used them to convey different meanings. When the referees made calls he didn't like, Duncan widened them to express shock. When a teammate missed a defensive assignment, he narrowed them and dropped his chin. Sometimes he'd lock his gaze on a teammate for two full seconds, or even three. His face might have been inscrutable, but his eyes never left any mystery about what he was thinking.

It was during timeouts, when he wasn't playing, that Duncan's eyes came fully alive. They were always moving—darting around to scan the faces of teammates and coaches, the referees, the video board, even the fans. Duncan had several timeout rituals. The moment the whistle blew, he'd pop up from the bench before everyone else and walk out to slap hands with the players as they came off the floor. Then he would vector over to the assistant coaches' huddle to have a look at their notes (something few NBA players do). When San Antonio's coach, Gregg Popovich, knelt down to address the team, Duncan would stake out a spot just behind his left shoulder. From this vantage point, he could see what "Pop" was scribbling on his dry-erase board and add his input when necessary. This vantage point also allowed him to monitor the body language of his teammates sitting in front of him.

After every timeout, when Popovich finished talking, Duncan would seek out one or two teammates, speaking with them softly but intently, sometimes wagging his finger as he explained a strategic point. He also touched them often, slapping hands or butts, tossing an arm around their shoulders, or, in lighter moments, playfully bumping them. As I watched him run this circuit, I realized that all of Duncan's movements were calculated. Like those charismatic connectors in the MIT study, he circulated widely among the team and was democratic with his time. He felt comfortable approaching everyone. He listened as much as he talked and never broke eye contact.

During this game in New Orleans, after the Pelicans jumped out to a 4–0 lead, Popovich called a quick timeout and threw what can only be described as a shit fit. The Spurs had played the night before and seemed tired. Popovich thought they looked lackadaisical and gave them an earful, angrily jabbing his clipboard with an erasable marker. He started by ripping into Duncan, who'd made a sloppy pass. Duncan pointed to himself defensively . . . "Me?" But Popovich reserved his fiercest rebuke for Tony Parker, the team's star guard, who had looked listless on defense. At the end of his talk, he said, "Tony, you're out." Parker seemed to take the benching in stride. He gamely pulled on his T-shirt and settled into a chair. But pulling him out was always a risky move—Parker had a tendency to get down on himself when criticized.

At the next break, Duncan sprang into action. He hurried off the court, walked straight over to Parker, put a hand on his head, and lifted it up in order to lock eyes with him. As Parker averted his, Duncan moved his hand to Parker's back and patted it. "You okay?" he asked. Parker nodded, looked up at Duncan, and flashed a faint smile. Duncan stood there for a moment, holding the pose and staring at his teammate for about three seconds. Only then did he take his seat.

Eight minutes later, when Popovich decided to put Parker back into the game, Duncan placed a palm protectively on his teammate's chest. In another timeout, Duncan walked up behind Parker, put his arms around him, and hugged him. He leaned over and whispered something in his ear with a smile. Parker laughed. Duncan put his left hand on Parker's shoulder and started kneading it. While Duncan had probably said all of five words, his message of support couldn't have been clearer.

After the game, Popovich wouldn't say why he'd sent Parker off so abruptly. Most of the Spurs bolted from the locker room without talking to reporters. I asked the Spurs guard Patty Mills if he'd noticed what Duncan had done. "Obviously he's been around Tony so long, he knows how to handle that situation," Mills said. "Tim always finds ways to get the message across, even if it's little, quick, and short. If something needs to be said, he'll say it. If not, he'll leave it alone. So when he does speak, everyone listens."

The great irony of Duncan's leadership was that even though he didn't like to talk, he worked hard to create an environment in which talking was encouraged. And he fashioned a role for himself inside the team as the player who facilitated this openness. He wasn't naturally expressive, but he learned to use the tools he had—especially his eyes—to send powerful signals at critical moments.

"He doesn't judge people," Popovich said of Duncan. "He tries to figure out who they are, what they do, and what their strengths are. He just has a very good sense about people. When we learned that about him . . . we knew we were going to be able to bring almost anybody here, unless they were a serial killer, and he was going to be able to figure out what to do with them. Tim Duncan touching you on the back of the head or putting his arm around you, or leaning over and saying something to you during a timeout, is big. He knows that the attention from him is just monstrous in their development and their self-confidence, and that recognition has made him the leader that he is."

I walked back to my hotel that night with a much clearer picture of how Duncan communicated with his teammates. He didn't deliver grandiose speeches or get in their faces to yell at them. He used words sparingly and purposefully to apply practical remedies as soon as problems flared up. And just like other Tier One captains, he made sure to reinforce these messages by touching his teammates and using his eyes to amplify the meaning of his words. Though "charisma" was the last word people associated with Duncan, he had turned out to be precisely the kind of charismatic connector that the MIT researchers had identified.

In addition to exploring the power of body language, the Harvard study of teaching fellows examined another idea—whether there was an ideal combination of gestures and expressions a person can make.

Ambady and Rosenthal noticed that the lowest-rated teachers had a tendency to sit, shake their heads, frown, and fidget with their hands. Those gestures seemed to be ones worth avoiding. The highest-rated teachers were generally more active than the others, but beyond that their gestures were all over the map. Some smiled, nodded, laughed, pointed, or clapped, while others did none of those things. It didn't matter, either, whether the speakers were attractive or their gestures were strong or subdued. Charisma was not some universal, repeatable, or even easily recognizable quality in a person. There was no "correct" set of mannerisms that increased one's odds of making a favorable impression. The most effective communicators had styles that were as distinct as their fingerprints. "Judges can identify whether a person is being warm or not," the researchers wrote, "although they might not be able to isolate the specific cues driving those perceptions."

In other words, whatever notions we have of what traits make somebody charismatic are implicitly wrong. It doesn't matter what kind of body language or speech pattern people use when communicating with others. What matters is that they develop a formula that works for them.

Most team leaders are conditioned to respond to a tough challenge by trying to think of the perfect words to use, and finding the ideal moment to deliver them. Tim Duncan, Yogi Berra, Carles Puyol, Carla Overbeck, and the other Tier One captains used a different approach. They engaged with their teammates constantly—listening, observing, and inserting themselves into every meaningful moment. They didn't think of communication as a form of theater. They saw it as an unbroken flow of interactions, a never-ending parade of boxing ears, delivering hugs, and wiping noses.

CHAPTER EIGHT TAKEAWAYS

- If faced with the task of trying to stiffen a team's resolve in the face of a grueling test, most of us will respond by finding a mirror and rehearsing a speech. Conventional wisdom tells us that the right words, delivered in the perfect moment, are the key to motivation. The captains in Tier One didn't simply fail to prove this idea—they suggested that it's patently false. They did not give speeches. They were often lousy interviews, too, or were considered to be quiet or even inarticulate. They led without fanfare.

- One of the great scientific discoveries about effective teams is that their members talk to one another. They do it democratically, with each person taking a turn. The leaders of these kinds of teams circulated widely, talking to everyone with enthusiasm and energy. The teams in Tier One had talkative cultures like this, too—and the person who fostered and sustained that culture was the captain. Despite their lack of enthusiasm for talking publicly, most of these captains, inside the private confines of their teams, talked all the time and strengthened their messages with gestures, stares, touches, and other forms of body language. The secret to effective team communication isn't grandiosity. It's a stream of chatter that is practical, physical, and consistent.

NINE

Calculated Acts

The Power of Nonverbal Displays

PITTSBURGH, 1976

Jack Lambert, the lanky, fair-haired, six-foot-four middle linebacker for the Pittsburgh Steelers, sidled into the locker room wearing his default expression, the sort of gunslinger's glower that prompted anyone in his path to step aside. Lambert was a man who seemed to be perpetually on the verge of exploding.

The Steelers had just finished throttling the Cincinnati Bengals 23–6, and Lambert had played a nearly flawless football game. In addition to recording eight unassisted tackles and a quarterback sack, he'd made an interception that resulted in a Pittsburgh touchdown and caused and recovered a fumble that set up a field goal. Lambert had not only spotted his offense ten points, he'd helped the defense keep Cincinnati out of the end zone. In a game with twenty-two players on the field, he'd single-handedly tilted the outcome.

The newspaper beat writers, in their rumpled khakis and dress shirts, had formed a semicircle in front of Lambert's locker, waiting to collect quotes. This was a job no one relished. For all the attention he attracted on the field with his expressive, high-energy play, Lambert loathed the press. He was openly contemptuous of reporters and didn't like being the center of attention. His scorn wasn't only reserved for people with tape recorders. Lambert could be hard on his teammates, too, barking at them if they lined up wrong or showed a lazy attitude. He once told the team's offensive captain, Sam Davis, it was time he went on a diet. As talkative as he was in the sauna, Lambert projected a solitary image by drinking alone at the hotel bar on road trips, reading novels in his room, or sitting by himself at the end of the bench. "I'm not a holler guy," he once said. "I may say something in the huddle, but for the most part I'm quiet. I've always felt you should lead by example, not lip service."

As Lambert arrived at his locker, the writers standing around him felt sheepish. Before the game, they'd pointed at the team's 1–4 record and piled on the eulogies, concluding that the Steelers wouldn't make the playoffs. Lambert's performance on the field had made them look like fools. Though nobody knew it, Pittsburgh would go on to win the rest of its games and set an NFL record by shutting out five opponents.

There was another reason for their silence, however. Bob Milie, the Steelers' assistant trainer, had also been waiting for Lambert, and as soon as he arrived, Milie set to work on his right hand with a pair of surgical scissors. A deep gash ran across his palm in an area where stitches were impossible to secure. The training staff had done its best before the game to dress the wound, but the bandages had failed and the gauze, the tape, and Lambert's ripped skin had become so mangled and blood-caked they were indistinguishable. The cut had bled out everywhere, creating crimson smears all over Lambert's white jersey and yellow uniform pants. He looked as if he'd just butchered a deer. The reporters had been transfixed by the gory spectacle.

"Well?" Lambert said, after a minute of silence. "Is anybody going to ask me anything or are you all just going to stand there?"

"What happened to your hand?" one of the writers finally asked.

Lambert lifted the shredded flesh up above his head so the writers could have a closer look. "It's just a little beat up," he said. "It's a rough game, you know."

American football is unique among team sports in that its teams are composed of two distinct units, offense and defense. These platoons do not interact. They have separate rosters and captains. When it came to the Steelers of the 1970s, however, the offense was just window dressing. It was the team's Steel Curtain defense—one of the best in NFL history—that made the Steelers so potent.

Though he wouldn't become a captain until the following season, there was no doubt in anyone's mind that Lambert was the engine of the defense. "Jack Lambert, without question, was the catalyst," said Bud Carson, the Steelers' defensive coordinator. "He was the guy that turned this from a very good football team and defensive team to a great defensive team. He was a very inspirational player, a tough player. I've never seen anyone like him. And without Jack Lambert I'm not sure we would have ever made it over the hump."

Lambert had been in the NFL for a couple of seasons, but his rapid ascent to stardom caught people by surprise. Not only was he slow-footed for a linebacker, but he was skinny, too, weighing in at just over two hundred pounds as a rookie—far less than the league average. When the Steelers drafted him, some NFL scouts and columnists compared him to a pool cue or a scarecrow and predicted he would never be a regular starter. Steelers scouts had given Lambert B grades for athleticism, quickness, strength, and agility.

His attitude score, however, had been off the charts.

From the moment he showed up at Pittsburgh's training camp in 1974, Lambert showed an uncanny ability to defy his physical limitations. While he wasn't big, he was blessed with superior balance and natural strength. His tackling technique—head up, hips squared—was ripped from a coaching manual. He studied so much film that he developed a sixth sense for the ball and always seemed to materialize in the perfect spot to make a play.

Lambert's most powerful weapon on the field, however, was something intangible. He scared the living shit out of people.

In high school, Lambert had lost several of his front teeth in a basketball game. Dentists had fitted him with a prosthetic, but on the field he never wore it. This toothless maw made him look like a deranged madman, or as *Sports Illustrated* famously described him, "Dracula in cleats." Before every snap, Lambert didn't assume the same frozen crouch most middle linebackers used—instead he pumped his legs maniacally, twitching with rage. He became famous for showing no mercy on quarterbacks, even when they scurried out-of-bounds to try to avoid him. Lambert would pound them into paste.

John Elway of the Denver Broncos, a future Hall of Fame quarterback, recalled looking up and seeing Lambert staring at him from across the line of scrimmage for the first time. "He had no teeth, and he was slobbering all over himself," Elway said. "I'm thinking: 'You can have your money back. Just get me out of here. Let me go be an accountant.' I can't tell you how badly I wanted out of there."

In reality, Lambert was an introverted, cerebral player who overcame his lack of size by poring over game film and honing his techniques. The general impression among fans, opposing players, and reporters, however, was that he was a frothing lunatic.

Lambert was well aware of his persona. Football was an emotional game, he said, and sometimes he needed to do things to fire up his team. But he also made sure to add a caveat—he wasn't violent. "I don't sit in front of my locker thinking of fighting or hurting somebody," he said. "All I want to do is be able to play football hard and aggressively, the way it's meant to be played." Lambert also rejected the idea that he was out of control. "I'm really not that wild, either. I'm emotional, but I know what I'm doing. It's a series of calculated acts."

There was no good reason why Lambert's hand injury in that crucial Cincinnati game had to become such a gruesome mess—or that his uniform should have become soaked in blood. The trainers could have wrapped the wound with fresh bandages every time he came off the field. When asked about this, Bob Milie, the trainer, said his staff had learned never to approach Lambert to treat one of his bloody injuries. Whenever they did, Lambert would scream at them not to touch him. "He was probably the biggest intimidator on the team," Milie said. "He *liked* having blood on his uniform."

In the previous chapter, we saw how Tier One captains like Tim Duncan improved their teams by keeping up a constant stream of practical communication and employing gestures, touches, and eye contact to bolster their messages. Jack Lambert did some of this, too. As the quarterback of the Steelers' defense, he called the signals, and he also challenged his teammates during games and gave them blunt feedback in the sauna afterward. Yet Lambert had anther quality that set him apart from Duncan. On the field, he went out of his way to project extreme passion and emotion. This seemed to me like an altogether different impulse—a more primal form of communication that belonged in a separate category.

On the morning of July 15, 1927, Elias Canetti, a twenty-one-year-old graduate student, climbed on his bicycle and went for a ride through the streets of Vienna, only vaguely aware of the bubbling political drama that had gripped the city. As he rode past the Palace of Justice, the building that housed Austria's Supreme Court, he saw thousands of members of the Social Democratic Party massing outside its doors. The crowd, outraged by a jury verdict in a murder case, had been gathering steam all morning, scooping up compatriots as it veered from one civic building to the next. As Canetti watched from his bicycle, the protest exploded.

Protesters smashed the building's windows and climbed inside. First they destroyed the furnishings. Then they pulled out books and files and set them on fire. As the building erupted in flames, firefighters arrived, but the rioters cut their hoses. Eventually the Vienna police chief, seeing no other alternative, armed his officers with rifles. They would end the protest by shooting eighty-nine protesters dead.

Canetti had pedaled away before the worst of the carnage, but the sight of the mob, whipped into a frenzy of looting and burning, had left a deep impression. He had been terrified by the spectacle but also fascinated by the way the crowd had seemed to develop a mind of its own.

In the coming years, as fascism and war gripped Europe, the notion of mobs, driven by a uniformity of thought and a thirst for violence, became a subject of global concern. As he watched these events unfold, Canetti returned to that scene in Vienna, where he had seen this animal power up close. The subject of mobs became the focus of his scholarly research. He would become one of the world's leading authorities on the psychology of crowds.

In his 1960 book, *Crowds and Power*, Canetti described the way an emotion could sweep rapidly and wordlessly through a group of people, creating an irresistible impulse to join in. "Most of them do not know what has happened and, if questioned, have no answer; but they hurry to be there where most other people are," he wrote. "There is a determination in their movement which is quite different from the expression of ordinary curiosity. It seems as though the movement of some of them transmits itself to the others." In the crowd, "the individual feels that he is transcending the limits of his own person."

Canetti believed that people didn't decide to join mobs; they were moved to do so by an emotional contagion that seeped into them unconsciously, creating a simultaneous alignment of their biology. That contagion would drive them to pursue some unified course of action, even at the risk of injury or death. A crowd, Canetti wrote, "wants to experience for itself the strongest possible feeling of its animal force."

For three decades, Canetti's observations remained the definitive work on the subject. Scientists conducted experiments to try to better understand the neurological forces he'd described but with limited results. In the 1990s, however, with the aid of advanced brain scanners, researchers in Italy made a significant breakthrough.

A group of neuroscientists at the University of Parma discovered, quite by accident, a class of cells inside the brains of monkeys that would fire up when the monkeys were watching other people perform various tasks, such as eating an ice cream cone. The researchers went on to identify neurons in the brains of these primates that mimicked, or mirrored, what others do. The discovery of these reactive cells, or mirror neurons, as the scientists called them, offered the first physical evidence that the phenomenon of brain interconnectedness that researchers had observed in groups might be the result of a complex, hardwired neurochemical system in our bodies that operates below consciousness. It also suggested that this pipeline could be manipulated by others and that humans could be forced to feel powerful emotions. In other words, what Canetti had observed in that Viennese mob was biology at work.

Since the discovery of mirror neurons, scientists have learned a great deal more about the nature of emotional "transfers" and just how quickly they can overtake us. In 2004, *Science* published an article based on the work of the University of Wisconsin neuroscientist Paul Whalen and his colleagues, who discovered that when it comes to looking at images that convey powerful emotions like fear, the human brain registers them and begins to buzz with activity in just seventeen milliseconds. Before we're even aware that we've seen a fearful image, our brains are already processing it.

Scientists still don't know what happens inside the body after these triggers are pulled or whether there might be a connection to the way people perform physically. Yet dozens of experiments done under the umbrella of "emotional intelligence" have made one thing clear: Many effective leaders can—and do—use this subconscious system to manipulate the emotions of their followers. Daniel Goleman and another psychologist, Richard Boyatzis, writing on this subject in 2008, said they believe that great leaders are the ones "whose behavior powerfully leverages this system of brain interconnectedness."

One method for doing this is something scientists call surface acting. This occurs when a person puts on an expression, or takes some subtle action, to try to influence the people around them. Another method, described as deep acting, occurs when a person doesn't pretend to feel something but alters their actual emotions instead.

To engage in deep acting, people need the capability to control, manage, and modify their feelings, and also to project them. Several laboratory experiments and field studies have shown that when team leaders display these deep emotions effectively, they can have a strong impact on the thoughts, emotions, and actions of subordinates. Studies have shown that a team leader who is in a positive mood can increase a group's enthusiasm, help it to channel anger more constructively, and even coax it to perform better on specific tasks, such as assembling a jigsaw puzzle.

What all of this research shows is that anyone who wants to change the emotional composition of a group—whether it's a Viennese mob or a football team—can do so by tapping into an invisible network that connects all people together. Strong leaders, if they are so inclined, can bypass the conscious minds of their followers and communicate directly with their brains.

Jack Lambert's bloody-uniform game in 1976 was hardly a unique event in the annals of Tier One captains. Most of them had, at some point when the stakes were high, performed acts that can only be described as aggressive displays. These moves weren't aimed at reaching any one person or solving any problem in particular but to release some emotional force into the atmosphere.

During pregame introductions, for example, Bill Russell would stride onto the court with maximum cockiness, glowering at the other team. Once he joined his teammates, he'd fold his arms regally, high up on his chest, as if he were the king of all he surveyed. Russell later said he struck this arrogant pose on purpose.

The Tier One captain who stood above the rest in terms of aggressive displays was New Zealand's Buck Shelford. On the rugby pitch, Shelford's persuasive *mana,* combined with his unforgettable toughness at Nantes, left no questions about his passion to win. One of Shelford's most memorable qualities as captain was his dedication to a pregame ritual known as the haka. New Zealand's native Maori tribe were renowned warriors, famous the world over for their intimidating facial tattoos, their skill at wielding giant staffs made of wood or whale-bone, and celebrating victories in battle by eating the roasted hearts of their enemies. The haka, which is basically a group dance, was an ancient component of Maori warcraft, a tightly choreographed spectacle of ignition performed in a variety of circumstances but mainly before battle. The haka was meant to paralyze the enemy with dread by conveying the idea that the warriors had come under the influence of the gods. It was also used to create a collective frenzy among the warriors that put their bodies into perfect sync. The message it sent, as the haka expert Inia Maxwell put it, was that "we're going to battle and we're not really expecting to come back alive or injury-free, so let's throw everything at it."

In the mid-1880s, when New Zealand's national rugby team first began traveling to play abroad, the All Blacks would entertain the crowds before kickoff by doing a haka. The version they used most often over the decades was a haka known as Ka Mate. To perform it, the All Blacks lined up at the halfway line before kickoff in a wedge formation facing the other team. The ritual began when the haka leader, standing in the center, shouted, *"Kia rite!"* ("Be ready!") At this, the performers put their hands on their hips, thumbs pointing forward. Then the leader shouted a series of preparatory commands:

"Ringa pakia!" ("Slap the hands against the thighs!")

"Uma tiraha!" ("Puff out the chest!")

"Turi whatia!" ("Bend the knees!")

"Hope whai ake!" ("Let the hip follow!")

"Waewae takahia kia kino!" ("Stamp the feet as hard as you can!")

Once the pack was in position, with each player's muscles flexed and lungs expanded to maximum volume, the dance would begin, accompanied by a thunderous group chant:

"Ka mate, ka mate?" ("Am I going to die, am I going to die?")

"Ka ora, ka ora?" ("Or will I live, or will I live?")

As the guttural sounds poured out of them, and as they stomped the turf, slapped their bodies, and punched the air, the players would add their own terrifying enhancements—sticking out their tongues, distending their mouths, and rolling their eyes until only the whites were visible. At the end, the entire team leaped into the air.

Opposing players did not understand a word the All Blacks were saying, but they didn't need to: Their body language left no mystery. In 1884, when the All Blacks visited Australia, a Sydney newspaper reported that "the sound given in good time and union by eighteen pairs of powerful lungs was sometimes tremendous" and had scared the Aussie players "out of their wits." The Australian player Dave Brockhoff, who witnessed the haka for the first time in 1949, said he believed the ritual gave the All Blacks "a physical, mental supremacy."

When Buck Shelford took over the captaincy in 1987, the haka was withering from neglect. A series of captains of European ancestry, who saw it as an obligation, had been performing it lifelessly for years. Shelford, a Maori, arranged for his teammates to visit a Maori college in New Zealand where they could learn about the haka's history and see it performed correctly. "I can still remember driving into the school that afternoon and the ground was rumbling as the whole school was doing the haka," Sean Fitzpatrick recalled. "It was wonderful." Shelford forced the All Blacks to practice the ritual, and then practice it some more. As the weeks rolled on, his team became increasingly engrossed in the performance. "It started to mean something to them," he said.

It would be naïve to suggest that a pregame dance was the primary reason the All Blacks continued their unbeaten streak for three more years, but Shelford's reinvigorated haka clearly became a source of energy for the team and a problem for its opponents. Some rival teams became so anxious about its effects that they called meetings to discuss how to respond to it. New Zealand's players also came to understand and appreciate its power. "It's a big advantage," Fitzpatrick told me. "Done properly, it can be very motivating."

Whether or not performing the haka made the All Blacks play better rugby, it was the kind of thing that might strengthen their resolve.

It also put Buck Shelford front and center where his teammates could see, hear—even feel—the aggression pulsing through him. The haka, like Lambert's bloody uniform or Bill Russell's arrogant pose, was the sort of thing that might fire people's mirror neurons. It was an excellent way for a captain to broadcast his fanaticism to his own team—to create the sort of contagion that Canetti described.

On the general topic of communicating with teammates, the one captain I struggled to get a handle on was the ice-hockey legend Maurice "Rocket" Richard.

Among his Captain Class peers, Richard was an outlier in one respect—he hardly interacted with anybody. Teammates say Richard would sit through entire six-hour train trips staring out the window, sphinxlike, without saying anything. On some game days, the total number of words he spoke could be counted on two hands. Though Richard didn't keep up a constant stream of banter like Didier Deschamps and didn't seem to be a charismatic connector like Tim Duncan, his Montreal Canadiens teammates still found him to be profoundly inspirational. The legendary center Jean Béliveau once wrote that Richard "embodied a force, an energy, something that rubbed off on many of his teammates and carried us to five straight championships."

"The Rocket was more than a hockey player," his former coach Dick Irvin said. "It was his fury, his desire, and his intensity that motivated the Canadiens."

Richard wasn't a physically imposing man, a skilled stickhandler, or, despite his nickname, a particularly fast skater. There is no question that he had a fiery temper (more on that later) and played a passionate and relentless brand of hockey. What people remember best about Richard is the intensity in his eyes. Though they were actually brown, people who saw them up close said they appeared black. Beneath Richard's bushy eyebrows, his eyes were the focal points of a narrow, triangular face that tapered into a prominent chin.

Because he played in the era before helmets with face shields were mandatory, his eyes were constantly on display, and people said the "fire" in them, especially when he got worked up, was unforgettable. Frank Selke, Montreal's general manager during those years, described it as a "piercing intensity," while sportswriters called it "the Rocket's red glare." William Faulkner, a hockey rube who once covered a 1955 Canadiens game for *Sports Illustrated*, was immediately transfixed by the intensity he saw in Richard, whose presence he described as having the "passionate glittering fatal alien quality of snakes."

Opposing goaltenders talked about Richard's eyes, too. When he swooped toward them with the puck, the snarl on his lips and the stern set of his jaw were terrifying enough, but it was his eyes that spooked them. "When he came flying toward you with the puck on his stick, his eyes were all lit up, flashing and gleaming like a pinball machine," said the former goalie Glenn Hall. "It was terrifying." While Tim Duncan's eyes were infinitely expressive, Richard's had exactly two settings— placid and stormy.

Richard didn't give locker room speeches, but according to one teammate, George Gross, he did have a peculiar ritual. Inside the dressing room in the final minutes before the game, Richard would swivel his head methodically from one side of the room to the other, stopping to stare at each of his teammates until they met his eyes. When he was done, he would make some clipped statement, like "Let's go out and win it." Given what we know about emotional contagion, deep and surface acting, mirror neurons, and the speed at which the brain registers strong emotions, this tactic suddenly takes on a different cast. It's as if Richard knew that by locking his beams on people and making them see his face, he could download his own intensity right into them.

Richard was, in fact, the silent type. He didn't engage in constant interactions and wasn't able to reach his teammates the way Tim Duncan did, by serving as his team's charismatic connector. Yet he might have realized that there is more than one way to communicate.

In a supercharged environment like the NHL, where the challenge to the athletes is both mental and physical, this deeper form of communication—based on displays rather than words—seems to have been a perfectly effective substitute.

The Tier One captains were not students of Elias Canetti. I would be shocked if any of them were steeped in the Italian study of mirror neurons or cared much about the scientific nuances of deep acting. If the aggressive displays they made to their teammates were intentional, as they seemed to be, this must have been something they intuited. It was another form of competitive intelligence.

If there is a pathway into the minds of human beings that bypasses consciousness and absorbs the emotions of others; and if this pathway can be activated by the sight of a bloody uniform, a hair-raising tribal dance, or just a deep stare; and if these displays can propel a team to run faster, jump higher, hit harder, and push through pain and exhaustion, then these captains must have been masters of the art.

It's hard to imagine how aggressive displays might be useful on the average team in the workplace. Trying to fire up one's sales team by performing a one-man haka would only earn a visit from the HR department. Making some kind of emotional statement seems better suited to "performance" teams, like flight crews or orchestras, that work together in situations where they only have one chance to get things right. In the realm of sports, however, there is plenty of evidence that such displays make a difference.

Philipp Lahm, the German football captain who, like Deschamps, led two different teams into Tier Two (more on him in a moment), summed it up well. Lahm believed that without passion, even the best teams won't win, and that the passion of one player could elevate the performance of an entire unit. When a leader does something dramatic on the field, he said, "it releases energies you didn't even know you had."

CHAPTER NINE TAKEAWAYS

- The greatest misperception about communication is the idea that words need to be involved. In the past few decades, a wave of scientific breakthroughs has confirmed something that most of us already suspected. Our brains are capable of making deep, powerful, fast-acting, and emotional connections with the brains of people around us. This kind of synergy doesn't require our participation. It happens automatically, whether we're aware of it or not.

- Time and again, I found examples of Tier One captains who had done dramatic, bizarre, and sometimes frightening things during or right before an important competition. These incidents had two things in common: First, they did not involve words; second, they were intentional. None of the captains in Tier One had read up on the science of emotional contagion. Yet they all seemed to understand that there were times when practical communication wasn't enough.

TEN

Uncomfortable Truths

The Courage to Stand Apart

As the Soviet-built Il-62 passenger plane cut through the frigid February air above the Atlantic en route from New York to Moscow, there wasn't a person on board who looked forward to landing. The primary occupants of the rear cabin were twenty of the Soviet Union's best ice-hockey players, slumped against their chairs in various stages of vodka ingestion. Despite having been heavy favorites to win the gold medal at the 1980 Lake Placid Olympics, the vaunted Red Army team had fallen apart.

Missing out on a gold medal at an Olympics—one held in the United States in the middle of the Cold War, no less—was humiliating enough for a team that had won fourteen of the last seventeen World Championships and four consecutive gold medals. Losing in the medal round to the Americans by the score of 4–3, as they had done, was a recipe for eternal despondency—or worse. The fact that the American team had been composed of a bunch of long-haired collegiate amateurs had made this one of the biggest upsets in sports history, a game forever remembered in the United States as the Miracle on Ice. The

Soviet players were so disgusted by their silver medals they hadn't bothered to have them inscribed.

The result was a colossal embarrassment for the Kremlin, which had forced the players to train slavishly for eleven straight months, driven by a tyrannical coach handpicked to ensure that something like this would never happen. The day after the defeat, *Pravda,* the paper of the regime, didn't even acknowledge the game had taken place.

After the plane reached its cruising altitude, one of the Soviet players, the veteran defenseman Valeri Vasiliev, grew tired of wallowing in misery. He, too, had been gutted by the loss, but in his ten years on the team Vasiliev had been through a few of these disappointments. He had known plenty of hardships in his life and wasn't one to mope. He left his seat and headed up to the flight deck to chat with the pilots.

Vasiliev had grown up in Gorki, about 250 miles east of Moscow. His father had been shot to death in a fight before he was born, leaving him and his siblings to the care of an overwhelmed mother. "We were raised by the street," he once said. Vasiliev was a tough kid, a hoodlum by some accounts, with a fondness for drinking and smoking, a dim view of authority, and a thick accent that betrayed a lack of schooling. Though he was ruggedly handsome, his broad bumpy nose bore the telltale signs of more than a few blunt impacts. His teammates loved to spin yarns about how Vasiliev could punch holes through wooden boards with his fists, bend nails around his fingers, or catch birds with his bare hands. "He was like a folk hero," his fellow defenseman Viacheslav "Slava" Fetisov told me. "There was a story that he once bit the head off a pigeon. I don't know where that came from."

One of the legends about Vasiliev wasn't a legend at all. During the 1978 World Championship in Prague, the Red Army team's hopes had come down to a decisive game against the tournament's hosts, the Czechs. The Soviets, who needed to win by two goals to secure the title, had jumped out to a quick 3–0 advantage, but the home team battled back to cut their lead to two. The Czechs had upset the Soviets the year before, and the pace of the game was exhausting even for the fittest players. Late in the third period, Vasiliev felt a lump in his throat and began struggling to breathe. When he came off the ice at the end of his shift, the pain was so intense he had to lie down. Still, when it came time to go back on the ice, he grabbed his stick and popped over the boards. The Soviets held on to win 3–1.

Back in Moscow, Vasiliev went for a checkup to figure out why he'd felt so gassed late in the game. The doctors ran some tests and came back with their diagnosis. He hadn't just played through some routine malady. He'd suffered a *heart attack*.

On the Soviet team, the stars of the show were the team's lightning-quick forwards, who were renowned for carving balletic circles around opposing defenses. Vasiliev, by contrast, had an awkward skating style and little interest in scoring. Though slightly undersize for a defenseman at five foot eleven and 190 pounds, he was the team's enforcer, famous for inflicting pain on rival forwards by sending them airborne with perfectly executed hip checks. He was so feared in the Soviet leagues that some teams pulled their best forwards when he came into the game to prevent them from being injured. NHL players who faced him in exhibitions called him Iron Ass or Lord of the Taiga. The great Bobby Hull once admitted that when he saw Vasiliev approaching, he got rid of the puck as quickly as possible.

"He was a simple guy who didn't play games," said Vladislav Tretiak, the Soviet goalkeeper. "He was a real Russian man—strong, straightforward. He said little but his actions spoke volumes."

In his 1987 memoir, *The Real Men of Hockey,* Anatoly Tarasov, the Soviet coach who built the mighty Red Army team, once raved that Vasiliev "remained simple and kind to his comrades, warlike and terrifying to his opponents. He was one of those players who, without a word and with only the strength of his actions, could rally the guys for an attack."

On the long flight to Moscow, as he sat with the pilots in a cockpit jump seat, Vasiliev heard a familiar voice. It belonged to his coach, Viktor Tikhonov, who was seated in the first-class cabin. A thin, unsmiling man with a boyish thatch of sandy hair, Tikhonov had taken control of the team three years earlier at the behest of the Soviet sports ministry, after it concluded that the previous coaches were too soft on the players. Tikhonov had a reputation as a stern taskmaster, and he had already collected a pair of World Championship wins and a 2–1 victory over the NHL's best players in a 1979 exhibition in New York City. But now, after the debacle in Lake Placid, his fate was uncertain, too.

In the final team meeting before leaving Lake Placid, Tikhonov had beseeched the players not to point fingers. The story they would tell in Moscow, he said, was that they'd lost as a team. As he sat in first class, however, flanked by his assistant coaches and various Soviet dignitaries, Tikhonov expressed a markedly different view. He ripped into the team's veterans, especially the forward Valeri Kharlamov and the captain, Boris Mikhailov. Not only were they old and slow, he complained, they were resistant to his coaching methods.

"Why did we bring them?" he wondered. "We lost because of them."

What Tikhonov didn't realize was that the cockpit door was open, and Valeri Vasiliev could hear every word he was saying.

Vasiliev, who died in 2012, never gave any formal account of what happened next. Tikhonov, who passed away two years later, never discussed the episode publicly, either. But according to one witness, Vasiliev popped out of his seat in the flight deck and came barreling through the cockpit door, headed straight for Tikhonov. "We agreed that we lost as a team!" Vasiliev shouted. Then he grabbed Tikhonov by the back of the neck and started shaking him. "I will throw you out of this airplane right now!"

Vasiliev was eventually separated from his coach and hauled back to the rear cabin to cool off. What would happen to him back in Moscow was anyone's guess. This wasn't the first time he had gotten into trouble. He had often defied the team's strict and abstemious training regimen by sneaking cigarettes and showing up to practices and games at the tail end of a bender. Given his disciplinary record, the disaster that had just transpired at Lake Placid, and the number of sports ministry officials and politburo members aboard that plane, the Soviets could easily have chosen to make an example out of him.

But Vasiliev wasn't sent to Siberia. Even though Tikhonov eventually followed through with his threats and benched or purged several of the team's veterans, including the forward Kharlamov and the captain, Mikhailov, Vasiliev kept his job. The following year, when the players were instructed to elect a new captain, they voted for Vasiliev— and the Kremlin allowed the decision to stand. From that point forward, the Red Army team, which competed at the pleasure of an authoritarian political regime, would have a captain who did not hesitate to speak truth to power.

The exodus of veterans from the Red Army team should have brought on a fallow period. When Vasiliev took over, however, the team began to feed off his toughness and coalesce around his leadership. With Vasiliev directing the defense, Tikhonov's new group of five young, freakishly fast and talented forwards felt safe enough to play with abandon, knowing they would be protected and that their occasional mistakes would be mopped up. The result was something nobody could have predicted.

The Red Army team did not struggle. It got better.

In their next major competition, the 1981 World Championship, the Soviets demolished Sweden, on Swedish ice, by the score of 13–1. It would go on to win the tournament by scoring sixty-three goals and allowing only sixteen. The Soviets then traveled to Canada to play in an exhibition series against one of the strongest Canadian teams ever assembled—a unit packed with NHL superstars including Guy Lafleur, Ray Bourque, Denis Potvin, and a young turk named Wayne Gretzky. In several previous attempts, the Soviets hadn't been able to hold off the Canadian professionals, who pounded away at them to the delight of howling, jingoistic crowds. This time, Vasiliev's Red Army team crushed them 8–1.

Over four seasons, the Soviets ripped off a Tier One spree of excellence in which it won or drew 96 percent of its games and captured twelve of thirteen possible titles—the most dominant run in the history of international hockey.

The winning might have continued for many years. But in 1983, Vasiliev was summoned to the office of a Communist Party apparatchik who made him an offer, he said, "that was incompatible with the way I lived my life." The official "wanted me to be the snitch on the team, to tell him what was going on within the group." Vasiliev wasn't interested. "I punched the guy and left," he said. "After that, they started to squeeze me out."

Following Vasiliev's involuntary retirement that same year, another defender, Slava Fetisov, was asked to take over as captain. The team continued its torrid pace through the 1984 Olympics but cooled after that, finishing third at the 1985 World Championship.

In his short three-year tenure as captain, Vasiliev had exhibited all the classic Captain Class traits. He was dogged on the ice, carried water for others, and played to the edge of the rules. He didn't give speeches, but teammates say he was constantly advising the coaches and counseling the players without ever raising his voice. "When there were no coaches around, he would talk to the players," Tretiak told me. "He always said the right thing in the locker room and on the ice."

In 1980, after two decades of dominance capped by the catastrophe in Lake Placid, the Soviets had seemed ripe for a fall. Some sports dynasties collapse simply because the players get old and satisfied and lose their edge. In other cases, the culprit is a personal clash that spirals out of control and destroys its unity. This has happened so often, in fact, that fans, reporters, and sports executives have come to view acts of dissent or disagreement inside teams as potentially fatal calamities. Modern teams are so hell-bent on tamping down confrontation that players who create it are usually sent packing.

Yet Vasiliev's extreme act of rebellion hadn't injected any of these toxins. Rather, it set in motion a series of events that brought his teammates closer, cemented his leadership, and paved the way for the team to reel off one of the sixteen most dominant streaks in sports history. There was a strong circumstantial case to be made that the moment Vasiliev attacked his coach was the moment his team made its turn toward greatness.

The archetypal captain of my imagination—and I suspect I'm not alone in this—was not the sort of person who would threaten to throw his coach out of an airplane. But all of the Tier One captains, to varying degrees, stood up to management during their careers. In 1995, the U.S. Soccer Federation locked the women's national team out of training before the Olympics rather than meet the salary demands of Carla Overbeck and her teammates. Yogi Berra, Mireya Luis, Buck Shelford, and Syd Coventry also clashed with team authorities over money. Once, when the Pittsburgh Steelers tried to put the players on a healthier, less meat-intensive diet, Jack Lambert took a paper cup outside, filled it with acorns, twigs, and dirt, and placed it on the desk of his head coach, Chuck Noll. "We changed the menu back to the way it was," said the team's chairman, Dan Rooney.

Of all the Tier One captains, Carles Puyol seemed—from the outside at least—to enjoy the most harmonious relationship with management. When there were conflicts, he said, he tried to keep them out of public view. Still, Puyol said, he believed that one of Barcelona's strengths was its tradition of electing captains. This, he said, prevented the manager from simply appointing someone "who will do everything he tells him to."

In the business world, this kind of institutionalized dissent is becoming fashionable. Rather than discouraging gadflies, some companies have given them exalted status. To avoid groupthink, some have adopted a method called "red teaming," in which a team working on a project will designate one person, or a small group of people, to make the most forceful argument they can muster for why the idea that's currently on the table is a bad one. By embracing dissent in this way, these companies believe they're better able to protect themselves from thoughtless agreement and complacency.

The general pattern of behavior I'd seen from Vasiliev and other Tier One captains suggested that some dissent is a good thing—a strong leader should stand up for the team. Vince Lombardi once said that a captain's leadership should be based on "truth" and that superior captains identify with the group and support it at all times, "even at the risk of displeasing superiors." Nevertheless, there's a line between a level of dissent that's effective for a team and a level of dissent that destroys its cohesion. If a captain constantly challenges management, resists consensus, and creates turbulence, the team will come to a point where it can no longer win. In baseball, where teams can spend up to eight months together, players like these—who reflexively dig in on their principles to the point of irritation—are known, pejoratively, as "clubhouse lawyers."

By taking on his coach to defend the other players, Valeri Vasiliev wasn't being a lawyer. He was making a powerful gesture of support and protection. It wasn't surprising that his teammates appreciated his courage, loved him for it, and rallied around his captaincy. The risk he took was that the coach would kick him off the team, or would make life so unbearable for the players that they would lose their will to win.

A few captains in my study, however, had engaged in a different, more explosive kind of dissent. They hadn't just spoken out against their coaches or managers, they had also publicly criticized their teammates. This was something quite different than the airplane incident. In these cases, the leader had not sought to support and defend the honor of the group but to prod the others into improving by calling them out.

MUNICH, 2009

The imperial seat of power in German football maintains an actual, physical address. It is located a few miles south of central Munich, at 51–57 Säbener Strasse, the site of a sprawling training complex belonging to Bayern Munich.

At the start of the 2009 season, the display cases on this leafy campus held the trophies from the twenty-one German league championships Bayern had won since 1900, the year it was founded. In 2009, however, the most distinct thing about the Bayern trophy case was what it didn't contain: recent trophies earned by beating the top clubs from the rest of Europe. After dominating the continent in the mid-1970s, Bayern had only won a single Champions League title—and that was eight years earlier.

In the minds of everyone inside the Säbener Strasse complex, the moment to rectify this problem had arrived. Thanks to a global boom in the football business, Bayern had never had so many resources at its disposal. Four years earlier, the team had moved into the 340-million-euro Allianz Arena, a futuristic monolith built just for them, with illuminated white, red, and blue polymer panels that could be seen from the mountains in neighboring Austria fifty miles away. During a season when club revenues closed in on three hundred million euros for the first time, Bayern had hired the renowned Dutch manager Louis van Gaal and spent fifty million euros to obtain two marquee goal scorers, the German forward Mario Gómez and the Dutch winger Arjen Robben. Before the 2009 season began, the roster was so loaded with talent that Franz Beckenbauer, the former Bayern star and a member of the team's governing board, called it the finest team Bayern had ever fielded.

Nevertheless, thirteen matches into the Bundesliga season, Bayern's superteam was a disorganized shambles. It had managed to win only five league matches and had been humiliated in an 0–2 Champions League group-stage loss to lowly Bordeaux.

Because league regulations forbid private ownership of sports teams, Bayern was technically a public trust owned by its 270,000 stockholders. In reality, the team's baronial board of directors kept tight control over its operations—from negotiating television deals to hiring the manager and selecting players. The board wasn't some collection of out-of-touch bureaucrats. Its members were former Bayern stars like Beckenbauer, Uli Hoeness, and Karl-Heinz Rummenigge. It was German football's Mount Olympus.

As fans and columnists grumbled about the team's dreary start, the board stayed silent. It had set a course and planned to stick to it. The board demanded obeisance and craved order, and the players knew better than to criticize its decisions. Speaking out against the Bayern board was the third rail of German sport.

Before the season, Bayern's manager, van Gaal, had made an unconventional move by appointing Philipp Lahm as the team's new vice captain—second-in-command to the principal captain, Mark van Bommel. A defensive midfielder or fullback who was only twenty-five years old, Lahm was not at an age when leadership is typically bestowed on a player. And at five foot seven, with a Paul McCartney mop and a boyish face, he didn't look the part.

Starting in the late 1960s, when Bayern pulled off one of the most dominant runs in football history, its fans had come to expect the team's captains to be giants of German manhood. Beckenbauer, who became captain in 1968, had been the clay model. An imperious figure with dashing looks and an alpha personality, he had a flair for going on long scoring runs from his position in central defense and using his speed and elegant, effortless ball skills to overpower defenders. He'd earned the nickname der Kaiser. Beckenbauer had helped Bayern win four German Bundesliga titles and three consecutive European Cups while also captaining the German national team to victory in the 1974 World Cup. Like France's Didier Deschamps, he was one of only three captains to lead two different teams—his club team and his national team—into Tier Two.

After der Kaiser, there was Lothar Matthäus, a volatile and handsome playboy whom the Argentine superstar Diego Maradona once identified as his toughest-ever opponent; Stefan Effenberg, a blond, six-foot-two midfielder nicknamed der Tiger who collected a league-record 109 yellow cards and once had a scandalous affair with a teammate's wife; and the goalkeeper Oliver Kahn, who was so prone to explosions that fans called him the Volcano (sportswriters preferred der Titan). The Germans had even come up with a pleasingly German term for this sturdy red-blooded brand of captain: die Führungsspieler. Translated literally, it means "the players' guide," but in practice, it's meant to connote a fiery totalitarian who is completely unafraid to scream at his teammates to play harder.

Standing next to these men, Philipp Lahm might have been mistaken for a teenage autograph seeker.

Though he earned a spot with Bayern's junior training program at the age of eleven and won raves from his coaches there, Lahm's path to the Bundesliga hadn't been an especially charmed one. Some German clubs, unimpressed by his small stature, had turned down opportunities to take the player on loan. A self-described local boy from Munich, Lahm didn't have a flashy bone in his body. He avoided nightlife, got lots of sleep, and once told an interviewer that he kept his money in a fixed-interest bank account. On the field, Lahm wasn't a big scorer or an aggressive tackler—in fact, he told me he'd never earned a red card in his career. "I don't think I've ever been close," he said. Unlike the Bayern leaders who came before him, Lahm wasn't an autocrat. He wore his authority loosely—speaking to teammates in calm, clear tones. "My style is to have a lot of conversations. It's important to address many issues, especially on the training field. That's the style that suits me the best."

While other German captains had been high-profile superstars, Lahm was perfectly content to supply his teammates with passes. "Since earliest childhood, my game has been about serving the team," he said. The best nickname the fans could dream up for him was Zauberzwerg (Magic Dwarf).

Lahm's sense of space, his ability to anticipate play, and his knack for launching attacks with pinpoint passing required some tactical knowledge, and lots of videotape, to appreciate. While almost nobody noticed, he was once credited with completing 133 passes during a game without a single miss. Even more remarkably, he didn't play a set position. Depending on the team's tactical needs at any given moment, he would switch between defense and midfield, from the left side to the right. "The only position Lahm can't play is goalkeeper," Beckenbauer told me, "because he's too short."

As Bayern opened the 2009–10 season with a lousy record of five wins, two draws and four losses, Lahm seethed over the Bayern board's personnel strategy. After one difficult draw, he gave a postmatch TV interview in which he ticked off a couple of reasons why he thought the team hadn't played well, mainly its lack of organization at midfield.

After the interview, Lahm was summoned to meet with the board. This hadn't come as a big surprise to him—one year earlier, in 2008, after Lahm had turned down an offer to transfer to Barcelona, he had told them that he would like to be invited to give his input on tactical matters from time to time, a condition it had accepted. As he walked into the room, he was prepared to engage in a frank discussion about the team's struggles. The board members didn't want to hear his opinions, however. They told him to stop criticizing the team on television and showed him the door.

Lahm was stunned by the rebuke—but rather than being chastened, he became even more determined to air his views. The only question was how to do it. The Bayern board hated disloyalty. Other Führungsspielers, as bold as they had been on the field, had never dared to train their fire at management. Not only that, but Bayern's rules expressly forbid players from speaking to the press without the club's prior approval. In November, however, with the team limping into a crucial league match against Schalke, Lahm decided that the consequences of staying silent were greater than the risks of breaking protocol. He asked his agent to arrange a sit-down with the Munich newspaper *Süddeutsche Zeitung*.

European football teams did not take a liberal position on player interviews. With the exception of a few postmatch comments, or the occasional anonymous leak, stars rarely said much of anything to the media until after the season—and even then, candor was in short supply. So when Munichers opened their newspapers on the morning of Saturday, November 7, just a few hours before Bayern's match against Schalke, they were shocked to discover that the team's vice captain had given the team a full-page, unauthorized, uncensored in-season critique. The next day, the *Guardian* called it "the most frank, no-holds-barred player interview imaginable."

Lahm had started off gingerly, telling the paper he believed the club had the power to fix the mess it was in. As a lifelong Bayern fan, he insisted, he had the club's best interests at heart. "But if I believe the team is doing nothing," he said, "or that it is lost somehow, then I will intervene and raise uncomfortable truths."

The main reason Bayern wasn't winning, Lahm continued, was a profound lack of strategic thinking. The board had loaded up on expensive scorers like Gómez and Robben without considering that the two men were accustomed to playing in different formations. Meanwhile, the team was a mess in midfield, where its players lacked versatility. Some had the ability to control the ball, but they didn't have the skill to launch attacks—while others had the opposite problem. "If you want to compete with Barcelona, Chelsea, and Manchester United, then you need a playing philosophy," he said. Top European clubs like these chose a system, then went out and found the right personnel to implement it. "One cannot simply buy players because they are good."

The Bayern board was predictably steamed.

"Deputy captain Philipp Lahm's interview . . . has violated internal rules in a flagrant and inexcusable manner," it said in a statement to the press. "It is an absolute taboo to express criticism of the club and one's coaches and teammates in public." The board promised that Lahm would receive the largest fine it had ever levied on a player.

The following day, after a 1–1 draw with Schalke, the Magic Dwarf was hauled before the board. The meeting lasted two hours. "In a very open, detailed, and constructive discussion, Philipp Lahm has apologized for his comments and the way he chose to make them public," the board said in another statement. "Lahm has accepted the fine imposed by the board and, for both sides, the issue from the weekend has been dealt with."

Though he didn't say so then, Lahm had a different take on the proceedings. He told me he apologized for how things went down but not for what he said. "It's not easy to go against the club that employs you. It's also difficult to come out against your teammates. Many people keep it behind closed doors, and that's certainly the best approach—to speak internally. But sometimes you have to use the public for help to be heard."

The day after the interview ran, a few of Lahm's teammates spoke out in support of his prescriptions. But others, especially the midfielders whose play he'd criticized, were furious with him—both for what he said about them and for his premeditated act of rebellion. Stefan Effenberg, the former Bayern captain and textbook Führungsspieler, thought Lahm had taken his criticism too far. "It is going to be brutal for Lahm," he told a reporter. "His performance is going to be scrutinized after every game now."

At the least, one would assume that Bayern's players had been distracted by their vice captain's interview and that their performance would have either continued to disappoint—or gotten considerably worse. But after holding Schalke to a 1–1 draw on the day the interview ran, the opposite happened. Bayern won nine of its next ten matches. Despite its terrible start, the team went on to claim the 2009–10 Bundesliga title.

Lahm's act of insubordination might have been more divisive than Vasiliev's, but the effect was the same. It made his team better.

Richard Hackman, the Harvard organizational psychologist who studied performance teams and extolled the virtues of functional leadership, had also observed the role leaders play in helping groups navigate conflict. All of his research supported one strong conclusion—all great leaders will find themselves right in the middle of it. In order to be effective, Hackman wrote, a team leader "must operate at the margins of what members presently like and want rather than at the center of the collective consensus."

Hackman believed that dissenting wasn't just a crucial function of a leader but a form of courage. Leaders who disrupted a team's established norms and routines often paid a substantial personal toll for doing so—a phenomenon that later researchers would describe as "the pain of independence."

Hackman's research left little doubt that teams need some internal push and pull in order to achieve great things. But it still didn't offer any explanation for my earlier question—the difference between positive dissent and the negative, destructive variety. To explore that, I turned to the research of one of the foremost authorities on group conflict, the management professor Karen Jehn.

During her long career, with stops at Stanford and the University of Pennsylvania, Jehn had conducted studies on teams that showed that certain kinds of disagreements didn't have a negative effect—in fact, teams that had high levels of conflict were often more likely to engage in open discussions that helped them arrive at novel solutions to problems. The worst outcomes came when groups engaged in thoughtless agreements. Nevertheless, hundreds of experiments by other researchers had concluded that conflict was harmful to a group's performance.

In 2012, Jehn and two colleagues published a meta-analysis of sixteen different experiments based on 8,880 teams. The paper's goal was to test a theory Jehn had developed about the nature of group conflict. Jehn believed that "conflict" needed to be better defined. She believed that dissent inside teams took several different forms. One was something she called personal or relationship conflict, which is defined as the manifestation of some personality clash—an interpersonal ego-driven showdown between a team's members. This kind of dispute was distinct from another form, task conflict, which is defined as any disagreement that isn't personal but arises from, and is focused on, the actual execution of the work at hand. There was a difference, she believed, between teams that squabbled because the members didn't like one another and teams that fought over their different views of how to solve a problem they were working on.

Jehn and her colleagues divided the 8,880 teams between those where personal conflict had arisen and those where task conflict was the predominant force to see if there was any variation in how well they performed. The differences were stark. Teams that had engaged in personal conflict had shown significant decreases in trust, cohesion, satisfaction, and commitment—all of which had a negative impact on their performance. For teams that had undergone task conflict, however, the effect on their performance was basically neutral. Arguing about the job at hand hadn't helped them, but it hadn't hurt.

There was one exception, however: teams that operated in highly pressurized environments. These teams were different from the others in that their work yielded immediate, quantifiable results—such as financial performance—that left no mystery about how successful their efforts had been. On teams like this, which received instant feedback through some system of scorekeeping, the presence of task conflict wasn't neutral at all. It made their performances about 40 percent better than the average. "We have found that task conflicts are not necessarily disruptive for group outcomes," the authors wrote. "Instead, conditions exist under which task conflict is positively related to group performance." In other words, teams that get quick, concrete feedback on their work, as they do in sports, got better results when they battled over the details.

As I read the full transcript of Lahm's interview, I noticed that his criticisms hadn't been driven by ego or malice. He avoided personal attacks and made it clear that he believed the team's management was perfectly capable of solving its problems. Rather than lashing out, Lahm kept his censures narrowly focused on tactics. He spent as much time offering remedies for these flaws as he had pointing them out.

Not long after the Bayern board punished Lahm, it began taking steps to follow the exact blueprint he had given. The earlier orgy of acquisitions in which the team loaded up on potent scorers fell away— replaced by a patient multiyear effort to shed some of its mismatched forwards and stock the midfield with players who had the ball skills to play the more creative, attacking style Lahm had described. As it did this, it improved.

After the following season, when van Bommel left the team, Bayern made Philipp Lahm its new captain. The season after that, with its rebuilding effort complete, Bayern finally realized its potential, winning the first of four consecutive German titles and capturing the grand prize that had eluded it for twelve years—the Champions League trophy. The following summer, with Lahm serving as its captain, too, the German national team won the 2014 World Cup in Brazil. That team finished the year with the highest Elo rating of all time—topping the record set by the Hungarians sixty years earlier.

The Magic Dwarf not only survived the turbulence of 2009, he helped his team make a turn toward historic excellence. He also prospered personally. By leading both a club and a national team into Tier Two, he joined Didier Deschamps and Franz Beckenbauer as the only captains to ever do so.

In the winter of 2015, inside the Bayern training facility on Säbener Strasse, Lahm told me that even though the fallout from his interview had been difficult, he considered his act of rebellion a worthy investment in the team's future. "The interview helped, because now we're going where we want to go with the club," he said.

Conventional wisdom tells us that teams perform better when they enjoy a high level of mutual love and harmony. Before writing this book, I would have lumped task conflict on the same pile with every other locker room carcinogen. Lahm's example suggested that tranquillity isn't more important than truth—at least the kind that's told by a captain who is known to be fiercely committed, who labors in the service of the team, and who avoids attacking people on a personal level. To lead effectively, Lahm believed, a captain has to speak truth not only to power but to teammates as well. "It's a totally romantic idea that you have to be eleven friends," he said.

Lahm might not have fit the profile of a hypermacho German football Führungsspieler who could put a team on his shoulders and lead it to glory. But while he wasn't the kind of leader German fans were accustomed to, his unemotional, calculated, and precise act of dissent against the board—aimed squarely at shoring up the team's tactics—had been far more courageous, and effective, than anything his predecessors had done.

Like most German football fans, Lahm said he'd grown up believing "that the team was the captain and the captain was the team." When he first made the senior Bayern squad at the age of nineteen, the mere sight of then-captain Oliver Kahn filled him with awe and "unbelievable respect." But over time, he said, his perspective shifted. He began to think the Führungsspieler was a show business creation that didn't have any real teeth. "Maybe," he said, "I have a different definition of what a leader is."

As much as we might be conditioned to fear it, dissent inside a team can be a powerful force for good. It's also clear that great captains have to be willing to stand apart when they believe it's necessary—to endure that "pain of independence" the researchers describe. There are limits, of course. No team can sustain itself for long if the captain, or anyone else, stokes the kind of conflict that's based on petty hatreds or personal beefs. The principled stands they take must be aimed at defending their fellow players, the way Valeri Vasiliev did, or by keeping the camera pointed squarely at tactics, as Philipp Lahm did by dissecting Bayern's personnel decisions.

All of this suggests that in any high-pressure team environment, even beyond sports, dissent is a priceless commodity. A leader who isn't afraid to take on the boss, or the boss's boss, or just stand up in the middle of a team meeting and say, "Here's what we're doing wrong," is an essential component of excellence.

CHAPTER TEN TAKEAWAYS

- Three words that are guaranteed to strike fear in the hearts of sports team executives are "locker room drama." As strong and tough as elite athletes are, the conventional wisdom is that teams are fragile units. A change in temperature of even a few degrees can rearrange their chemistry in a way that renders them ineffective. Team executives tend to eliminate rancor and cast out the players who spark it. Yet the captains of the greatest teams in sports history not only did defiant, dissenting, and potentially divisive things—they did them habitually.

- Studies on the effects of conflict inside teams have reached every imaginable conclusion—it's bad, it's good, it's somewhere in between. The truth is that it depends on what kind of conflict we're talking about. There are, in fact, several varieties. These include "personal" conflict, which is driven by hatred or dislike, and "task" conflict, which happens when an argument breaks out within a team about the way it's conducting its affairs. On teams in competitive environments, personal conflict is the toxin— but that's not what these elite captains engaged in. When these men and women broke china, they either did so to defend their teammates against management or to make a practical point about what the team was doing wrong. These were not acts of petulance driven by ego. They were acts of personal courage aimed at helping the team play better together.

ELEVEN

The Kill Switch

Regulating Emotion

In the afterglow of France's 27–22 victory over Denmark in the semifinals of the 2009 world handball championship, Jérôme Fernandez, the team's newly installed thirty-one-year-old captain, barely had time to celebrate. After stripping to his underwear to dunk himself in a giant plastic garbage can outfitted as a makeshift ice bath, he had to get packed for the flight to Zagreb for the final. There was one thing Fernandez did make time for, however. As soon as he had a free moment, he called his parents back in Bordeaux.

When his mother, Brigitte, picked up the phone, Fernandez knew from the sound of her voice that something was terribly wrong.

For weeks, his parents had been keeping a secret from him, hoping to spare him so he could focus on the tournament. They couldn't wait any longer. "Jérôme," his mother said, "your father is dying. He is in the hospital. He may not live more than a few days."

Fernandez was too startled to speak. His father, Jacques, had undergone an operation two years earlier to remove tumors in his lungs, but the doctors had told the family he had made a full recovery. As Jérôme's career took off and he juggled the schedules of the French national team and his club team in Spain, his father's illness had drifted to the back of his mind. He had no idea that the cancer had returned.

Jacques and Jérôme Fernandez had the kind of bond that few fathers and sons ever manage to achieve. Jacques had been only twenty when Jérôme was born, and the closeness in their ages had helped them form an unusual "fusion," as Jérôme described it. They didn't talk much, because talking wasn't necessary. Each knew what the other was thinking. "It was a close relationship," Jérôme said. "We had very little difference."

Their focal point was, and had always been, handball. Jacques Fernandez loved the sport; he had been a fairly good player himself and had taught the game to Jérôme and his two brothers. As Jérôme grew to six foot six, it became clear that he was a prodigy. Since his son made the national team in 1997, Jacques had watched every match he'd played. Before it became clear that his condition was grave, he had refused to check into the hospital, because its televisions didn't carry the World Championship.

On the phone, when he finally recovered the ability to speak, Jérôme told his mother he would come home immediately. "But she said to me, 'You must play for your father,'" he recalled. "'You must win, and you'll have time to come back to speak with him and tell him goodbye with a medal. But you must win for him.'"

His father's condition had put Fernandez in a wrenching bind. A few months earlier, he had been named France's captain, but he was still growing into the role. Some of his teammates had wanted the job, and weren't convinced that he was the correct choice. With a narrow, oblong face and dark, close-cropped hair, Fernandez had a friendly and innocent smile that was never far from the surface. He wasn't one for speeches, and when he did address teammates he did so in low, measured tones. He did not convey the intensity of a warrior.

If he went home, and France failed to win the final, there would be questions about his leadership. "I didn't want that," he told me.

With the match just twenty-four hours away, Fernandez went to see his coach, Claude Onesta, to tell him what was going on. Onesta, who had known Fernandez for years, was sympathetic—to a degree. "I understand," Onesta said, "you are very young to lose your father. But you also have the finals of a World Championship." If Fernandez chose to play, he would have to put his father out of his mind. If he chose not to, Onesta added, "tell me now and I'll pull you out and you'll go back to France. But you must decide."

Fernandez had no idea if he was capable of playing through this, but he made up his mind right there: *"Je veux jouer pour mon père,"* he said. ("I want to play for my father.")

As Fernandez steeled himself for the final against Croatia, he grappled with another problem—what to tell the team, or whether to tell them. He worried that the news might distract the other players or cause them to treat him differently on the court. "If a teammate says, 'My father is dying,' that can disturb the entire group and cause the team to lose," he said. As much as he could have used their support, he decided to leave them in the dark.

In any game, on any day, some participant will be coping with a painful personal distraction. In extreme cases, when an athlete is dealing with the death of a family member or a sick child at home, everyone knows about it. Teammates give them hugs. The fans give them a warm ovation. The TV commentators salute their courage. The gravity of the situation is acknowledged. The situation Fernandez faced was both unusual and extreme. The final against Croatia was, to date, the biggest match of his life. Not only would he have to set aside his emotions, he would have to behave, in front of his teammates, as if nothing was the matter. By not hurrying home to say goodbye to his father, he had chosen to make a dangerous gamble. How would he feel if his team lost and he arrived home too late?

The modern sport of handball traces its roots to 1906, when a Danish gym teacher named Holger Nielsen published the first official rules.

The basic concept behind it was a rather cheeky idea—that football might be more lively if its rules were inverted. The players were restricted to using their hands and forbidden from using their feet.

Early on, the game was played outdoors on grass, but it eventually migrated to indoor hard courts, where it borrowed the dribbling and floor tactics of basketball and the narrow goal nets and physical contact of hockey. The spectacle of players setting picks, throwing elbows, shoving one another, and whipping the coconut-sized ball around at speeds approaching ninety miles per hour made it one of Europe's most popular games. The heart of the sport has always been the competition between national teams, and next to the Olympics the biggest prize is the biennial World Championship.

France's opponent in the 2009 final was the host team, Croatia, which would be playing at the Arena Zagreb in front of a raucous partisan crowd of fifteen thousand. The Croats had blown through the tournament field without a loss and, just five days earlier, had defeated France 22–19 in a nondecisive match in the preliminaries. The French had won their first Olympic title in Beijing the year before, but few had tipped them to beat Croatia at home. The London bookmakers had given the Croatians a 16 percent edge.

The moment France emerged from the tunnel, the Croatian fans, packed in to the gills, began pressing their home-court advantage by belching air through the orange plastic noisemakers that had been handed out at the doors. The noise, which sounded like a swarm of bees trapped in a phone booth, made it impossible for the players to hear their sneakers hitting the floor.

As 129 million viewers tuned in around the world, the French team—drawing on its indefatigable defense—managed to keep the match competitive in the first half by bottling up Croatia's most prolific scorer, the nine-fingered winger Ivan Čupić. At halftime, the French trailed by a point, and with twenty minutes left in the second half they clawed their way to a tie. With a little over two minutes to play, the French found themselves with an improbable three-goal lead, the ball, and an opportunity to seal the win.

In the center of the court, about fifteen feet in front of the Croatian goal, Fernandez received a pass in heavy traffic. He leaped into the air with his right arm cocked to shoot. Just as he left his feet, however, a Croatian defender lowered his shoulder, nailed Fernandez in the ribs, and knocked him violently backward.

The Croatian goalkeeper, expecting a shot to come quickly, charged out of his crease to block the ball—but Fernandez had another plan. He'd decided to wait. As he plunged to the floor, his body barely two inches from thumping down on the court, Fernandez fired a desperate off-kilter shot across his body. The ball darted under the goalkeeper's outstretched arm and one-hopped into the empty net.

His goal gave France an insurmountable 23–19 lead.

The arena fell silent. The Croatian players, so full of fire early on, looked heavy-legged, angry, and utterly beaten. As time expired, the French television commentator went bananas. *"C'est fini!"* he screamed, his voice hoarse from shouting over the din. *"Champions du monde!"* The jubilant French players rushed to the center of the court, where they locked arms and began dancing in a circle—all of them, that is, except one.

Though his acrobatic goal had sealed the victory, and though this was his first major competition as France's new captain, Fernandez had fallen to his knees. His forehead was planted on the floor and he was sobbing. The other French players, seeing their teammate in distress, rushed to his side. They thought Fernandez had injured himself. After a minute or so, they lifted him up and led him over to accept the trophy. After the ceremony, when the other players found out what their captain had been going through, they were stunned. "They didn't understand how I did it," Fernandez said.

The morning after the victory, Fernandez flew home and headed straight to the hospital with his young son. His father was still alive. Fernandez gave him his medal and they sat and talked for several hours—mostly about the World Championship but also about the past and the future. "He told me he was very proud of me," Fernandez said. Jacques took his young grandson into his arms. "I saw that my father was very sad," Fernandez said, "because he understood he wouldn't see him grow up." Jacques passed away five days later.

In the years that followed, with Fernandez as its captain, France completed its turn toward Tier One. It became the most dominant team in handball history by a thick margin: After winning back-to-back Olympic gold medals, France won three of four World Championships and two European crowns—the only team to hold all three titles simultaneously.

In an interview in the winter of 2015, when I asked Fernandez if he thought his decision to play that day had helped to make his team more formidable, he quickly dismissed the idea. The team could have won without him, he insisted. He did acknowledge that the 2009 final in Zagreb changed the way his teammates viewed him. "When they saw that we were able to win something together, and that I wasn't a personal captain—that I was a collective captain—they accepted my nomination. They said, 'Jérôme is a good captain and I can follow him.'"

In previous chapters, we have seen captains do many dramatic and selfless things at the beginning of their teams' Tier One streaks that seemed to have had a catalytic effect—they include acts of extreme competitive will or doggedness, small gestures of support, grand displays of emotion, and expressions of protection or dissent. But what Fernandez did in Zagreb was something altogether different. In this case, the captain's signature moment was a selfless demonstration of *emotional* strength.

In his graduate student days in the 1970s, Richard Davidson, a professor of psychology and psychiatry at the University of Wisconsin, set out to investigate one of the relative backwaters of his field—the nature of emotion. At the top of his list was emotional resilience. Why are some people able to bounce back quickly from setbacks while others feel defeated by them?

Davidson and his colleagues constructed mesh caps covered with sensors and placed them over the heads of their test subjects. Then they showed their subjects disturbing video clips or photos designed to elicit a strong negative emotional response. The researchers used the caps to map what happened inside their subjects' brains as they tried to process their feelings. The differences between people in this regard could be "seen" through the level of activity in an area of the brain known as the prefrontal cortex. The left side of the PFC, as we now know, is the brain's control center for positive emotions. The right side is the area where it processes darker, more negative ones. When Davidson's subjects became distressed, there was heightened activity on both sides. But there was one significant difference—the resilient people, the ones who were quicker to snap back to a neutral emotional state, showed greater activity in the left PFC.

In fact, the differences could be dramatic: A high-resiliency person could have up to thirty times more activity in this region than a low-resiliency person.

In later experiments, Davidson learned that resilient people also sent certain kinds of signals from the left PFC to another brain region—the amygdala, which is the brain's rapid action and response center for threats and danger. He theorized that the signals flowing through this pipeline were "inhibiting" messages telling the amygdala to settle down—that everything was going to be fine. People who scored low for resiliency had had fewer or weaker signals passing through this neural channel.

These differences seemed to be largely governed by what kind of cranial hardware a person had been born with. For those with strong, active PFCs with a left-side bias, these findings were highly encouraging—they had greater natural ability to set aside distracting, negative thoughts and forge ahead through adversity by staying focused in the moment. If these people made an error, for instance, they might be more likely to chalk it up to a lack of sleep, or a bad strategy, and to quickly return to normal.

Given how remarkably he'd fought through the dire news about his father during the final against Croatia, it might be safe to conclude that

Fernandez was one of these resilient people blessed with an enviable brain. In fact, all of the captains in Tier One—including Yogi Berra, Carles Puyol, Buck Shelford, Valeri Vasiliev, and Carla Overbeck—had demonstrated the same kind of emotional fortitude. Sometimes it was reflected in their ability to keep cool after a provocation. Other times it was the way they were able to play on through painful injuries that might have sidelined anyone else.

Yet there was one particular captain in Tier One whose battle with emotion stood out from the others. Her test didn't come in the form of a single wrenching episode—it wasn't something disturbing that appeared on a video screen then flittered away. It was a chronic situation that unfolded slowly over a period of eighteen months, one that would have tested anyone's ability to recover, no matter what kind of brain they had.

In February 1999, Ric Charlesworth, the head coach of the Australian women's national field hockey team, the Hockeyroos, asked Rechelle Hawkes to meet him for lunch at a café in the Subiaco district in the city of Perth.

There was nothing unusual about a coach and his captain huddling to discuss the upcoming season, especially with the 2000 Sydney Olympics a year and a half away. But Charlesworth's agenda was something nobody anticipated.

In the six years since Hawkes had assumed the captaincy of the Hockeyroos, there had never been a more dominant field hockey team, of either gender, in the history of the sport. Australia had captured seven straight major titles and maintained an unbroken number-one world ranking. The team had a reputation for destroying opponents by playing at an exhausting tempo with a machinelike efficiency—never complaining to the umpires, never taunting opponents, never betraying even the slightest vulnerability to pain.

At thirty-two, Rechelle Hawkes was already a legend in hockey circles. The daughter of a policeman from Western Australia, she was slim and toned with wide-set hazel eyes, dimples, and raven hair offset by the white headbands she wore on the field. Hawkes had all the classic traits of a Tier One captain. She didn't score much, wasn't exceptionally fast, and did not display dazzling stickwork. She focused on her conditioning and on perfecting the sport's quieter, more team-oriented skills—trapping the ball, passing, tackling, changing directions. She felt uncomfortable in the spotlight, never gave blustery speeches, and had a reputation for understatement. On the day she broke the Australian record for the most caps, or games played for the national team, she told reporters she was "pretty happy."

After struggling with injuries the season before, Hawkes considered retiring but decided to stick with the team for the chance to finish her career by winning a third Olympic title—this time at home in Sydney. Aside from the odd injuries, she had mostly floated through her hockey career on a cloud. That was about to change.

After an exchange of pleasantries, Charlesworth told his captain the reason he'd asked to meet: He wanted to make a change to the team's leadership. From that point on, he said, there would be a different captain named before every match. Sometimes it might be her, sometimes not. Charlesworth had come to believe that by eliminating the fixed captaincy, the other players would feel more responsible for the outcome, which would empower them to work harder on the field. He believed that a revolving captaincy would end any politics or jostling among the players for the role. He told Hawkes she shouldn't take it personally. "The captaincy is just a ribbon," he said.

The truth is, Hawkes wasn't shocked to hear this. Since the mid-1990s, Charlesworth had been conducting a series of experiments on the Hockeyroos, all based on the advice of a psychologist who had told him about the phenomenon of "social loafing" that the French scientist Maximilien Ringelmann first observed. To make sure that his players worked just as hard in the team context as they would alone, Charlesworth had gone to great lengths to tamp down individual differences and push everyone into taking a leadership role. He required the players to change their shirt numbers constantly and forced everyone, even the stars, to sit out games occasionally in order to keep them hungry and motivated. In 1996 he had named four players, including Hawkes, as permanent members of a "leadership group," which was later expanded to six. The members of the group would take turns filling the captain's role on the field.

Hawkes had never seen the point of these maneuvers. She'd rolled her eyes whenever Charlesworth banged on about how the captaincy was an "anachronism," a relic of the nineteenth century, when the world was a more hierarchical place. She tried not to let it bother her. She kept on leading the way she always had, pulling her teammates along when things got tough. Her fellow players and the Australian media still considered her the leader anyhow—and in match programs, she still had the letter C printed next to her name.

What Charlesworth proposed at the café, however, was more drastic. There was no guarantee Hawkes would ever lead the team again.

Hawkes wasn't just any captain—she was the most decorated leader in her sport's history. For six years she had done nothing but serve her team selflessly. Now, heading into a home-soil Olympics where the hopes of a nation would ride on her team's performance, she felt truly pushed aside. She was being demoted.

Hawkes had every right to feel humiliated. Nobody would have blamed her for quitting on the spot. But Hawkes was a not a typical athlete. "I've got an ego, but I don't have a huge ego," she told me during an interview in 2016. "Whilst I liked the thought of being captain, I didn't think I had any right to demand that I stay captain. I thought: Am I being selfish? By saying 'Hang on, I think I should remain captain,' is that a selfish approach? Shouldn't this be all about the team anyway?"

When Charlesworth finished his spiel, Hawkes sat for a moment, considering her response. She didn't think the move would have a big effect on the team's performance, but she also knew the mindset of her coach. Handsome and articulate with piercing pale blue eyes, Charlesworth was a revered figure in Australian sport. He had won renown as a four-time Olympian who was considered one of the best male field hockey players in history. A polymath who was also a physician, a federal politician, and a high-level cricketer, Charlesworth was famous for his innovative tactics on the field and Svengali-like motivational powers off of it. When it came to the Hockeyroos, he exercised absolute authority. "There's no arguing with Ric," Hawkes said. "He generally doesn't listen to what other people say."

In the café that day, Hawkes reasoned that there was no point in protesting. "I told him: 'If that's what you want, there's nothing much I can do about it.'"

When the news got out, the Australian media was considerably less restrained than Hawkes had been. In a country that holds its sporting captains in high esteem, Charlesworth's experiment was viewed as sacrilege. Sportswriters mocked his notion of a "leaderful" team. One columnist called him hockey's Communist coach.

Once the season began, the open captaincy became a source of tension. The players suspected one another of lobbying for the honor, and when match captains were announced there were sour faces in the dressing room. Cliques hardened. By the time the team traveled to Holland the following season for the 2000 Champions Trophy tournament, the last major international competition before the Olympics, it was in disarray. For the first time in nine seasons, the Hockeyroos failed to bring home the gold. "The wheels fell off a little bit," Hawkes recounted. "I don't know if I can put it down to leadership. Subliminally, maybe I took a step back. Maybe the loss of the captaincy did have a psychological effect on me that I wasn't aware of."

Charlesworth didn't believe the captaincy situation was the problem. He told reporters he'd deliberately rested star players in crucial matches to see how younger players withstood the pressure. He blamed the loss on the referees.

With the Sydney opening ceremony just weeks away, Charlesworth drove his players harder than ever. He berated them after sloppy performances and refused to set the Olympic roster, leaving everyone—

even veterans like Hawkes—wondering if they would make the cut. After one match, Charlesworth ripped Hawkes in front of the team, something he'd never done before. The pressure grew so intense that on an off day she took a ferry to a remote island to get her head together. "My confidence was at a low point," she said. "I didn't want to quit, but it wasn't enjoyable."

As the Sydney Games began, the Hockeyroos played tentatively in their first two matches, narrowly defeating England and playing an inferior Spanish team in a 1–1 draw. Gradually, however, they found their footing. They beat South Korea 3–0 in their final pool match, and then, in the medal round, throttled their archrivals the Netherlands 5–0 and steamrolled China 5–1 to earn a spot in the final. Hawkes could see the finish line. She felt as if she had endured the worst of it—and survived. But her troubles weren't over.

On September 29, hours before the final match against Argentina, Hawkes appeared at the team's pregame meeting. Since it would be her last game, she knew the cameras would be following her. Already, the tribute machine had snorted to life. At the opening ceremony, Hawkes had been tapped to take the Olympic Oath on behalf of all the athletes, which she'd done to thunderous applause. With a win, she would have taken home a gold medal in three Olympics, tying an Australian record. Whether she liked it or not, *she* would be the story.

The meeting took place in the living room of a house the team shared during the Games. The players took their places on the chairs and sofas, which were turned to face one end of the room. Charlesworth walked to the front. He began the meeting, as always, by reading the starting lineup and naming the match captain. That's when Charlesworth turned to the team's veteran defender Renita Garard and said six words nobody had expected.

"Renita will wear the armband today."

Every set of eyes in the room turned to Hawkes. It had been a foregone conclusion that she would lead the team onto the field for the final. "I couldn't believe it," the team's star striker, Alyson Annan, told me. "It was Rechelle's fourth Olympic games, she was the most capped player, and this was her last game for Australia. I thought, out of re-spect to her, she should have been captain. We all saw her as our leader."

Hawkes wasn't sure how to process the snub. At first, she reacted the way she always did, by choking back her feelings. "I just thought, 'Ah, that's pretty crappy.'" When the meeting ended, Hawkes walked back to her room without saying a word. As she closed the door and lay down on the bed, the full weight of the humiliation landed. "I felt hurt," she said. "It was a kick in the teeth to me, because I sort of led the team along that journey. There was a spiritual leadership going on, and I felt let down by that." Hawkes put her headphones on and escaped into music. A few hours later, she packed her gear and boarded the team bus.

As the final began, the Australians were jittery. They missed several early chances to score, their shots glancing off the goalposts or flying over the crossbar from point-blank range. Nine minutes in, Annan charged the goal in traffic and punched the ball past a diving Argen-tine goalkeeper. The score was 1–0.

The Australians had been saving up a few special plays for the final, and when they earned a corner in the closing minutes before halftime, they decided to unveil one of them. The play had been drawn up for Hawkes.

The initial pass came to the defender Jenny Morris, who stood at the top of the Argentine goal circle. Morris reared back to unleash a shot, but as she followed through she intentionally skimmed the ball—sending it dribbling over to Hawkes, positioned just to her left. The Argentine defense bit on the fake, giving Hawkes a clear look at the net. The pressure in that moment was immense. Hawkes drew back her stick and let go.

It wasn't exactly a storybook ending. Hawkes's shot was deflected and bounced off the right post, but one of her teammates, Juliet Haslam, alertly slammed it home to put Australia up 2–0.

After the goal the television cameras found Hawkes, panning in on her face as she jogged back to the centerline. She smiled as a pair of teammates congratulated her. A few seconds later, the smile fell away.

She looked down at the grass, her thoughts pouring in. She sucked in a deep breath, tilted her head back, and blew it out. "That was a watershed moment," she said, "because I knew that we'd pretty much got the game."

In the second half the two teams traded goals, but the outcome was never in doubt. As the final seconds expired, Hawkes leaped into the air, arms raised, a picture of joy and emotional release—an image that ran in newspapers all over the world the following day. Rechelle Hawkes had had her moment after all.

When I asked Ric Charlesworth about his decision to name Renita Garard captain for the final, he said he hadn't given it much thought; he hadn't considered, or known, the effect it would have on Hawkes. He'd gone with Garard because she seemed to have the clearest head and the fewest distractions weighing on her.

When it came to effective team leadership, Charlesworth told me, he didn't believe that one person could ever possess all of the necessary qualities. "Some people do inspirational things on the field, some people set a tone at training, some people are very emotionally aware and gregarious off the field," he said. "All of that stuff is leadership, but not everybody does it all." Hawkes, he said, was "a bit superficial and scattery," and wasn't socially adept enough, or intellectually engaged enough, to be the team's "permanent" leader.

It's impossible to know whether Rechelle Hawkes or Ric Charlesworth was the primary engine that powered the Hockeyroos. After the Olympics, when they both left the team, the spell was broken—the Hockeyroos failed to win the 2001 Champions Trophy and came fourth in the 2002 World Cup. One thing is clear, however. Even though her coach questioned her fitness to lead, Hawkes had the strength of character to block out her humiliation, remove her own concerns from the equation entirely, and continue leading the players in the face of enormous pressure. "This wasn't about me not running out on the field first," she said. "This was about the collective of a team—and I wouldn't play on a team if I wasn't one for giving to the team. I do reflect on [the snub] sometimes. I've been interviewed about it and I've always said: 'Well, at the end of the day, what do people remember? They remember that the Hockeyroos won that gold medal in Sydney.'"

For Hawkes, the Olympic final was—to some degree—less of an athletic accomplishment than an emotional one. After eighteen months of humiliation, just a few hours before it was set to end, she had to cope with the biggest setback of her career. She may have had the right sort of brain to handle these things—it might be as simple as that. But when I asked her about this ability, she didn't see it as a sign of her exceptional biology. Emotional control, she told me, was just another form of discipline.

"You have to regulate emotion," she said. "You can bring it back at some later stage, but when you know you've got something to do, you can remove it from your thoughts, put it in a vault, and get on with what you need to get on with."

As he travels the world giving lectures about his research on emotion, Richard Davidson, the Wisconsin scientist who studied resilience, is quick to point out that the way a person's brain is wired isn't deterministic. Even people whose genes suggest a tendency to be swamped by negative emotions like anxiety or depression won't necessarily respond that way in real-life situations. Inside our DNA, he said, "each gene has what we can think of as a little volume control that goes from low to high. That volume control is highly dynamic, and how we are in the world—our demeanor, the activities in which we engage, our emotional lives—all affect those volume controls and can regulate our genes." In other words, a person's emotional tendencies can be muted.

After meeting the Dalai Lama in India in 1992, Davidson decided to turn his attention to a more practical question. He wanted to know whether people could train themselves to be more resilient. Over the years, Davidson had become a strong believer in the concept of neuro-plasticity, the idea that people's brains will physically change over time and that those changes can depend on their life experiences. For most of us, this transformation happens unwittingly, at a level below consciousness. What Davidson wanted to know was whether people could make positive changes intentionally.

He set out to explore a theory he'd long suspected to be true—that meditation, especially the long, grueling kind that Buddhist monks engage in, might cause this kind of brain rewiring to occur. Are people who meditate better at recovering from adversity?

Davidson invited two groups into his laboratory to serve as subjects for an experiment. The first consisted of fourteen experienced meditation practitioners, each of whom had at least ten thousand hours of practice. The second was a control group of fourteen people who did not meditate matched to the meditation experts by age and gender. Each participant, in turn, was placed inside an MRI scanner, where the scientists could observe their brain activity.

Before the experiment began, the researchers used a device called a thermal simulator to deliver a painful (but not dangerous) heat sensation to a spot inside each subject's left forearm. Once inside the scanner, the participants were told they would be receiving the heat blast but would be given fair warning: The pain would come ten seconds after they heard an audible tone. When the experiment was finished, the researchers looked at the data to see what was happening inside the brains of both groups before, during, and after the stimulus.

The moment the members of the control group heard the tone indicating that the pain was coming, Davidson said, "their brains went haywire . . . without the actual pain being delivered." Then, once the stimulus was over, their brains continued to run on overdrive. "Their pain circuits kept activating—they didn't recover," he said.

The meditation experts were similar to the control subjects in one respect—they also had elevated brain activity while the heat was being delivered. But as they anticipated the pain, and after it ended, their responses were vastly different. Their brains were dramatically less active. The meditation experts, Davidson said, "exhibited something that we have identified as one very important constituent of well-being, which is the ability to rapidly recover from adversity."

While this field of science was still in its infancy, Davidson's research suggested that the brains we're born with are not necessarily the same ones we carry throughout our lives—there is no unalterable blueprint. It may be possible for us to find a better path or, as Davidson puts it, to "reframe adversity" in a way that makes it feel less extreme or enduring. In other words, it may be possible for people who have been overcome with negative emotions in the past to teach themselves to become more resilient.

The only Tier One captain who seemed to have any significant experience with meditation was Barcelona's Carles Puyol. Late in his career, he began practicing yoga and studying the teachings of Tibetan Buddhism. "It's a very interesting philosophy," he said. "They are always very calm. They try to avoid conflict—to make their path by doing well without hurting anyone—and I think that's very good." On several occasions on the field—including one incident in which an opposing player slapped him in the face—Puyol had shown a phenomenal ability to avoid retaliating.

The only trouble with Puyol's example was that from what I could tell, he'd *always* been able to control his emotions. In fact, most of the Tier One captains had displayed the same level of mental stability early in their careers as they had at the end.

There was, however, one notable exception.

On March 13, 1955, with his team trailing the Boston Bruins 4–2 in the third period of a crucial late-season game, Maurice Richard, the star forward for the Montreal Canadiens, received the puck behind the centerline and swooped into the Boston zone. Desperate to spark a comeback, Richard had only one man between him and the Boston goal—a bespectacled Bruins defender named Hal Laycoe.

Richard knew that Laycoe wasn't quick enough to stop him one-on-one. The two men had once been teammates. They had already exchanged a few nasty blows earlier in the game and Richard knew Laycoe would probably try to pull something—shoving him, grabbing his jersey, even diving on the ice to slow him down. As Richard prepared to blow past him, Laycoe lunged forward and grabbed him around the waist with one arm. As Laycoe struggled to hold on, the stick in his opposite hand swung around and nailed Richard above the left ear.

Richard stopped his attack. The head blow had given him a concussion and he felt woozy. He pulled off a glove, ran his hand through his hair, and examined his fingers. He saw blood. Then Laycoe made the mistake of calling him a "frog."

By 1955, getting mauled on the ice was nothing new for Maurice Richard. The Rocket was already the NHL's all-time leading goal scorer, and other teams went to extreme lengths to try to neutralize him. It wasn't unusual for the Rocket to take a shot on goal from his knees with one or even two defenders draped on his back. As the former NHL referee Red Storey once said, "No hockey player in history was held or hooked or high-sticked the way he was."

Richard wasn't big or especially durable. He'd broken so many bones in his junior career that he'd twice failed the entrance physical for the Canadian military. Early in his career, after a string of injuries kept him out of the lineup for weeks at a time, the Canadiens concluded that he was too fragile for the NHL and removed him from their reserve list, allowing any other team to poach him if they wanted to.

Richard's lack of size and goal-scoring talent weren't the only reasons teams targeted him, however. He had so much trouble controlling his temper that they often tried to provoke him into fighting back and drawing a retaliation penalty—which he usually did. In the 1954–55 season, Richard spent more time in the penalty box than all but four other players in the NHL.

After hearing Laycoe's insult, Richard went berserk. He chased after Laycoe and clubbed him so hard across his back that his stick broke. The referees pulled Richard away, but he wriggled free and landed a shot on Laycoe's cheek, knocking off his glasses. As they watched the two men trade punches, the crowd at the Boston Garden was stunned. They had seen plenty of fights before, but this level of mayhem was something new.

In the middle of the melee an official named Cliff Thompson grabbed Richard and held his arms. When Laycoe saw that Richard couldn't defend himself he skated up and landed a punch of his own. Richard became even more enraged. He warned the official to let go of him, but Thompson held on. Then Richard broke free, wheeled around, and punched Thompson in the face. Twice.

Laycoe was given a five-minute major penalty, which was doubled after he threw a bloody towel at the referee. Richard was ejected from the game and led back to the locker room, where he would receive five stitches to his head. He was later hospitalized on account of the head injury. The Boston police came to the locker room threatening to arrest Richard for assault, but his coach barred the door. The next day, the *Boston Record* ran a photo of the altercation with a banner headline: "Richard Goes Insane."

There was no question that the NHL would suspend Richard—assaulting an official was a major offense bordering on unthinkable. Richard had already been fined and put on notice three months earlier for a brawl in Toronto in which he'd slapped an official with his glove. The only question was how severe the penalty would be. The Canadiens desperately needed Richard in the lineup. The team was clinging to a one-game lead over Detroit with just three games to play in the regular season.

Given that he'd been provoked by Laycoe, the consensus in Montreal was that Richard ought to be suspended for the rest of the regular season—no more. After the Canadiens returned home, the NHL president, Clarence Campbell, called all parties to a meeting at the league office. In his defense, Richard said he'd been disoriented. He was bleeding and concussed and wasn't sure who had been pinning his arms, or if that person was trying to hold him so Laycoe could hit him.

Later that same day, Campbell handed down his verdict: Richard was suspended for the rest of the season *and* the playoffs. "The time for probation or leniency is past," the commissioner wrote. "Whether this type of conduct is the product of temperamental instability or willful defiance of the authority in the games does not matter. It is a type of conduct which cannot be tolerated by any player—star or otherwise."

The suspension cost the Canadiens dearly. Without their leading scorer, they would be hard-pressed to hold on to first place, much less win the Stanley Cup. For the team, Richard's explosion was a call to action. The Rocket needed to learn how to manage his rage.

Maurice Richard did not possess the kind of emotional control that Fernandez, Hawkes, and other Tier One captains had displayed. Without looking into the matter any further, it would be easy to conclude that Richard had some kind of anger disorder and deserved every ounce of his heavy punishment. But it wasn't quite that simple.

There was a backstory.

In the early 1950s, Montreal was a tense, divided city. Three-quarters of the population was French Canadian, but its ruling class was almost exclusively English-speaking, and the laws were written and enforced by Anglophones. French Canadians in Montreal were treated as an underclass. They were only a third as likely to graduate from high school and far more likely to live in poverty. In French-speaking Montreal, the period from 1936 to 1959 is known as La Grande Noirceur (the Great Darkness).

Richard, a ninth-generation French Canadian, shared the perception that the city's civic institutions discriminated against his people; not only that, he suspected the bias extended to the NHL. In his mind, the owners of the other teams, together with Campbell, the league's Anglo-Canadian commissioner, conspired against the Canadiens. He was convinced that the referees held their whistles after cheap shots against Montreal players and punished them more severely when fights broke out. These weren't opinions Richard kept to himself. Two years earlier, in 1953, after one of his teammates was suspended for a fight he hadn't started, Richard penned a column in a French-language newspaper calling the suspension a "farce" and accusing Campbell of being a dictator who discriminated against French Canadian players. "If Mr. Campbell wants to throw me out of the league for daring to criticize him, let him do it," he wrote. His defiance of Campbell made Richard a hero in Montreal.

When the French Canadian fans heard Campbell's verdict, their pent-up frustrations boiled over. Fans who called in to radio programs threatened to blow up Campbell's office. "Tell Campbell I'm an undertaker," said one. "He's going to be needing me."

The evening after the suspension, on March 17, Montreal was scheduled to host Detroit in what would be the season's most impactful game. It was St. Patrick's Day, and two hours before face-off a well-lubricated crowd of protesters gathered outside the Forum, chanting "Down with Campbell!" and carrying signs that said "Injustice au Canada Français." Not long after the game began, just minutes into the first period, Detroit scored two quick goals. Then the situation took a bizarre turn. Campbell, who was a regular at Canadiens games, strode into the building and took his seat.

At first there were only jeers and catcalls. But when Detroit scored two more unanswered goals to go up 4–0, the fans began throwing things in Campbell's direction: peanuts, programs, hard-boiled eggs. Finally, as the first period wound down, somebody set off a tear gas canister. As the fifteen thousand fans evacuated the Forum, they fell in with the protesters still gathered outside. The crowd quickly turned violent. A mob cut a path from the arena straight down Saint Catherine Street, setting fires, overturning cars, smashing windows, and looting stores. More than a hundred people were arrested, and more than thirty were injured.

The disturbance on the evening of March 17, 1955, known as the Richard Riot, was a watershed moment in Montreal's history. Rather than denouncing the violence, the city's French Canadian leaders angrily blamed Campbell—both for his punishment of Richard and his provocative decision to attend the game. Many historians believe that the Richard Riot was the moment Canada's French-speaking minority found its voice and began to advocate for better treatment.

Without Richard, the Canadiens would end up falling out of first place and going on to lose the Stanley Cup. Yet most French-speaking Montrealers did not care. They considered Richard's outburst a justifiable expression of righteous indignation. To them it wasn't a loss of control but a courageous act of civil disobedience.

Justified or not, Richard's explosion had crossed a line—and the Canadiens had to do something to rein in his temper. After the season, the team fired Dick Irvin, the hard-nosed coach who had often encouraged Richard to retaliate against opponents, and replaced him with Toe Blake, a forty-three-year-old former Canadien. Though Blake had limited coaching experience, he was half French Canadian and bilingual, and had earned Richard's trust. Blake was given one express order: Prevent the Rocket from blowing his stack.

The following season, Blake kept up a running monologue, reminding Richard that his behavior had hurt the team, lecturing him about the virtues of keeping his cool, and urging him to redirect his frustration in positive ways. "If you want to win you have to control your temper like you control the puck," Blake told him. "Get a grip on yourself. Put your anger into shooting the puck."

It wouldn't take long for Richard to be tested. In January 1956, a New York Rangers player punched Richard's little brother, Henri, who had recently joined the team, and then set after Richard, hitting him twice and bloodying his face. The old Richard would have lost it. The new Richard simply locked eyes with his coach and retreated to the locker room to have his injuries treated. Later, when he retuned to the bench, Blake pulled him aside. "Maurice, you aren't allowed to get mad," he said. "But if you do get mad, then slam that puck in their net."

Though his progress was sometimes halting, Maurice Richard slowly became a different kind of hockey player. In the 1955–56 season, his penalties fell to 1.3 minutes per game from a career high of 1.9

the year before. As he stopped worrying about bearing so much of the team's scoring burden, his point total fell slightly—to second on the team and third in the NHL. None of this did any damage to the Canadiens or to the way Richard was perceived in the locker room. In fact, Montreal went on to win the Stanley Cup that season.

The following year, Richard was named captain.

As he became the leader, Richard continued his transformation. Rather than trying to finish every attack, he began to feed more passes to his linemates, dropping his point totals to sixth overall in the NHL. His growing tendency to spread the puck around gave opponents fewer opportunities to provoke him, and his penalty minutes declined again. In his final season, 1959–60, Richard was hardly penalized. While he still played hockey with fierce intensity, his teammates found him to be different off the ice—calmer, more patient, more content. Richard and his wife, Lucille, were busy looking after their seven young children, and Richard doted on them. He spent nearly all of his free time horsing around with them, taking them skiing, even coaching their baseball teams.

In Richard's farewell game in 1960, Montreal set an NHL record—and earned a spot in Tier One—by winning its fifth consecutive championship.

Maurice Richard, who passed away in 2000, never spoke at length about his effort to control his temper. It's possible that the riot, which opened the eyes of the world to the discrimination against French Canadians, relieved some of the pressure he felt to stand up for his people. Former Montreal players say the NHL's referees also began to take it easier on them, removing one of the primary triggers for Richard's eruptions. It's also possible that while he sat on those long train rides, staring out the window, the Rocket was mimicking the meditation experts Davidson studied in his laboratory. Maybe he was able to rewire his brain to help it override negative thoughts.

What we can say, however, is that the moment the Canadiens began the winning streak that established them as the greatest team in NHL history corresponds precisely to the beginning of Richard's attempt to keep a lid on his emotions.

The three captains I've discussed in this chapter—Jérôme Fernandez, Rechelle Hawkes, and Maurice Richard—all showed, in their different ways, that a leader's emotional control can have a profound impact on a team in a decisive moment. Although I narrowed the focus to these three, the same rule applies evenly to all of the captains across Tier One. We saw it in Yogi Berra's stoic endurance of the taunts and insults he heard during his rookie season with the New York Yankees and in the way Mireya Luis tried to break up the fight that broke out after Cuba beat Brazil at the 1996 Olympics.

We will never know if these captains were simply born with superior brains or whether this kind of self-regulation was something they developed through practice. Maybe their extraordinary commitment to their teams was some kind of mutation that crowded out every other self-focused impulse running through them.

There is one thing we can say with certainty, however: At times when they were flooded with negativity, these captains engaged some kind of regulatory mechanism that shut those emotions off before they could have deleterious effects. In other words, they came equipped with a kill switch.

CHAPTER ELEVEN TAKEAWAYS

- There's no doubt that great captains use emotion to drive their teams. But like aggression and conflict, emotion comes in more than one flavor. It can enable, but it can also disable. During their careers, the Tier One captains all faced some issue that stirred up powerful negative emotions—an injury, a rebuke, a personal tragedy, even a climate of political injustice. These captains not only continued playing through setbacks—they excelled. They walled off these destructive emotions in order to serve the interests of the team.

- A person's ability to regulate emotion is largely governed by the kind of brain wiring they're born with. Nevertheless, our genes provide us with a little wiggle room, and our brains do possess the ability to change over time. Scientists also believe it's possible that we can force them to change through patience and practice. The Tier One captains suggest that this might be true. They displayed and, in one case, developed a kill switch for negative emotions.

PART III

THE OPPOSITE DIRECTION

Leadership Mistakes and Misperceptions

In every nation that keeps reliable television ratings, the most-watched live broadcast in the past fifty years has been a match between two sports teams. The event might be a Super Bowl; a World Cup final in football, rugby, or cricket; or an Olympic gold medal match in ice hockey or women's volleyball. The audience could be from the United States, Canada, England, India, New Zealand, or Japan. The specifics really don't matter. The fact is that in the history of human events, nothing draws a larger and more diverse audience than two elite groups of athletes competing.

There's clearly something more to this than a simple desire to be entertained. The kinds of teams that play for these championships are at the summit of their ability. They are finely calibrated and battle tested. They aren't just exciting to watch, they're also deeply evocative. Part of what makes us human is the desire to join a collective effort. That's why our brains are wired together. In America, it's a notion that's printed on every dollar bill on a banner held in the beak of a bald eagle: *E Pluribus Unum*, "Out of Many, One."

Most people don't get a lot of opportunities to compete on masterful teams in situations when everything is on the line. We might experience a paler version at work, or in a pickup basketball game at the gym, but that's about it. To satisfy our urge for collaboration, we turn to spectator sports. Stadiums are where we go to be pulled out of the narrow confines of our lives and into the guts of a unified body chasing a worthwhile goal.

But there's another aspect to these astronomical ratings numbers, one that's rarely acknowledged. Part of our desire to join a great collective stems from the desire to be nobly led. We want to be inspired. We are programmed to respond to brave, steadfast, and fiercely committed leadership—the kind we see on great sports teams.

The characteristics of a superior captain, as we saw in Part II, are not the ones most of us take for granted. That's not to say they're a mystery—in fact, these qualities seem to be predictable and eminently repeatable. It doesn't matter what team sport we're talking about, or what country the participants come from, or whether the athletes are men or women. On the sixteen best teams in history, the presence of a captain who belongs to the rare species I've described is the only unifying element.

As I wrote this book, however, it became clear to me that the world is turning its back on this idea. The disconnect between the evidence I was gathering and the perceptions of sports fans and even business experts was growing larger and the conventional wisdom about team leadership was undergoing a fundamental shift. The emerging philosophy didn't just question our assumptions about how teams should be constructed, it extended to the basic question of whether teams need captains at all.

In Part III, I'll examine three questions:

1. Why do so many teams pick the wrong captains?
2. Why is the concept of captaincy falling out of vogue?
3. Are great leaders made or born?

TWELVE

False Idols

Flawed Captains and Why We Love Them

TURIN, 1999

The Juventus forward Filippo Inzaghi scored the first goal just six minutes after kickoff, a nifty little tap-in off a left-side cross. Five minutes later he struck again, this time with a deflected chip shot over the goalkeeper's head. Before the match had properly begun, the score was Juventus 2, Manchester United 0. The slaughter was on. The sixty-nine thousand fans at Turin's Stadio delle Alpi broke into a pounding chant: "*Ale, ale, ale, La Juve!*"

To the United faithful, it all seemed too familiar. Despite having been in business since 1878, owning a long and glorious record in English football, and being arguably the world's most popular team of any kind, United had two pressing sources of embarrassment: One, it had never won a match on Italian soil; two, it hadn't won a European title since 1968. On this damp and chilly late-April evening, United's players knew the task ahead was a tall one. This was the semifinals of the Champions League. To make it to the final in Barcelona and the chance to win their first European title in thirty-one years, they would have to score three unanswered goals against a team renowned for its defense, in the belly of one of the loudest stadiums on earth. They would also have to defy history.

United's Irish-born captain, the twenty-seven-year-old midfielder Roy Keane, had been in this situation once before. Two years earlier, United had lost in the Champions League semifinals to Germany's Borussia Dortmund by a 2–0 aggregate score. Keane was determined that this time United would break through.

Just thirteen minutes after the second Juventus goal, when David Beckham took a corner, Keane charged into the box, headfirst, guiding the ball off his forehead and into the net to make the score 2–1. Ten minutes later, United tied the match. In the final seven minutes of normal time, after Juventus botched a clearance, United's Dwight Yorke dribbled between defenders and into scoring range before he was taken down. United's Andy Cole rushed over to collect the ball and tap it into the net, sealing the improbable 3–2 victory. Manchester United's dramatic comeback had earned it a spot in the Champions League final, or, as one television commentator described it, "the gates of football heaven."

Roy Keane had been, hands down, the hero of the night. Every time the camera found him, he'd been running. He had blocked every passing opportunity, challenged every ball, and launched a dozen attacks with pinpoint passes. As he left the pitch, thoroughly spent, the Italian fans were so awed by his performance that they stood and applauded. Alex Ferguson, United's manager, said Keane had competed "as if he would rather die than lose."

After the match, the United players poured into the dingy visitors' dressing room, shouting, hugging, and posing for photos. "Well played, boys!" someone shouted. Ferguson was so caught up in the moment he'd forgotten to take off his raincoat. As his teammates exchanged piggyback rides and whipped tape balls at one another, Roy Keane took a seat in front of his locker. He chugged the contents of a plastic water bottle, staring off at nothing in particular. A thought registered on his face and his eyes dropped to the floor.

Nine minutes after scoring his captain's goal, Keane had made a late, reckless tackle on the Juventus midfielder Zinedine Zidane, for which he'd been given his third yellow card of the tournament. The booking, under Champions League rules, meant he would have to sit out the next match—the final. Incredibly, Keane's most majestic feat as a player and captain had come within a few minutes of his most egregious lapse in judgment.

On any European football forum, when the subject of captains comes up there is always someone who proffers the view that the problem with team X is that its players need a swift kick in the arse from a captain like Roy Keane.

At five foot ten and 179 pounds, Keane was not *physically* intimidating. As a teenager he'd been so small, skinny, and brittle-looking that most top English clubs wouldn't even give him a tryout. By the age of sixteen, he'd fallen out of football entirely, forced to live at home and take a job working in a potato field.

After fighting his way up the ranks to sign with Manchester United, however, Keane's ferocity captured the imagination of the football world. He became the showroom model for a certain type of leadership, the Roy Keane school of captaincy. Nearly everything about this man, from the way he looked to the way he played, was ripped from the pages of Tier One. He wasn't a big scorer or a showy controller of the ball. He wasn't a speech-giver, although teammates say he talked constantly and, by all accounts, constructively on the pitch. He hated attending club events, avoided the press whenever possible, preferred the company of his family, and had no patience for the trappings of stardom, which he described as "the bullshit of celebrity, fame, and associated nonsense." On the night when Beckham married the former Spice Girl Victoria Adams, Keane blew off the celebrity-studded affair to drink alone at his local pub, the Bleeding Wolf.

On the pitch Keane was, by his own description, a "driven bastard" who never tapped the brakes. His managers were astounded by how much ground he covered. His inner fire was so abundant, and his posture so tightly wound, that he seemed more like a boxer than a footballer. His coal-black eyes, which sat just below the straight unforgiving line of his brow, locked hard on any target of his ire, and his face, with its strong jaw and permanent black stubble, was engineered for snarling. A master of aggressive displays, Keane once said that when he sensed his team getting too comfortable, he would make a reckless challenge or a bruising tackle just to "inject some angry urgency into the contest."

In one famous incident, before a 2005 match against Arsenal, Keane pushed his way through the tunnel toward the Arsenal captain, Patrick Vieira, who had been trying to bully one of his teammates. "I'd shut my mouth if I were you," he shouted, motioning to the pitch. "I'll see you up there." As a referee blocked his path and told him to cool it, Keane, chest puffed out, complained that Vieira had "shot his fucking mouth off." United, fired up by their captain, clawed back from 0–1 to win 4–2 in a match in which several usually mild-mannered United players contributed to a total of six yellow cards and one red. "They were a big team, and in the tunnel they were even bigger," Keane said. "So I said to myself, 'All right, let's go.' Aggression must be met with aggression."

Like the captains in Tier One, Keane never hesitated to speak out against anything that stood in the way of winning—a list that included opponents, referees, teammates, his manager, and even United's increasingly well-heeled fans, whom he once accused of being too preoccupied with their "prawn sandwiches" to properly support the team. After a tough loss in a 2002 Champions League semifinal, Keane ripped his teammates for the way they'd played and even the way they primped in the dressing room mirror. They had become so caught up in the trappings of wealth and celebrity, he said, that they "forgot about the game, lost the hunger that got [them] the Rolex, the cars, the mansion." When Keane captained the 2002 Irish World Cup team, he became so incensed by the lackadaisical approach to training and the poor quality of the facilities booked by the Football Association of Ire-

land that he lit into the team's manager in the dressing room and ultimately flew home rather than continue to play. "You're a fucking
wanker and you can stick your World Cup up your arse," he said. On
its face, Keane's combative nature wasn't unusual for an elite captain.
What was different about it, and what made it stand out from the
crowd, was its pervasiveness. During matches his hair-trigger temper
not only attracted special attention from the referees, it made him a
target for opposing teams, which tried to provoke him into blowing his
stack. Keane was booked almost seventy times in his Premier League
career, with thirteen red cards, racking up a list of offenses ranging
from berating referees to stomping on opponents as they lay on the
turf. On three particularly infamous occasions, he elbowed an opposing player in the face, stood on a goalkeeper to prevent him from getting up, and threw a ball at the back of an opponent's head. When
Keane got riled up, Ferguson wrote, "his eyes started to narrow, almost
to wee black beads. It was frightening to watch." Oftentimes, his aggressive style of play was often too much for his body—producing several ankle injuries, a season-ending torn knee ligament, and a chronic
hip ailment that led to a 2002 surgery.

Keane also had a nasty habit of getting into trouble off the pitch. In
May 1999, one month after the victory in Turin, he got into a brawl
with some Manchester pub-goers who were pestering him. At ten P.M.
he was stuffed into the back of a police van and taken to jail under
suspicion of assault. His team paid a price, too: In the FA Cup final
four days later, Keane—who later admitted he wasn't feeling fit—
injured his ankle and hobbled off after eight minutes. One year earlier,
during a preseason tour of Asia, Keane got into a drunken fight with a
teammate, the Danish goalkeeper Peter Schmeichel, who later showed
up at a press conference with a black eye.

There is no question that Keane was an effective leader. During his
eight-year captaincy, Manchester United earned a place in Tier Two
by winning four Premier League titles in five seasons, including three
consecutively. During the 1998–99 season, United became the only
team in English football history to win the league title, the FA Cup,

and the Champions League in the same year, an achievement known as the treble.

To his many supporters, Keane was the epitome of the "Captain, Leader, Legend" species—an inspirational Führungsspieler whose passion to win and contempt for opponents gave his team a backbone. They believed that his glorious record absolved him for his frequent outbursts. "Sport is not a place for flawless people," Gary Neville, a teammate, wrote. He believed that Keane's "fight and passion" helped pull his fellow players along. "The idea that my role model should be a football-playing angel who never gets booked is alien to me."

Keane's critics took a different view. Given Manchester United's fan base and financial resources during his captaincy (a league-topping $230 million in revenue in 2000), its historical prestige (fifteen English titles prior to 2005, when he left), its legendary coach (Ferguson), and its rare abundance of young talent (David Beckham, Nicky Butt, Ryan Giggs, Paul Scholes, and Gary and Phil Neville), they believed his teams should have achieved more.

The case of Roy Keane was a curious one. No captain of his stature, as far as I could tell, had ever done so many egregious things on the field or gotten into so much trouble away from it. He did not seem to possess the ability to neutralize his negative emotions and his lack of restraint often had negative consequences for his team. No top-tier leader I studied had ever been so beloved yet so widely viewed as a problem child.

Most athletes understand that on the field of play, they enter a zone of "bracketed morality" where they might do things they would never do in polite society. In this setting, there are two flavors of aggression: one that is "instrumental," in that its purpose isn't to injure but to further some laudable goal; and one that is "hostile," revealing itself when someone sets out to inflict harm, regardless of the consequences.

The rampant aggression that made Roy Keane such an icon was the same quality that made him different from the Tier One captains. On the field or off, he was unable to regulate his ferocity. In the heat of a match, it was difficult to tell whether he was acting out of indiscriminate hostility, a desire to fortify his team, or both. Unlike Maurice Richard, whose anger seemed to stem, at least in part, from the unfair treatment he felt he'd received as a French Canadian, Keane really had no excuse. He seemed to be bubbling with malevolence nearly all the time.

In sports, the term of art for when an athlete removes whatever brakes they may have on aggression is that this person "plays angry." In 2016, a Rutgers sports psychologist named Mitch Abrams, who had worked with professional sports teams, decided to survey all of the research he could find about violence and aggression in sports and tie it all together in a position paper that, he hoped, would clarify the state of thinking on this issue. Abrams began by citing a number of studies that suggested that athletes who play angry do reap some benefits. "Anger can be an emotion of action as the physiological surge of the sympathetic nervous system can lend itself to an increase in strength, stamina, speed and a decrease in perception of pain," he wrote.

But when taken as a whole, Abrams found that the studies presented more evidence that playing angry can produce negative returns. It wasn't just that anger could draw sanctions from the referees. Intense anger, he wrote, could also harm a player's performance "due to impairment in fine motor coordination, problem-solving, decision-making and other cognitive processes."

In 2011, a pair of researchers from Stanford and Dartmouth published a study in the journal *Athletic Insight* that attempted to explore the competitive strengths and weaknesses of aggressive athletes. The researchers gathered five full seasons' worth of data from the NBA and ranked every player in the league by the rate at which they earned technical fouls. Unlike routine fouls, technical fouls are called when players aggressively step out of line—either by confronting referees, fighting, hurling insults, or making excessively hard or blatant contact with an opposing player.

After controlling for variables like position and minutes played, the researchers found that "aggressive" players—those with the highest technical foul rates—were, in fact, different from their colleagues. Some of their qualities were positive: They were more likely to excel at tasks that required power and explosive energy, such as rebounding and shot blocking. They also tended to take, and make, more field goals. The "energy" that a technical foul creates, or the angry disposition behind it, "may facilitate successful performance in some aspects of the game," the researchers said.

Yet the data also showed that these players were no better—or were considerably worse—at the aspects of basketball that involve "precision and carefulness." While they took more foul shots, they were no better at converting them. When it came to taking, and making, three-point shots, the players who competed in a "high-arousal state" struggled mightily. The aggressive players also showed a greater propensity to commit turnovers. "Aggressive players may be prone to recklessness, which is consistent with research showing that angry people tend to engage in risky decision-making," they said.

This study, along with others like it, didn't suggest that "playing angry" was a scourge to be avoided. But the researchers did suggest that it might be more helpful in sports where people spend more time banging into one another. As much as playing angry might have made Keane a more vigorous athlete, his sport required a combination of physical force *and* precision.

Keane was well aware that his temper sometimes crippled his team. "Ever since I was a kid, small for my age, my instinct has been to look danger in the eye rather than turn the other cheek," he once explained. Because he lived in a state of perpetual aggression, he believed he possessed a "self-destruct button" that led to incidents with negative consequences. Sometimes other people pushed it. Sometimes he did.

The captains in Tier One were certainly not immune to destructive outbursts. Inside their case files, I'd found nearly a dozen examples of incidents where they had let their emotions get the best of them, usually in situations where the pressure was high. Among them, there were two that stood out—but for different reasons.

On August 28, 1951, the New York Yankees and the St. Louis

Browns were in the fifth inning of a late-season game. The outcome only really mattered to the Yankees, who were locked in a tight race for first place in the American League.

With St. Louis at bat, the home-plate umpire, Ed Hurley, made what seemed to be a routine ball-four call. But because the bases were loaded, it allowed the Browns to walk in a run, cutting the Yankees' lead to three. Yogi Berra, the Yankees' catcher, never had any trouble objecting to calls made by umpires. On this occasion, however, he did more than just argue. He whipped off his catcher's mask and started berating Hurley. He bumped chests with him and, by some accounts, grabbed his arm. His stunned manager and teammates, who rushed over to restrain him, thought Yogi was about to throw a punch.

Berra was ejected from the game, and his teammates and the fans feared what the umpire might put in his game report. Berra was the team's most indispensable piece—he was on his way to winning the American League's Most Valuable Player award. If the league suspended Berra, the Yankees knew, they would be hard-pressed to make it to the World Series.

As luck would have it, the league went easy on Berra—he was fined fifty dollars but not suspended. If his teammates hadn't intervened, however, there was a chance that Berra's loss of control might have torpedoed the season and eliminated the Yankees from Tier One.

The second peculiar outburst by a Tier One captain came at the tail end of a 1994 World Cup qualifier between the U.S. women's football team and Trinidad and Tobago.

During this era in women's football, the Americans were one of only a handful of truly competitive teams. As such, the Americans spent most of their time going through the motions against overmatched rivals. Trinidad and Tobago was one of the worst teams the United States played on a regular basis, but the routine thrashings had begun to wear on the players. With the game well in hand and Overbeck controlling the ball in midfield, one of the Trinidadians came after her, landing a forceful, studs-up tackle. Then, after they'd both gotten up, the Trinidadian player punched the U.S. captain in the back of the head.

Unlike Berra, whose team was in a tight race for the American League pennant, Overbeck had no compelling reason to strike back—the score at the time was 10–0. But on this day, she wasn't having it. She not only smacked the player in the face, she tackled her and started punching her on the ground. "I lost it," she told me. "I'd never lost it like that."

Overbeck should have been booked. Had they wanted to, football officials could have slapped her with a suspension. But the match referee didn't seem to have a firm grasp on what had happened. In the end, one of Overbeck's teammates, who'd been trying to break up the fight, was ejected instead.

On the surface, these aggressive acts seemed as if they'd been ripped from the book of Roy Keane. The closer I looked, however, the more different they were. It wasn't what happened in the heat of the moment but what took place afterward.

As soon as the St. Louis game was over, for example, Yogi Berra parked himself outside the umpires' dressing room to apologize to Ed Hurley and make clear that he hadn't meant any harm. Hurley accepted his apology and suggested a light punishment.

When I asked Carla Overbeck about the fight with the Trinidadian player, she explained that she was emotionally spent; the U.S. team had been on the road for two months straight and resented having to play yet another qualifying match against a wobbly opponent. Moreover, she said, she was mortified by what she'd done. "Everyone was like, 'That was awesome,' and I'm like, 'No, it wasn't.' I pride myself on being in control. Here we are, crushing them 10–0, and I let her get to me. Afterward I was sobbing."

Time and again, after Keane had lost his temper on the field, his response was the polar opposite—he rarely showed remorse, even long after the fact. If anything, Keane was known for holding grudges and waiting years to get revenge. In his 2002 memoir, Keane described the motives behind a brutal tackle he'd put on one longtime nemesis, the Norwegian defender Alf-Inge Håland, who had taunted Keane on the field after he'd injured his knee four years earlier. "My attitude was fuck him," he wrote. "What goes around comes around."

The more I studied Roy Keane, the more I wondered why—if he knew that his team paid a price for his loss of control—he didn't try harder to do what Maurice Richard had done: learn to turn his anger on when it was helpful and shut it down when it wasn't.

Researchers have spent a lot of time looking at the question of why some people are more aggressive than others. They have suggested that these people have different kinds of brains, suffer from cognitive impairment or immaturity, or possess a "warrior gene" that predisposes them to risky behavior. One psychologist, Michael Apter of Georgetown University, theorized that aggression is driven by the pursuit of a pleasure sensation that comes from seeing a rival's fortunes reversed.

Another idea, backed by laboratory experiments, is that some people have chronically hostile and irritable personalities—they possess a "hostility bias" that makes neutral actions seem threatening and prompts them to react angrily to challenges. People who have this bias struggle to come up with explanations for the motives of others that don't involve hostility and to respond in ways that aren't violent.

I suspected Roy Keane might be one of them.

There was one small problem, however: If Keane's aggression was driven by a hostility bias, then what explained the occasional violent outbursts I'd seen from the captains in Tier One?

A possible answer to this question came in the form of a paper written in 2000 by a trio of researchers at Case Western Reserve University. These researchers believed, as Richard Davidson did, that every person is born with a different mechanism for controlling negative emotions. Some people have robust systems for restraining them, while others do not. But the Case Western scientists believed that restraint wasn't some machinelike force; it was a resource—a form of energy people kept in reserve. The levels of these reserves varied not only between people but within them. In other words, our restraint tanks will either be empty or full at any moment, depending on how often we've been forced to draw from them.

The key argument this study made was that restraint is finite. The more we're forced to employ our self-control, the less of it we have; and the less we have, the less able we are to inhibit our worst impulses. It's not clear that this theory is true—later experiments haven't always backed it up. But it's still fair to say that the ugly things Yogi Berra, Carla Overbeck, and the other Tier One captains did on the field might have been anomalies. It's possible that they had ample reserves of restraint, but in those particular moments their tanks were down to fumes. The difference between these captains and Roy Keane was that for them, these incidents were exceedingly rare.

In 2001 and 2002, the momentum that Manchester United had built over three dominant seasons began to fade. The team finished third in the Premier League and failed to make it to the Champions League final for a third straight year. Early in the following season Keane started taking pain injections in his hip, and at the beginning of the next season, after he was suspended for five games for what he'd written about Håland, he opted for surgery.

When he returned to the team in December 2002, Keane vowed to become less confrontational on the pitch—both for the sake of his body and the performance of the team. "I'd come to one firm conclusion, which was to stay on the pitch for ninety minutes in every game," he explained. "In other words, to curb the reckless, intemperate streak in my nature that led to sendings-off and injuries . . . to find the balance between unbridled and controlled aggression." Finally, it seemed, Keane had turned the corner to become a calmer, more deliberate player—and under his steadier leadership, United rallied to win the 2002–03 Premier League title.

The following year, United's David Beckham left for Real Madrid, and the team struggled to incorporate a new wave of players. Suddenly surrounded by young stars like Cristiano Ronaldo, Keane grew more distant and remote. He resented the way the new generation of players fixated on their clothes, their hair, their flashy cars. United finished third in the league again and bombed out of the Champions League in the round of sixteen.

By November 2005, with the team struggling and Keane nursing a foot injury, his vow to keep a lid on his temper finally gave way. Keane gave an interview in which he ripped into his teammates, accusing them of arrogance, self-absorption, and a shortage of character. "It seems to be in this club that you have to play badly to be rewarded," he said. "Maybe that is what I should do when I come back. Play badly."

In one sense, Keane was just doing what Philipp Lahm and other great captains would have done—taking a stand for what he thought was right. He insisted that the interview had been a calculated decision. But while the motivation for speaking out might have been a good one, Keane showed another reason why he didn't fit the Tier One profile. His comments hadn't been task-oriented at all. He wasn't dissecting the team's strategy on the field the way Lahm had done. His comments about his teammates were aggressively personal. He had taken a bad situation and made it toxic.

After the interview, Alex Ferguson decided he'd had enough. Keane left the team by "mutual consent" and retired as a player soon after.

Since he left the game, Keane has bounced between managing jobs and from one angry confrontation to the next—he was hauled into court over an alleged road rage incident (he was found not guilty) and got into an altercation with a fan at a hotel bar in Ireland. He was accused of angrily ringing the doorbell of a former player for fifteen minutes in an attempt to confront him about malicious rumors he believed the player had spread about him. None of this leaves much doubt that he possesses the hostility bias scientists described.

Roy Keane wasn't a failure as a captain. Not by a long shot. He had so many of the right traits that it's no surprise he's so fondly regarded. There is no question, however, that he was a flawed captain. He lacked a kill switch to regulate his emotions, and he had a penchant for making personal attacks on teammates.

The bigger problem, when it comes to Roy Keane, is that the least effective parts of his character are what he's most admired for—the fighting, the lack of contrition, and the unyielding barrage of hostility he directed at everyone around him. From the outside, these things made him so vividly different from other captains that they seemed to be the hallmarks of his success as a leader. They overshadowed the things he did that actually helped his team: his dogged play, his water carrying, and his unrivaled talent for making displays of powerful emotion to shore up his teammates.

When football fans say their team needs a captain like Roy Keane, what they're really saying is that it lacks an enforcer on the pitch who intimidates the opposition, or that the players are too soft and comfortable. These things sound good in online forums, but the evidence suggests they're not the kinds of qualities that turn teams into long-standing Tier One dynasties.

Before this book was published, whenever I told people that its subject was the captains of the world's greatest sports teams, they would always come back at me with the same response: "Oh, so you're talking about Michael Jordan and the Bulls."

To state the obvious, Michael Jeffrey Jordan was a magical athlete, an otherworldly leaper who seemed to hang in midair on the basketball court. But there was more to it than that: Jordan could rebound, defend, handle the ball, slash to the basket, and score from any distance. Another thing that's rarely acknowledged is how fast he was. Jordan's college coach said he once ran the forty-yard dash in 4.3 seconds. This unprecedented cocktail of skills produced ten NBA scoring titles and five MVP awards.

On the surface, Jordan's leadership record seemed equally impressive. He was the Chicago Bulls' co-captain during each of the team's six NBA title runs. Like Roy Keane, Jordan had a lengthy list of Captain Class traits. He was tough, focused, and dogged on the court, playing and practicing with relentless intensity. During the 1997 NBA Finals, he battled through a raging stomach bug to score thirty-eight points and hit the clinching shot, only to collapse after the buzzer. Jordan didn't have the kinds of violent episodes Keane did, but he was still highly aggressive, constantly probing the limits of what the referees would allow, especially in the area of shit-talking opponents.

There is no doubt that the Bulls were one of the best basketball teams in history. In the two seasons between 1995 and 1997, Jordan's team recorded the two highest NBA Elo ratings of all time, as compiled by FiveThirtyEight.

If public opinion mattered, it would be no contest. Michael Jordan would be one of the greatest captains in history, period. But there are two powerful reasons why this may not be the case. The first is that his teams never made it to Tier One. The second is that Jordan did not match the Captain Class blueprint.

Though it's often overlooked, Jordan's first six years in the NBA were not a triumph. Even as he became known as the league's most electric player, the biggest star in sports, and his team's undisputed leader, the Bulls did not make it to the NBA Finals. In his first three seasons, the team had a losing record and bombed out in the first round of the playoffs. When Phil Jackson arrived in 1989, he was Jordan's fourth coach. As captain, Jordan led mostly by needling and belittling his teammates, who lived in perpetual fear of his famously sharp tongue. When Jordan lost confidence in a player, he would lobby management to get rid of him.

In 1988, the Bulls acquired Bill Cartwright, a veteran center. Though he was clumsy and unflashy, had terrible knee problems, didn't block many shots, and couldn't catch passes unless they were thrown directly at his nose, Cartwright had excellent footwork and knew how to neutralize the league's top big men. He could score twenty points a game if called upon but had played alongside enough NBA stars in his nine-year career with the New York Knicks to know how to make space for them. He had no problem carrying water.

Cartwright was quiet and remote in public, with a perpetually pensive, slightly sad expression. He didn't do speeches, but he was an enthusiastic mentor to the younger players, who called him Teach. As Sam Smith wrote in his book *The Jordan Rules,* Cartwright had a remarkable work ethic and no illusions about anything coming easily. As Cartwright once put it: "You just play until there's no game left in your uniform."

Jordan could not have been more different. On the court he was emotional and animated. Off the court, he was congenial and charming, with stunning good looks and a fondness for finely tailored suits. The first thing that made him stand out from the captains in Tier One was his enthusiasm for celebrity. Beginning with his groundbreaking work for Nike, Jordan would become the most prolific product endorser in sports, building a portfolio that eventually brought in an estimated one hundred million dollars a year. Jordan didn't just like being a celebrity; he became the model for what a sports celebrity is.

The second difference was the way he played basketball. Jordan rarely labored in the service of his team. He ran the Bulls' offense as he wished, to the exclusion of the supporting cast, and judged everything the organization did by how much it helped him.

When the Bulls acquired Bill Cartwright in 1988, they traded away the forward Charles Oakley, Jordan's closest friend on the team. Jordan told the Bulls' general manager, Jerry Krause, that he virulently opposed the move. Furious about losing Oakley, Jordan went out of his way to make Cartwright feel unwelcome. He mocked him in the locker room, often while Cartwright was within earshot, at one point labeling him Medical Bill for his persistent knee problems. On the court, Jordan sometimes ignored Cartwright when he was open.

Behind the scenes, Cartwright made it known to teammates that he wasn't a fan of "Michaelball." Eventually, the tension came to a head. According to Smith, Cartwright confronted Jordan for the things he'd said about him and for telling other players not to pass him the ball. "Michael could walk over just about anybody because he was so overwhelming with his talent," the former Bulls scout Jim Stack said. "But Bill held his line."

In 1990, at the beginning of Jordan's seventh season, the Bulls were on the cusp of putting it all together. They had made three straight trips to the conference finals but couldn't seem to finish the deal. When the team got off to a sluggish 7–6 start, Phil Jackson decided it was time to do something to heal the locker room. In a stunning move, he announced that Cartwright would join Jordan as co-captain.

The idea of Jordan sharing power was shocking—the fact that he'd be sharing it with Medical Bill was hard to fathom.

Jackson told the *Chicago Tribune* he'd tapped Cartwright for the role because he was the kind of communicator who could help convince the other players to buy into their roles. "It was about stability," Cartwright told me. "I'm the guy who was always there early for practice, never late, stayed after, talked to guys, and took care of myself. It was more about the example for the young guys."

The team responded to Cartwright's captaincy immediately with a five-game winning streak. The Bulls would go on to finish the season 61–21, sweep through the playoffs with a 15–2 record, and at long last win their first NBA title. It was only then that Jordan finally acknowledged Cartwright's contributions. "I loved having Charles [Oakley] on the team," Jordan said, "but Bill made the difference."

The 1990s Bulls were known as Michael Jordan's team, and he was credited with leading it to glory. He became a global model for leadership among sports fans—and also for a generation of teams and athletes. But the fact remains that the Bulls hadn't been able to make their "turn" until Bill Cartwright joined Jordan in the captaincy. It was Bill Cartwright who carried the water, put in the work, and provided the practical communication. He was, in short, the kind of Captain Class presence the team hadn't had.

Setting aside Jordan's leadership ability, there was another reason the Bulls never managed to put together a winning streak worthy of Tier One. In 1993, while still in his prime, the thirty-year-old Jordan retired from basketball. Though he would return to the team eighteen months later, Jordan's hiatus put the Bulls in a tough spot. After three straight titles, they bowed out in the quarterfinal round of the playoffs in the next two seasons.

Of all the ways Michael Jordan strayed from the profile of Tier One leaders, this one was the most baffling and the hardest to unravel. How could he quit?

At the time of his retirement, Jordan was coping with his own devastating personal loss: the death of his father, James, who was murdered in a botched car robbery at a highway rest stop in North Carolina. Jordan had shared a close bond with his dad, and the twists and turns of the investigation consumed him. It would be easy to understand if Jordan had retired because he couldn't focus on basketball—but Jordan didn't explain it that way. "Before my father passed, I was thinking about quitting anyway, not quitting but retiring, because I just kind of lost my motivation for the game of basketball," he said. In another interview, he explained that he'd become "a little bit bored."

To the public, this was a confounding admission. After all, nobody loved competition more than Jordan. Whether he was playing Horse with teammates after practice, or golf, or table tennis, or poker, he couldn't bear to lose. In a 1993 interview with Oprah Winfrey, Jordan conceded that he might be a "compulsive competitor."

Jordan's obsession with winning never shut off. It was a permanent condition that seemed to be driven by deep emotional forces. Basketball had proved to be a good conduit for a while, but it hadn't been enough. After retiring, he barely took a breath before setting off on a new challenge: trying to make the roster of Major League Baseball's Chicago White Sox. Jordan played 127 games in 1994 for the minor-league Birmingham Barons, hitting a measly .202 with 114 strikeouts. Not until baseball's players went on strike the following summer did Jordan, suddenly idle again, return to the Bulls.

On the field, the captains in Tier One shared Jordan's relentless drive. Off the field, however, they were basically homebodies—intense competition seemed to be the last thing on their agendas. Early in his career, Bill Russell retreated to his basement after games to play with his model trains. Maurice Richard spent nearly all of his free time with his family and sometimes slept twelve hours a night. Jack Lambert's teammates accused him of being antisocial on road trips because he spent so much time buried in a book. Carles Puyol, no fan of nightlife, once said: "I consider myself a very quiet, family-oriented person. There are many things that can make you lose focus, and so I have tried to avoid all of that."

Jordan wasn't wired this way. He was gripped by an insatiable desire to compete in every waking moment—the longer the odds were against him, the sweeter the victory. Basketball was just one outlet. When he wasn't on the court, he turned to other pursuits—golf outings, high-stakes poker games, and endorsement deals.

The great mystery of Michael Jordan, the one that made his story so unusual, was why the greatest player basketball has ever seen felt such an overwhelming need to keep proving himself.

Michael Jordan's induction into the Basketball Hall of Fame, which was held in Springfield, Massachusetts, in September 2009, began with a video tribute. The lights at Symphony Hall dimmed, and soon the audience was treated to a montage of Jordan in his familiar scarlet uniform, launching his body at baskets, pumping his fists after nailing game-winning shots, and, of course, hoisting trophies. By the time he strode up to the podium in a loose-cut putty-colored suit with a black tie and a white pocket square, Jordan was in tears. "Thank you," he said, drying his watery eyes with long strokes of his thumb and index finger. It took eighty seconds for the cheering to stop. "I told all my friends I was going to come up here and say thank you and walk off," he began. "I can't. There's no way. I've got so many people I can thank."

Jordan began with a few touching tributes to former teammates, coaches, and heroes he'd looked up to. About five minutes in, as he was talking about his siblings, he made the first reference to his "competitive nature." At the six-minute mark, the speech took a strange turn. Jordan told a story about his high school coach, who hadn't promoted him to the varsity basketball team as a sophomore. "I wanted to make sure you understood," Jordan said. "You made a mistake, dude." The crowd laughed and applauded. Jordan poked out the famous tongue, as if he'd slipped back into game mode.

Most Hall of Fame induction speeches follow a pattern. The player thanks his family, heaps appreciation on teammates and coaches, and praises God for giving him the talent to have such a blessed career. Jordan dispensed with all of that rather quickly. His speech devolved into a long catalog of ancient beefs as he took shots at former NBA players, coaches, and executives who'd disrespected him. It wasn't the speech of a legend. It was the speech given by an underdog who succeeded despite everyone else's best efforts.

The reviews of Jordan's address were resoundingly negative. The NBA writer Adrian Wojnarowski likened it to "a bully tripping nerds with lunch trays in the school cafeteria." Jordan, he wrote, "revealed himself to be strangely bitter."

Four years later, Jordan answered his critics in a TV interview. "I was really explaining to people about my competitive nature," he said. "Most people say that was the worst speech? Okay. That's from your perspective. . . . I'll go to my grave thinking, 'I said what I wanted to say.'"

What the speech revealed is that throughout his basketball career, Jordan had spent a great deal of time nourishing every narrative in which he'd been dismissed. Like Roy Keane, Jordan played angry, but his anger wasn't the kind that pushed him to violence—he rarely lost his temper on the court. Jordan's anger was an elaborate fabrication. To play his best, he needed to feel slighted, which, in turn, fired him up to go out and try to prove the doubters wrong. "That's how I got myself motivated," he once said. "I had to trick myself, to find a focus to go out and play at a certain level."

To keep the fire of bitterness burning hot, Jordan had to dig deep. He vacuumed up every ancient snub or critical newspaper column he could remember and tossed it into the furnace. The captains in Tier One seemed to have a kill switch to block negative emotions. Jordan had rigged his control box to supply them with fertilizer. The problem with Jordan's approach is that when the games ended and the arena lights shut off, his emotional appetite did not. He set off to find another game, another kind of challenge—preferably one in which he would be underestimated.

The reason Jordan quit basketball in his prime after winning three NBA championships is that nobody dared to question him anymore. He wasn't bored, he'd simply run out of fuel. In the end, he wasn't so much a star as a meteor. When his anger finally burned out, so did the Bulls.

Michael Jordan was one of the shiniest objects sports has ever seen. And because his play received so much attention, his personality was so magnetic, and his teams won so many trophies, people assumed he was the leader of the Bulls and was doing a bang-up job of it. The fact is that he wasn't a superior captain.

By the time Jordan returned to the Bulls in 1995 for his second tour, Cartwright had left the team. Jordan shared the captaincy with Scottie Pippen, who'd filled in during his absence. Jordan said that he knew that he had some work to do as a leader—but after the team struggled that season, he reverted to his old ways. Jordan's constant criticism so rankled the veteran guard Steve Kerr that the two men got into a fistfight during preseason training camp.

Those Bulls teams would go on to win another three titles, bringing Jordan's career haul to six. Yet without Bill Cartwright—and later, Scottie Pippen—sharing the captain's role, it's not clear Jordan would have won anything.

Michael Jordan deserves to be celebrated for his sublime athletic ability, his burning will to win, and the extent to which he reimagined celebrity. That's all fair and appropriate. The notion that he was also an elite leader is not only wrong, it does a disservice to the institution of captaincy. As much as the fans admired and enjoyed their behavior and equated it with surpassing leadership, Jordan and Roy Keane were false idols. As leaders, they were not purebred members of the Captain Class. For teammates, coaches, and executives, their captaincies were the stuff of a thousand migraines.

The best leaders in sports history were not mesmerizing characters. They didn't always make for great television. That's what we've come to expect, however. So that's what we continue to get. The chief reason teams choose the wrong people to lead them is because the public judges every captain against this distorted picture.

In the next chapter, we'll examine another consequence of these mistakes and misperceptions. It's the increasingly popular notion that leadership is something we've outgrown.

CHAPTER TWELVE TAKEAWAYS

- The general opinion among sports fans is that leaders of spectacular teams should operate at a fiery temperature. In recent decades, this logical bias has gone in search of bodies, and it has found them in the person of two men: Roy Keane and Michael Jordan. Both of these captains are considered leadership icons. But a close examination shows that the traits they're most widely renowned for, and that are most often identified as the key factors that made them outstanding leaders, did not fit the profile of the captains in Tier One.

- The problem with these flawed captains is that they have distorted the picture of what enlightened leadership looks like. They have set a standard that is not only impossible to meet but does not produce the best results. The danger is that people who are charged with choosing leaders will end up promoting people who have the wrong characteristics. But it also increases the chances that after they fail, they will start looking for ways to eliminate the role of a captain entirely.

THIRTEEN

The Captaincy in Winter

Leadership's Decline, and How to Revive It

For seven years, Christie Rampone had captained the U.S. women's national football team, serving as the tireless, selfless nucleus of the defense. She'd won two Olympic gold medals and the 2015 World Cup, assembling a record nearly as impressive as Carla Overbeck's. She was forty. The moment had come to let the next generation run things.

To take her place, Jill Ellis, the U.S. coach, appointed a duo of captains: midfielder Carli Lloyd, the breakout star of the World Cup; and the team's most solid defender, Becky Sauerbrunn. "They are two extremely professional players in both game and training environments and they embody the DNA of this program," Ellis said.

When U.S. Soccer posted the news on Twitter in January 2016, the responses came pouring in. Most of the comments were expressions of support and congratulations to the team's new leaders. Down the list, however, I noticed that someone had put forth a different view.

"Captains? What is this, high school?"

At roughly the same time I began writing this book, the sports world's perceptions of captains took a dark turn. The first sign of trouble came in 2007 when the NFL convened a committee to set some leaguewide guidelines for team leadership. The committee decided that the designated captains of each team should be allowed to wear a C on their jerseys and that all teams be required to choose captains before playoff games. But it also decided that teams should have the right to avoid naming any captains during the regular season. Sure enough, five years later, the NFL's New York Jets took them up on it. Matt Slauson, one of the team's veteran linemen, said the absence of captains "kind of forces guys to step up and take ownership." After posting an 8–8 record the season before, the Jets dropped to 6–10.

Two years later, in 2014, the NBA's Boston Celtics—Bill Russell's Boston Celtics—not only traded away their captain, they decided to leave the post vacant. Three months after that, when Derek Jeter retired, the New York Yankees suggested they might retire the captaincy altogether. "We have a number of different people that are very strong leaders and high-quality individuals," said the team's general manager, Brian Cashman. "That doesn't mean you have to put a C on it."

By 2016, the tradition was in full retreat. At the start of the NHL season that fall, four teams hadn't bothered to select captains, even though the league's rules expressly required them to do so. "Today's game is led by core groups of players," explained Brooks Laich, a veteran center who'd played for the suddenly leaderless Toronto Maple Leafs. "It's not done by one individual."

Even in England, where the captaincy has long been seen as a vital tradition, the same kind of thinking crept in. When Chelsea initially declined to renew longtime captain John Terry's contract after the 2016 season, the *Guardian* declared it "a potentially defining moment for the entire Captain, Leader, Legend species, whose very existence appears under threat." The column went on to declare that the value of captains in football was "debatable."

During this period I noticed another troubling development. Many teams began naming captains for reasons that had nothing to do with their leadership ability.

In 2011, after his team finished fourth in the English Premier League, Cesc Fàbregas, the captain of Arsenal, decided to leave the team for Barcelona. Faced with naming a new leader, Arsenal's manager, Arsène Wenger, made a curious move. At the time, the team's most prolific scorer, the striker Robin van Persie, was only signed through the following season. Wenger knew there would be many offers for van Persie's services and was desperate to keep him on the roster. He believed that his best hope was to try to shore up van Persie's allegiance to the team—so he named him captain.

Arsenal did not prosper under van Persie's command. They finished third in the league table, bowed out in the early rounds of the Champions League, and failed to win any trophies. Despite being given the armband, van Persie not only left Arsenal the following season, he decamped to a rival, Manchester United.

Despite this debacle, Wenger's opportunistic (some would say cynical) view of the captaincy not only survived, it started popping up in unlikely places. In 2014, after Brazil imploded spectacularly at the World Cup, the national football team's new coach decided to strip the captaincy from the center back Thiago Silva and bestow it upon the country's latest young impresario, the twenty-two-year-old goal-scoring prodigy Neymar da Silva Santos, Jr., whose confidence had been shaken by his team's poor showing at the World Cup. Giving the armband to the brightest young star, rather than a water carrier, ran counter to everything Brazil had learned in those years when Pelé had avoided the role. "I confess I did not understand the choice," said the former Brazil captain Carlos Alberto Torres. "Maybe someday Neymar will be ready to be a good captain, but not now."

Building up a player's loyalty, or giving him a vote of confidence, was one thing. But in many cases, teams made a more fundamental mistake. They convinced themselves that the captaincy was the natural right of the player with the highest market value.

Take, for instance, baseball's New York Mets. After signing their star third baseman David Wright to a $138 million multiyear deal in 2012 and making him captain at the same time, the team left no mystery about its rationale. "I think the decision was made when we gave him the contract," said the team's co-owner Jeff Wilpon. "When you commit that kind of money and resources to a guy like this, you want to make sure he's the leader."

If I had to give out a prize for the most baffling captaincy logic, it would go to the NHL's hapless Edmonton Oilers, who in 2016 decided to bestow their captaincy on a center named Connor McDavid. It's not that McDavid lacked talent or didn't have the potential to develop into a fine leader. What's disturbing is that on the day he accepted the job, he'd only been alive for nineteen years and 266 days. He became the youngest team leader in NHL history.

To Arsenal, Brazil, the Mets, the Oilers, and a host of other teams, the captaincy had come down to which superstar's ego needed stroking, or which player cost the team the most money, or which promising teenager they hoped to build around. It had ceased to be a matter of which player was the most fit to lead.

This radical shift in philosophy coincided with an era in which broadcast, cable, and satellite television companies all over the world had started bidding enormous sums for the rights to carry live sporting events. The piles of revenue this generated had made teams, leagues, and international sports federations wealthy beyond their wildest imaginings—in 2016, the sports industry took in an estimated ninety *billion* dollars, a sum not too far behind the global market for cancer treatments.

The amount of cash pouring in was so substantial that it changed the underlying motives of the business. From the earliest days of organized team sports, the surest path to financial success was to win. In the new economy, the chief goal was to turn your games into appointment television.

The primary beneficiaries of this new order were the rarest commodity in sports—the kind of bankable superstar players and coaches that people will tune in to watch. By 2016, the average salary for an NFL coach had ballooned to nearly five million dollars, while the highest-paid NFL player earned more than thirty million—both about five times what their equivalents had been in the 1990s. In the English Premier League, the spending accelerated even more rapidly. The sixteen-million-dollar annual salary Manchester City reportedly agreed to pay Pep Guardiola in 2016 was nine times what Manchester United's Alex Ferguson earned in 2000. Over the same period, the Premier League's highest-paid players saw their incomes rise by a factor of more than six.

As they became richer, more sought after, and more essential to putting on a good show, these celebrity coaches and athletes started throwing their weight around. On many teams, two opposing power centers found themselves vying for control. Basic decisions about how a team competed, and even whom it signed, became a game of tug-of-war between an indispensable star player and a marquee coach. Under this new paradigm, the old hierarchy of a team fell away.

On the Tier One teams I studied, the typical pecking order put the coach at the top, the talent on the bottom, and a water-carrying captain in the middle who served as an independent mediator between them. In this new order, where power and popularity went hand in hand, the middle manager's role had been squeezed out. Unless the captain was the superstar, the captain was a bystander.

Some of the same forces have come to bear in the business world, where many companies in thriving talent-dependent industries embraced a new workplace ethos in which hierarchies were softened and office floor plans were reengineered to break down the walls that once kept management and talent separated. One emerging school of thought, popular among technology companies in Silicon Valley, is that organizations should adopt "flat" structures, in which management layers are thin or even nonexistent. Star employees are more productive, the theory goes, and more likely to stay, when they are given autonomy and offered a voice in decision-making. Some start-ups have done away with job titles entirely, organizing workers into leaderless "self-managing teams" that report directly to top executives.

Proponents of flatness say it increases the speed of the feedback loop between the people at the top of the pyramid and the people who do the frontline work, allowing for a faster, more agile culture of continuous improvement. Whether that's true or not, it has certainly cleared the way for top executives to communicate directly with star employees without having to muddle through an extra layer of management.

As I watched all this happen, I started to wonder if I was really writing a eulogy. Just as I was building a case for the crucial value of quiet, unglamorous, team-oriented, workmanlike captains who inhabit the middle strata of a team, most of the world's richest sports organizations, and even some of its most forward-thinking companies, seemed to be sprinting headlong in the opposite direction.

The gap between what I was learning about leadership and what was transpiring in the world led me back to a question I'd first considered at the beginning of the process. After all this time, and all the energy we've spent studying team leadership, why haven't we figured it out? Why are we still tinkering with the formula?

One of the first scholars who attempted to build a composite model for enlightened leadership was the historian James MacGregor Burns. In his 1978 book, *Leadership,* Burns used the stories of figures like Moses, Machiavelli, Napoleon, Mao, Mahatma Gandhi, and Martin Luther King, Jr., to figure out what linked them together.

Burns concluded that there were two distinct types of leadership—one that was "transactional" and another that was "transformational." Transactional leadership occurred when the person in charge cared most about making sure their underlings followed orders and that the hierarchical lines of an organization were strictly maintained. There were no appeals to higher ideals, just a series of orders given and carried out. The more desirable model, transformational leadership, only came to pass when leaders focused on the values, beliefs, and needs of their followers, and engaged them in a charismatic way that inspired them to reach higher levels of motivation, morality, and achievement. The secret of transformational leadership, Burns wrote, is that "people can be lifted into their better selves."

Management experts have since embraced transformational leadership and expanded its definition to include a longer list of attributes. Great leaders, the canon says, show a talent for navigating complexities, promoting freedom of choice, practicing what they preach, appealing to reason, nurturing followers through coaching and mentorship, inspiring cooperation and harmony by showing genuine concern for others, and using "authentic, consistent means" to rally people to their point of view.

The captains in Tier One displayed many of these traits. They were conscientious, principled, and inspirational, and connected with their teammates in ways that elevated their performances. Yet there were things about the way they led their teams that didn't square with the definition Burns put forward. These men and women were often lacking in talent and charisma. Rather than leading from the front, they avoided speeches, shunned the spotlight, and performed difficult and thankless jobs in the shadows. They weren't always steadfast exemplars of virtue, either.

Truth be told, transformational leadership seemed like a grab bag into which every imaginable positive trait had been thrown. It presented an idealized view of leadership, one that was less attainable than aspirational. Of course, maybe that's the whole point: Leaders cut from the same cloth as Moses, Gandhi, and Napoleon come along so infrequently that no rational person should expect to meet one. The best we can do is to try to understand them, and to help the inferior leaders we settled for make incremental improvements.

The trouble with setting the bar so impossibly high is that we risk doing damage to the entire concept of leadership. After a while, people get tired of waiting for a unicorn to wander into the building, so they start looking for new ways to construct teams that don't require unicorns at all.

The captains in Tier One, as a whole, did not convey the idea that they were born to lead. They didn't have extreme talents that were readily apparent to everyone. Beyond the way they led, they had little in common. They lived at different times in different countries and did not share a common gender, language, culture, religion, or skin tone. They could be tall, beautiful, short, or homely, immensely skilled at their craft—or not. There is nothing about them that suggests they were one-in-a-billion natural leaders whose greatness was genetically predetermined.

I started to suspect that the real reason we can't agree on the formula for elite team leadership is that we've overcomplicated things. We've been so busy scanning the horizon for transformational knights in shining armor that we've ignored the likelier truth: there are hundreds upon thousands of potentially transformative leaders right in our midst. We just lack the ability to recognize them.

In 1982, Reuven Gal, a former Israeli army colonel, was allowed to review the personnel files for 283 Israeli soldiers who had won medals for gallantry on the battlefield during the 1973 Arab–Israeli War. He set out to see what qualities they shared.

Gal noticed that the medal-winning soldiers had received higher marks for physical fitness, intelligence, motivation, devotion, decisiveness, and perseverance under stress than the members of a control group. He also noticed that a surprising number (64 percent) were officers, suggesting a possible link between a person's leadership qualities and their motivation to do brave, selfless things under fire.

Gal's most surprising finding about the medal winners, however, was how much they did not have in common. Some were old, some young. Some were professional soldiers, others reservists. While many were officers, some came from lower ranks. Psychological tests showed that their personalities were all over the grid. "The heroes of the Israeli Defense Force do not form any unusual or deviant group," Gal wrote. "They are certainly not a group of 'supermen.' . . . They are not born heroes, either; they become heroes."

Gal and his research partners were surprised by these results, but they were also encouraged. Heroism clearly wasn't coded into a person's genes, but it did seem to be closely correlated with leadership. By developing better leaders, they reasoned, it should be possible to create an army that does more heroic things.

After conducting interviews with dozens of soldiers, they formulated a simple equation to explain their findings: Leadership = $P \times M \times D$.

Gal told me that the first variable—the P—stood for potential, which he defined as a person's God-given leadership ability. This was a natural gift that couldn't be taught, he said, and would start to become evident in a person's behavior as early as kindergarten. But it also wasn't excessively rare; many members of an army unit might have these skills.

To become a leader, however, a person with potential also needed to possess the next variable: M. "The prerequisite to be effective is motivation," he said. These two variables were something of a twin set. People who had leadership potential often had the motivation to fulfill the role. But it was the third variable in Gal's equation that caught my attention: D for development.

Here, Gal believed, biology played no role. Any leadership candidate, no matter how gifted, had to make an effort to learn the ropes and to prove that they had the right qualities. "You have to earn your leadership over time, to prove that your charisma is used the right way and that it flows in a positive group-oriented direction." Leaders must learn how to become a "prism" through which the group's perceptions are filtered and to learn how to manipulate these emotions in a way that lifts others, rather than unsettling them by confirming their fears. "Take three guys and put them in exactly the same situation," Gal said. "One of them will view it as desperate and hopeless. One will appraise it as stressful but challenging. But the third one will view it as a fascinating opportunity for excitement." Gal believed that the ability to frame these kinds of situations in a positive light was partly a reflection of a leader's personality but also a function of *experience*.

It might sound trite to compare the profiles of sports captains to those of combat heroes. Obviously, the threat of mortal injury will provoke a stronger response in most people than the prospect of losing a volleyball game. Yet Gal's view of development did not seem out of line with the stories of the captains in Tier One.

In Part II of this book, we saw how Yogi Berra dedicated himself to becoming a better catcher and, in doing so, learned how to manage and lead a pitching staff. We saw how Maurice Richard developed a kill switch to keep his temper in check, how Carla Overbeck built respect among her teammates by carrying their bags, how Valeri Vasiliev won the loyalty of his teammates by standing up to his coach, how Tim Duncan circulated among his teammates offering a constant flow of practical communication, and how Buck Shelford and Jack Lambert used nonverbal displays to transmit passion.

While these acts might have been intuitive to these men and women, there is nothing about them that required skill. They were functions of behavior.

More important, none of these Tier One captains were given the leadership role on their teams the day they arrived. In every case, some time had elapsed. They'd been given a chance to listen and observe and audition for the part. In other words, they'd developed.

None of this should suggest that it's easy to become an elite captain or that this stratum of leadership is within everybody's reach. As we also saw in Part II, these men and women did things in competition that most of us wouldn't consider. But I do think it's fair to say that by studying the leadership behavior of these captains it's within anyone's power to improve, and that the number of people who can become exceptional team leaders is larger than we realize. "Leaders are made, they are not born," as Vince Lombardi famously said. "They are made by hard effort, which is the price which all of us must pay to achieve any goal that is worthwhile."

To this point, *The Captain Class* has focused most of its attention on how captains led their teams. There is, of course, another important constituency—the executives, managers, and coaches whose job it is to assemble these units.

Most of us think of team dynamics in the same way we might ponder the vastness of space—it's something mysterious and unknowable. We can design a team intelligently, putting all of the pieces meticulously into place until there doesn't seem to be a competitive weakness. But at the end of the day, what happens in the room, or on the field, is beyond our control. The unit will either pop, or fizzle.

The first thing the sixteen teams in Tier One teach us is that leadership matters. It's not that having a captain of a certain kind was a bonus—it was the only common denominator. As a writer, the best analogy I can think of is that captains are like the verb in a sentence. The verb may not be as memorable as the nouns, as evocative as the adjectives, or as expressive as the punctuation. But it's the verb that does the yeoman's work—unifying the disparate parts and creating the forward momentum. In the closed unit of a great sentence, it's the only essential component.

It's true that many sports teams have soured on this idea. Captains have become unfashionable—like pleated slacks, Rollerblades, and gluten. People who build sports teams have started conflating talent, or market value, with leadership. They have eliminated hierarchies that allow team leaders to exist in a robust middle layer of management. They are afraid to choose leaders that defy conventional wisdom or whose penchant for creating friction inside the team works against their economic priorities. The simplest bit of advice I could give to team executives in sports and beyond would be to stop doing these things immediately.

The larger question, of course, is how to choose the *right* leader. In sports, the seven traits I've outlined in Part II should serve as an excellent guide. In the world beyond sports, where the parameters of competition are different and where teams do an infinite variety of things from building software to selling Toyotas, the prescription isn't so obvious.

The best set of instructions I have come across—the one that most closely matches my own observations about Tier One captains—was compiled by Richard Hackman, the late Harvard social and organizational psychologist, who spent decades observing teams of all kinds as they worked. While their goals were as different as landing a plane is from performing a piece of classical music, Hackman focused his attention on comparing how their preparations and processes affected their outcomes. By doing so, he pieced together the outlines of a theory on the nature of effective team stewardship, or as he put it, the "personal qualities that appear to distinguish excellent team leaders from those for whom leadership is a struggle."

Hackman's theory consisted of four principles:

1. Effective leaders know some things.

The best team leaders seemed to have a solid understanding of the conditions that needed to be present inside a team in order for its members to thrive. In other words, they developed a vision for the way things *ought* to be.

2. Effective leaders know how to do some things.

In "performance" situations, Hackman noticed that the most skillful leaders seemed to always sound the right notes. They understood the "themes" that were most important in whatever situation the team was in, and knew how to close the gap between the team's current state of being and the one it needed to reach in order to succeed.

3. Effective leaders should be emotionally mature.

Hackman understood that leading a team could be "an emotionally challenging undertaking." Great captains have to manage their own anxieties while coping with the feelings of others. The most mature leaders didn't run away from anxiety or try to paper it over. Rather, they would pour into it with an eye toward learning about it—and by doing so find the right way to defuse it.

4. Effective leaders need a measure of personal courage.

The basic work of a leader, Hackman believed, was to move a group away from its entrenched system and into a better, more prosperous one. In other words, a leader's job is to help a team make the turn toward greatness. To do this, he believed, a leader—by definition—had to "operate at the margins of what members presently like and want rather than at the center of the collective consensus." To push a team forward, a leader must disrupt its routines and challenge its definition of what is normal. Because this kind of thing produces resistance, even anger, leaders have to have the courage to stand apart—even if they end up paying a substantial personal toll for doing so.

The "strange" thing about Hackman's four rules, as he put it, was what they *didn't* include. There was nothing in there about a person's personality, or values, or charisma. There was no mention whatsoever of their talent. Leading a team effectively wasn't a matter of skill and magnetism, it was all tied up in the quotidian business of leadership. To Hackman, the chief trait of superior leaders wasn't what they were like but what they did on a daily basis.

The trouble with this idea is that it makes the job of identifying a worthy leader considerably more difficult. You could interview someone for hours and never know whether they have this kind of ability until they start doing the job.

There second challenge in choosing a leader—one that is no less vital—is knowing what kind of people to avoid.

Deborah Gruenfeld, a social psychologist at Stanford's business school, has spent most of her career studying the roles of individuals inside organizations. She is one of the world's leading experts on the psychology of power.

The conventional view, Gruenfeld says, is that people's achievements alone are rarely enough to allow them to acquire power. Most of us believe there are emotional and promotional components to being a leader that don't come through on a résumé. As a result, many people wrongly believe they can claim status inside an organization by "tricking" others into thinking they're entitled to it even if they might not be. It's an outgrowth of the old adage "fake it till you make it."

According to Gruenfeld, the research suggests that the opposite is true. In real life, she says, people often attain and hold power within an organization by downplaying their qualifications. "We gain status more readily, and more reliably, by acting just a little less deserving than we actually are."

The captains in Tier One were not poseurs. They didn't make speeches, didn't seek attention or acclaim, and were not comfortable wearing the cloak of power. Most of them took subservient roles and carried water for their teammates. In other words, they behaved precisely the way Gruenfeld describes. They won status by doing everything in their power to suggest they didn't deserve it.

In 2016, Bret Stephens wrote a column in the opinion pages of the *Wall Street Journal* in which he described a conversation he'd had with his eleven-year-old son. The subject was the difference between fame and heroism. His son's point of view on the subject was that famous people depend on what other people think of them to be who they are. Heroes just care about whether they do everything right.

Stephens went on to describe a modern phenomenon, fed by all forms of traditional and social media, in which people devote considerable energy to boasting about their talents and pretending to be great, even when they're not. He called this "posture culture."

When I read this, I realized that this is exactly the kind of mindset that has become tangled up with our views about captains. All too often, the people who propose themselves for positions of power are quick to trumpet their abilities. And those of us who make these decisions are often swayed by the force of their personality.

The truth is that leadership is a ceaseless burden. It's not something people should do for the self-reflected glory, or even because they have oodles of charisma or surpassing talent. It's something they should do because they have the humility and fortitude to set aside the credit, and their own gratification and well-being, for the team—not just in pressure-packed moments but in every minute of every day.

This instinct shouldn't be confused with the desire to make others *happy*. Scientists have shown that a team's perceptions of its work and of the efficacy of its leader often have no bearing on how well it performs. A great leader is dedicated to doing whatever it takes to make success more likely, even if it's unpopular, or controversial, or outrageous, or completely invisible to others. A leader has to be committed, above all else, to getting it right.

In about 600 B.C., the Chinese philosopher Laozi must have had a lot on his mind. It was a period of growing political independence throughout China as new leaders emerged and the old feudal system broke down. It was also a time of civil wars and bloodshed. In the middle of the upheaval, Laozi made a few observations about leadership that struck me as a fine note to end on.

"A leader is best when people barely know he exists, not so good when people obey and acclaim him, worst when they despise him," he wrote. "Fail to honor others and they will fail to honor you. But of a good leader, who talks little, when his work is done, his aims fulfilled, they will all say, 'we did this ourselves.'"

CHAPTER THIRTEEN TAKEAWAYS

- Captains have fallen out of favor in sports. In some cases, teams have opted to use the title as a tool to build loyalty. In others, they have simply bestowed it on the player who has the highest salary. Some teams have eliminated the role altogether. This trend mirrors an idea that has taken hold in business, where some companies are experimenting with ways of eliminating middle management to bring top executives closer to star talent. These ideas are practical responses to changing attitudes and economics, but there is no indication that they help create elite teams.

- Scholars who study leadership have done a fine job of identifying positive traits that all leaders aspire to, but they have set a prohibitively high bar. The captains profiled in this book did not always clear it. They were not abundantly talented or charismatic. Most of the things they did to help their teams become dynasties were functions of behavior and experience—of the skills they developed and the choices they made on the job. Great leaders do not need to be glamorous. They only need a knowledge of what a successful effort looks like and a plan to get there. They do not need to remind people how great they are. If anything, they should give the impression that they don't believe they're worthy of leading at all.

Epilogue

A regulation baseball is a hard object the size of an orange. It weighs at least five ounces—roughly the same as a billiard ball or a D battery. If one of these things hits your body after being flung at a high speed, it's likely to provoke some theatrics.

On the unseasonably chilly afternoon of July 24, 2004, a pitcher for the Boston Red Sox named Bronson Arroyo threw an eighty-seven-mile-an-hour slider directly at Alex Rodriguez of the New York Yankees. The five-ounce missile made landfall on Rodriguez's elbow, which, lucky for him, was wrapped in a protective sleeve. His body wasn't damaged. His ego was another story.

On his way to first base, Rodriguez stopped and glared at Arroyo, a six-foot-four, 190-pound beanpole with long, shaggy hair. "Throw that shit over the fucking plate!" he yelled. And then again, with added heat, *"Throw that shit over the plate!"*

Like Rodriguez, just about everyone in the stands at Boston's Fenway Park suspected that Arroyo, who had just given up his third run in three innings, had thrown at Rodriguez on purpose. In a game the night before, Rodriguez had singled in the winning run, and he had already scored once that afternoon. The Red Sox, who trailed the Yankees by three runs in the game and by nine and a half games in the division standings, might have figured they had nothing to lose by trying to rattle one of New York's best hitters.

Then again, they might have had deeper motives.

Since their founding in 1903, the Yankees had rung up twenty-six titles in thirty-nine World Series appearances, becoming one of the world's most successful sporting institutions. The Red Sox, meanwhile, hadn't won a title since 1918 and had found dozens of ways to permit the Yankees, their fiercest rivals, to humiliate them. One year earlier, I'd watched from the press box as a slumping Yankee infielder named Aaron Boone stepped to the plate in the eleventh inning of the seventh game of the American League Championship Series and, despite having hit only six home runs all season, sent Boston packing with a deep shot to left.

Beyond simply being a Yankee, Rodriguez made a tempting target for another reason. Before the 2004 season, he'd raised the city's championship hopes by agreeing to a tentative trade deal. Boston's players and fans had gone so far as to offer him a heartfelt welcome to town. But then, in typical fashion, the Yankees swooped in to sign him instead. Once again, the Red Sox had been humiliated. Rodriguez had wanted to wear Yankee pinstripes all along. Overnight, he had become public enemy number one.

As Rodriguez glared at Arroyo, Jason Varitek, the Red Sox catcher, entered the frame. One of a catcher's jobs is to protect his pitchers from large angry men carrying bats, so Varitek walked right up to the Yankees star, who towered over him, and delivered a message. "I told him, in choice words, to get to first base," Varitek said.

Rodriguez took a couple steps forward, his eyes narrowing to slits. *"Fuck you!"* he shouted. This sort of behavior was unusual for Rodriguez, who wasn't known as a hothead. Varitek stood his ground, so Rodriguez pointed a finger at him. "Come on!"

In 98 percent of these situations, the hitter settles down. The home-plate umpire might head over to have a word with the pitcher and his manager, but that's essentially it.

This instance would belong to the other 2 percent.

With a single furious motion, Varitek shoved his hands, one of them still attached to his catcher's mitt, straight into Rodriguez's face. The force of this lunging punch, combined with Rodriguez's forward motion, was strong enough to jar his head violently backward and to lift his feet off the ground. As the two benches emptied, Rodriguez threw Varitek into a headlock. The other players converged on the scene, setting off a spirited round of punches. One Yankee pitcher would leave the field with blood trickling down his face.

The 2004 Boston Red Sox were not a Tier One team, but they were special to me. It was their transformation from a half-assed bunch of jokers to legitimate contenders that convinced me to write this book in the first place. So after finishing my research, I decided to circle back—just out of curiosity—to see if there had been any one event that sparked their metamorphosis. The search didn't take long. It was the afternoon of July 24.

After the brawl ended, the energy in the ballpark was completely different. The brawl had brought Boston's fans roaring to life, and the Red Sox players seemed energized. "Huge adrenaline surge on our end," said the Boston pitcher Curt Schilling.

The statistical probabilities suggested that at this point, Boston had a 25 percent chance of winning the game. Yet by the bottom of the ninth inning, the Red Sox had battled back to trail the Yankees by a run. That's when Boston's third baseman, Bill Mueller, stepped in against the Yankees' legendary closer Mariano Rivera and, with one out and a runner on first, clouted a two-run home run to win the game. The ballpark erupted. As the Red Sox celebrated, a chant of "Yankees suck!" thundered from the grandstands.

After "The Punch," as it became known, the wandering, undisciplined vibe I'd seen in the Boston clubhouse melted away, replaced by a palpable sense of purpose. The Red Sox only won four of their next ten games, but managed to outscore their opponents by fifteen runs. On August 7, they went on a tear—winning nineteen of their next twenty-three games, including a streak of ten in a row. After squeaking into the postseason and shocking the Yankees in the American League Championship Series, they won their first World Series title in eighty-six years. Before the Punch, the Red Sox had won 54 percent of their games. Afterward, they won 69 percent.

The Red Sox went on to become baseball's best team over the next five seasons, making the postseason four times and claiming another World Series trophy in 2007. More significantly, they had finally stepped out of the Yankees' shadow.

Empiricists don't believe in the concept of "momentum" in sports. They find it ridiculous to think that a single display of emotion by a respected member of a team could produce a contagion powerful enough to upend the laws of probability. They will tell you that in a linear form of competition like baseball, a winning season is little more than a random event, a fortunate sampling of individual performances in which many players finish the season at the high end of their expected statistical range. As much as I love statistics, I knew that in this case they were wrong.

When the 2004 season began, Boston's de facto leader was the superstar shortstop Nomar Garciaparra, the team's most popular player. By July 24, however, Garciaparra was on his way out. Injured, aloof, and unhappy, he'd become a lump in the clubhouse. One week later, the Red Sox traded him.

At thirty-two years old, Jason Varitek was entering the downslope of his career. During the off-season, the Red Sox, pessimistic about his age, his numbers, and his prospects, had lowballed him on a contract extension. He wasn't expected to be playing there much longer. Though he had earned the respect of his teammates, Varitek had none of Garciaparra's star power. Quiet and unassuming, he kept an outdoorsman's goatee and a wardrobe full of unsightly extra-large sweaters. He handled the pitchers well, showed toughness on the field, and never said anything interesting to the media.

For years afterward, Varitek refused to sign photos of The Punch because he felt he'd embarrassed the game and set a bad example for kids. He insisted he'd only been doing his job. "I was just trying to protect Bronson," he said afterward. "For protecting a teammate, I'll take whatever comes."

The Punch generated a different response from Boston's fans. Even though Varitek was ejected that day, fined two thousand dollars, and suspended for four games, they viewed it as a justifiable act of gallantry—the moment the Red Sox finally stood up to their tormentors. Photos of the incident could be seen all over Boston, framed on the walls inside sports bars or clipped to the sun visors of taxicabs. The Boston sportswriter Dan Shaughnessy once used his column to write a fawning letter to Varitek, addressing him as "the man who turned a season around by shoving your mitt into the face of Alex Rodriguez."

By discarding the rules of polite society and making an aggressive display of force at a time when his team's confidence was collapsing, Jason Varitek had behaved precisely like a Tier One captain. In fact, everything about the man seemed to fit the profile. The Punch wasn't some random event, one of several million data points in a season. It was the work of an elite leader.

Even the Red Sox, one of the most ruthlessly quantitative teams in baseball at the time, seemed to come around to this point of view. After the season, they not only kept Varitek, they rewarded him with a four-year, forty-million-dollar contract extension.

They also named him captain.

Appendix

Tier One: The Elite

These sixteen teams passed all of the eight tests I designed to determine the greatest sports dynasties of all time (see Chapter One).

They had at least five members; they competed in sports where the athletes must interact or coordinate their efforts during competition while also engaging directly with their opponents; they competed in a major spectator sport with millions of fans; their dominance lasted for at least four years; they had ample opportunities to prove themselves against the world's top competition; and, finally, their achievements stood apart in some way from all other teams in the history of their sport.

Collingwood Magpies (Australian rules football),
  1927–30
New York Yankees (Major League Baseball), 1949–53
Hungary (men's football), 1950–55

Montreal Canadiens (National Hockey League),
  1955–60
Boston Celtics (National Basketball Association),
  1956–69
Brazil (men's football), 1958–62
Pittsburgh Steelers (National Football League),
  1974–80
Soviet Union (men's ice hockey), 1980–84
New Zealand All Blacks (rugby union), 1986–90
Cuba (women's volleyball), 1991–2000
Australia (women's field hockey), 1993–2000
United States (women's football), 1996–99
San Antonio Spurs (NBA), 1997–2016
Barcelona (men's football), 2008–13
France (men's handball), 2008–15
New Zealand All Blacks (rugby union), 2011–15

The "Double" Captains

Three outstanding soccer captains led more than one team into Tier
Two. Because of this rare achievement, they were given special consideration in the book.

Franz Beckenbauer; Germany (1970–74) and Bayern
  Munich (1971–76)
Didier Deschamps; France (1998–2001) and Olympique de
  Marseille (1988–93)
Philipp Lahm; Germany (2010–14) and Bayern Munich
  (2012–16)

The Judgment Calls

Three of the sports included in this study proved the toughest to analyze—and all of them forced me to make some controversial decisions. The first was professional football, which I discussed in detail in Chapter One. The other two are the National Football League and international cricket.

For the NFL, finding the most uniquely successful team wasn't a major challenge. By winning four Super Bowls in six seasons, Jack Lambert's 1974–80 Pittsburgh Steelers achieved the most concentrated burst of success in the sport's history, making them a lock for Tier One. The trouble was trying to decide whether another team should join them.

The obvious candidates were the 1981–95 San Francisco 49ers and the 2001–17 New England Patriots, which own the NFL's two longest streaks of general excellence. As of March 2017, both teams had won five Super Bowls and posted elite overall win percentages and Elo ratings. Over the years, these teams had many player-leaders who fit the Captain Class mold. The 49ers' captains included, at various times, Joe Montana, Ronnie Lott, Spencer Tillman, and Steve Young; while the Patriots enjoyed the guidance of selfless, inspirational athletes like Bryan Cox, Rodney Harrison, Devin McCourty, and Tedy Bruschi. The man at the top of the leadership heap, however, was New England's long-time offensive captain Tom Brady, who in 2017 became the only NFL quarterback to win five Super Bowls.

Though he was the team's best player, and one of the NFL's top celebrities, Brady's list of Captain Class traits is undeniable. He is a private, introverted sort who lives quietly off the field, is picky about endorsements, and doesn't provide tabloid fodder. While he leaves the locker-room oratory to his coach, he is constantly correcting and consulting teammates and is famous among them for the abundant passion he displays on the field—often by getting in their faces to motivate them. Before the 2016 season, Brady endured a long and humiliating legal battle with the NFL, and during the season, though he never mentioned it publicly, his mother began undergoing chemotherapy. Nevertheless, he led the Patriots to the Super Bowl, where he engineered the greatest comeback win in the game's history.

To many people, the fact that the NFL suspended Brady for four games in 2016 for allegedly conspiring with the team's equipment managers to deflate game balls (to make them easier to grip) represents a blot on his character. Yet this behavior would fall neatly under the Captain Class banner of playing to the edge of the rules and engaging in what scientists call "bracketed morality" (see Chapter Six).

Nevertheless, both the Patriots and the 49ers suffered from the same liability that kept them out of Tier One—their résumés were so similar that neither one achieved something truly unique. Should the Patriots go on to win another Super Bowl, or to continue playing at their current pace, they could still make the cut. But as of this writing, only the Steelers qualified.

In cricket, three teams belonged in the Tier One conversation. The first was the 1975–85 West Indies, captained by Clive Lloyd, which won two World Cups in three finals appearances and played twenty-seven straight international tests without a loss. The others are a pair of Australian teams: the 1998–2003 side, led by Steve Waugh, that won a World Cup, posted a record sixteen consecutive test victories, and dominated England in the Ashes; and the 2003–08 unit, captained by Ricky Ponting, which won two World Cups and matched the earlier Australian team's achievement of sixteen consecutive test wins.

Once again, the captains of these teams fit the mold. Disciplined early in his career for a drunken brawl in a bar, Ricky Ponting subsequently channeled his aggression against rivals. He led with brashness and competitive fire, and often challenged the spirit, and possibly the letter of the rules. Sledging (or trash-talking opponents) became a controversial art form, and on-field confrontations were not uncommon, even with umpires. Steve Waugh's ability to control his emotions while directing play earned him the nickname "the Iceman." He, too, engaged in on-field verbal sparring that on occasion threatened to become physical. Although not an obviously gifted player, his legendary resolve fashioned him into one of the leading batsmen of the side, and its competitive heart. During their reigns, the Australian teams were communicative groups that held regular sessions after matches where the players, still in their whites, would crack open beers and deconstruct the matches.

Among them, however, Clive Lloyd of the West Indies was the finest Captain Class prototype. He was not his team's star, or a particularly gifted athlete. He wore thick glasses (the result of an eye injury sustained as a child) and was vastly outshone by superstar teammates, including Vivian Richards. His calm, low-key, and open leadership style helped to unify a team composed of players from many Caribbean nations, and he often stood up to cricket authorities by taking principled stands—especially on matters of player pay.

Off the pitch, Lloyd held the players to a strict curfew and counseled them to be dull and to repress their passions. On the pitch, however, the story was different. While he discouraged the team from sledging, he adopted an aggressive and controversial tactic—using a rotation composed exclusively of tall, athletic "fast" bowlers who threw balls in excess of 90 miles per hour that were hard to control and even harder for batsmen to dodge. The strategy was designed to create fear, if not carnage. After West Indies bowlers put several batsmen in hospital during a 1976 test series, India's captain declared his innings early—essentially surrendering the test. To critics who said the strategy had no place in a genteel sport, Lloyd responded, "this is cricket, sometimes you have to take it."

In the end, however, no cricket team qualified for Tier One. The West Indies excelled in both forms of the sport—test and one-day international, or ODI—but its achievements were nearly all matched or exceeded by the Australian sides. Waugh's unit was arguably the finest test cricket team ever assembled, but it did not stand out in the ODI format. Ponting's team had the reverse problem: it dominated ODI cricket by winning two World Cups but had an inconsistent test record. In isolation, all three teams might have ranked as the best in history. Put together, however, none of their records could be considered uniquely superior.

Tier Two: The Finalists

Some of the most recognized and widely revered dynasties in global sports failed to make my list of the sixteen greatest teams in history. Though they were all extraordinary in their own ways and all met the basic criteria I devised for what constitutes a superior team (see Chapter One), they were excluded from the top echelon, or Tier One, for a couple of reasons. Either they lacked the opportunity to prove themselves fully, or they were outshone by the achievements of another team in the same genre of sport. I've listed these 106 Tier Two teams, along with their details, in the following chart.

Those teams with the most impressive credentials, which came the closest to Tier One, are noted with asterisks after their names.

Disqualification Codes

A.

These twenty-eight teams lacked sufficient opportunity to prove themselves. They played at a time when the best teams from different nations rarely met, or when major tournaments were scarce or did not include all the world's top teams. Some competed in sports in which they did not assemble to play together very often, while others played in leagues that did not allow them to play the champions of another, competing league.

B.

The sixty-six teams in this category had records that, while impressive and highly unusual, were eclipsed by another team that competed in the same genre of sport. In some cases, several teams had arguments for Tier One, but none clearly stood out above all others. In a few sports (see women's handball and men's water polo) the team with the best overall record simply hadn't put together a performance that was dominant enough to earn a spot.

C.

These twelve extraordinary men's professional soccer teams came within spitting distance of Tier One. Many of them were the greatest club teams their countries have ever produced. But they all fell just short of the top tier in some small, arguably forgivable way.

TEAM	DATES	COMMENTS	DQ CODE
American Football: National Football League			
Cleveland Browns	1946–50	Won four All-American Football Conference titles and one NFL title in five seasons under captain Lou Saban and others, but the AAFC was less highly regarded than the National Football League.	A
Green Bay Packers*	1961–67	Captained by Willie Davis and Bob Skoronski, this team won five NFL titles in seven seasons, including three straight, but the first three came before NFL champions began playing the champions of the rival American Football League.	A
Miami Dolphins	1971–74	Won two Super Bowls, four division titles, and 84 percent of its regular-season games and recorded the modern NFL's first undefeated season behind captains Nick Buoniconti, Bob Griese, and Larry Little but lost the 1971 Super Bowl by three touchdowns and lost in the conference playoffs in '74.	B

TEAM	DATES	COMMENTS	DQ CODE
San Francisco 49ers*	1981–95	Won five Super Bowls and eleven division titles in fourteen seasons through the 1995 Super Bowl and earned the highest single-season Elo rating for an NFL team in modern times under a collection of captains that included Joe Montana, Ronnie Lott, Spencer Tillman, and Steve Young. It fell short of the record of four titles in six years, had a similar long-term record as the 2001–17 New England Patriots, and posted a disastrous 3–6 record in 1982.	B
Dallas Cowboys	1992–95	Won three Super Bowls in four seasons while amassing the best overall Elo rating in NFL history for any team during a four-season stretch.	B
New England Patriots*	2001–17	Captained by Tom Brady and a group that includes defensive players Rodney Harrison, Bryan Cox, Devin McCourty, and Tedy Bruschi, this team won five Super Bowls and fourteen division titles in sixteen years and achieved the highest Elo rating in NFL history over a five-season stretch, winning 83 percent of its games and two of five Super Bowls (it nearly won a third). Yet this team fell short of the record of four titles in six years, missed the playoffs in 2002 and 2008 and, as of March 2017, its record wasn't appreciably better than the 1981–95 San Francisco 49ers.	B

TEAM	DATES	COMMENTS	DQ CODE
Australian Rules Football			
Carlton	1906–10	Won three titles in five Grand Final appearances while posting an 82 percent win rate under captains Jim Flynn and Fred Elliott.	B
Melbourne Demons*	1955–60	Won five of six titles between 1955 and 1960. Came within eighteen points of winning a sixth Grand Final but missed matching the all-time record of four championships in a row.	B
Baseball: Major League Baseball			
Philadelphia Athletics	1910–14	Won four division titles and three championships in four overall trips to the World Series over five seasons.	B
Boston Red Sox	1915–18	Won three World Series titles in four seasons behind captains Jack Barry and Dick Hoblitzell.	B
New York Yankees*	1936–41	Captained until 1939 by Lou Gehrig, this team won four World Series titles in a row and five of six but failed to match the record of five straight.	B
Oakland Athletics	1971–75	Won three straight World Series titles and five straight division titles.	B
Atlanta Braves	1991–2005	Won fourteen division titles in fifteen seasons and appeared in the World Series five times but only won it once.	B

TEAM	DATES	COMMENTS	DQ CODE
New York Yankees	1996–2000	Won four World Series titles in five seasons, falling one win short of the record. This team did not name a captain, although many say outfielder Paul O'Neill was its unofficial leader.	B

Baseball: Negro National League / Japan League

TEAM	DATES	COMMENTS	DQ CODE
Pittsburgh Crawfords	1933–36	Won four consecutive titles but failed to match the record of another Negro National League team. Racial segregation prevented them from taking on the top all-white teams of the major leagues.	A
Homestead Grays*	1937–45	Won eight titles in nine seasons and 89 percent of their games under captain Buck Leonard, but racial segregation prevented them from taking on the top all-white teams of the major leagues.	A
Yomiuri Giants (Japan)	1965–73	The "V-9" Giants won nine consecutive Japanese baseball titles but played in an era when Japanese teams did not compete against teams from Major League Baseball, which is widely believed to have been the superior league.	A

Basketball: National Basketball Association

TEAM	DATES	COMMENTS	DQ CODE
Minneapolis Lakers	1948–54	Won one BAA title and four NBA titles in six years behind captain Jim Pollard.	B
Los Angeles Lakers	1980–88	Won five NBA titles in nine seasons behind Kareem Abdul-Jabbar but lost in the first round of the playoffs in 1981.	B

TEAM	DATES	COMMENTS	DQ CODE
Boston Celtics	1983–87	Won two NBA titles in four straight Finals appearances under captain Larry Bird.	B
Chicago Bulls*	1991–98	Won six NBA titles in eight seasons with a 79 percent win rate in its title-winning seasons under captains Michael Jordan, Bill Cartwright, and Scottie Pippen but finished second and third in its division in '94 and '95 and dropped out of the quarterfinals of the NBA playoffs in those seasons.	B
Miami Heat	2010–14	Won two NBA championships in four straight Finals appearances with four captains, including LeBron James and Dwyane Wade.	B
Basketball: Women's National Basketball Association			
Houston Comets*	1997–2000	Captained by the great Cynthia Cooper, this team won four consecutive WNBA titles but never played against the champions of the competing American Basketball League in two of these seasons.	A
Basketball: Men's International			
United States*	1992–97	Captained at the outset by Larry Bird and Earvin "Magic" Johnson, the "Dream Team" won six straight major competitions, including two Olympic gold medals and a World Cup. But it rarely competed and had an inconsistent roster.	A

TEAM	DATES	COMMENTS	DQ CODE
Basketball: Women's International			
United States*	2008–16	Won three consecutive Olympic gold medals and two straight World Cups behind captains Lisa Leslie, Sue Bird, and others but rarely played together.	A
Cricket: Men's International			
West Indies*	1975–85	Captained by the legendary Clive Lloyd, this team excelled in the one-day international cricket format, winning two World Cups and losing in the final of a third. It set a record by playing twenty-seven straight international test matches without a loss. Its World Cup and consecutive test-win streaks were later topped or matched by other teams, however.	B
Australia*	1998–2003	Captain Steve Waugh's teams beat England in the Ashes test series three times, posted a record sixteen test victories in a row from 1999 to 2001, and won the 1999 World Cup, but lost the ICC Champions Trophy three times.	B
Australia*	2003–08	Dominated one-day international cricket by winning World Cups in 2003 and 2007 and an ICC Champions Trophy in 2006 while tying a record with sixteen consecutive test wins. Captain Ricky Ponting's team was inconsistent at times in major tests, however, including a 2005 loss to England in the Ashes series.	B

TEAM	DATES	COMMENTS	DQ CODE
Field Hockey: Men's International			
India*	1928–36	Captained for a time by the great Dhyan Chand, this team won three straight Olympic gold medals but disbanded for long stretches between events and rarely played outside the Olympics.	A
India	1948–56	After a break during World War II, this team won another three straight Olympic gold medals but disbanded for long stretches between events and rarely played outside the Olympics.	A
Pakistan	1978–84	Won one Olympic title, two World Cups, and two Champions Trophies, but its Olympic title came in a boycott year.	B
Netherlands	1996–2000	Won two Olympic gold medals but only one World Cup and three of five Champions Trophies.	B
Australia*	2008–14	Won two World Cups, two consecutive Commonwealth Games, and five straight Champions Trophies but lost the '12 Olympics and '14 Champions Trophy.	B
Field Hockey: Women's International			
Netherlands	1983–87	Won one Olympic title, two World Cups, and two European titles but fell short of Australia's marks.	B
Netherlands	2009–12	Won one Olympic gold medal, one of two World Cups, and two straight European titles under captain Maartje Paumen but won only one of four Champions Trophies.	B

TEAM	DATES	COMMENTS	DQ CODE
Football: Men's International			
Italy*	1933–38	Won consecutive World Cups and an Olympic gold medal but did so when many top teams and star players didn't participate in these tournaments.	A
Brazil*	1968–73	Lost only one match and dominated the '70 World Cup behind captain Carlos Alberto Torres but failed to win a second World Cup or match Hungary's overall wins and Elo rating.	B
West Germany	1970–74	Won one World Cup, finished third in another, and won one European Championship under captain Franz Beckenbauer.	B
France	1998–2001	Won one World Cup, one European Championship, and one Confederations Cup behind the captaincy of Didier Deschamps.	B
Spain*	2008–12	Captained by Iker Casillas, this team won one World Cup and two consecutive European titles but failed to win a second World Cup.	B
Germany	2010–14	Captained by Philipp Lahm, this team won one World Cup, went undefeated for twenty-eight straight matches, and achieved the highest Elo rating ever recorded for a men's international football team, but failed to win the 2016 European title.	B

TEAM	DATES	COMMENTS	DQ CODE
Football: Men's Professional			
Aston Villa (England)	1893–1900	Captained by Jack Devey, this team won five English titles in seven years and two FA Cups but finished sixth in one season and did not face the best teams from other nations.	A
Alumni (Argentina)	1900–11	Won nine league titles in twelve years but did not compete against other top international teams.	A
MTK Budapest (Hungary)	1916–25	Won nine straight league titles but never faced the top club teams from other nations.	A
Huddersfield Town (England)	1923–28	Won three straight English Football Association titles in five seasons and was twice runner-up under captain Roy Goodall. Failed to win the annual FA Cup.	B
Arsenal (England)	1930–35	Captained by Tom Parker and Alex James, this team won four English titles in five years and one runner-up but came up empty in the FA Cup competition, making it to only one final. Rarely faced top teams from abroad.	A
Juventus (Italy)	1930–35	Won five Serie A titles in five years behind captain Virginio Rosetta but rarely faced top teams from abroad.	A

TEAM	DATES	COMMENTS	DQ CODE
Torino (Italy)	1942–49	Won five league titles in a row in an era when top international teams rarely met (streak ended tragically when most of its members, including the captain, Valentino Mazzola, died in a plane crash).	A
Millonarios (Colombia)	1949–53	Colombia's best-ever team, the "Blue Ballet" won four of five league titles and one runner-up but played before 1960, when top South American teams began competing in the annual Copa Libertadores.	A
River Plate (Argentina)	1952–57	Won five league titles in seven years but played before the Copa Libertadores era of international play.	A
Real Madrid* (Spain)	1955–60	Won five European Cups in a row (a record) and an Intercontinental Cup and posted two of the top four Elo ratings in history behind captains Miguel Muñoz and Juan Alonso but failed to win the Spanish league in three of those five seasons.	C
Peñarol* (Uruguay)	1958–62	Captained by William Martínez, this team won five straight Uruguayan titles and two Copa Libertadores. It defeated Benfica (below) in the '61 Intercontinental Cup but lost decisively to Real Madrid (above) in the '60 Intercontinental Cup and to Brazil's Santos (below) in the '62 Copa Libertadores.	C

TEAM	DATES	COMMENTS	DQ CODE
Benfica (Portugal)	1959–65	Portugal's best-ever team, captained by José Águas, won five of six domestic titles, two domestic Cups, and two European Cups in four trips to the final but failed to dominate a relatively shallow domestic league and lost the '61 Intercontinental Cup to Peñarol (above).	C
Santos* (Brazil)	1961–65	Behind Pelé and captain José Ely de Miranda, or "Zito," this team won five straight Taça Brasil league titles, four of five São Paulo state championships, two South American titles, two Intercontinental Cups, and four major titles in a single season twice. Its only blemish was losing the '63 São Paulo state title to rival Palmeiras.	C
Internazionale* (Italy)	1962–67	Captain Armando Picchi's "La Grande Inter" won three league titles plus two European Cups (with a semifinal and one runner-up), plus two Intercontinental Cups over five seasons, and won or drew 70 percent of its matches in the Italian league. Nevertheless, it did not win its domestic league in two seasons, lost to Celtic (below) in the 1966 European Cup, and fell short of Barcelona's tallies in several key areas.	C
Real Madrid (Spain)	1965–69	Won four of five Spanish titles and one European Cup behind captain Francisco Gento.	B

TEAM	DATES	COMMENTS	DQ CODE
Celtic* (Scotland)	1965–74	Scotland's best-ever team, captained by Billy McNeill, won nine straight league titles and a '67 European Cup but played in a relatively weak league and lost the '67 Intercontinental Cup.	C
Ajax* (Netherlands)	1969–73	Holland's best-ever team, captained by the great Johan Cruyff, came within a hair of matching Barcelona. It won or drew 92 percent of its matches, winning three European Cups in four seasons (to Barça's two) in addition to one Intercontinental Cup and several domestic titles. But it finished number two in the Dutch league in '71, didn't win as many overall titles as Barça, and did not match Barça's Elo rating.	C
Bayern Munich* (Germany)	1971–76	Franz Beckenbauer's club team won three consecutive Bundesliga titles and three straight European Championships over five seasons but twice failed to win a domestic title, once finishing tenth.	C
Independiente (Argentina)	1972–75	Won a record four straight Copa Libertadores titles and one Intercontinental Cup but failed to win a single domestic league title.	B
Liverpool* (England)	1975–84	Won seven English titles and four European Cups in nine seasons under Emlyn Hughes, Phil Thompson, and Graeme Souness but stumbled to a fifth-place league finish in the 1980–81 season.	C

TEAM	DATES	COMMENTS	DQ CODE
Juventus (Italy)	1980–86	Won four of six Italian titles and one European Cup in two finals appearances but didn't match the records of other clubs.	B
Steaua București (Romania)	1984–89	Won five of five Romanian titles (including a 104-match unbeaten streak) and one European Cup in two finals appearances behind captain Tudorel Stoica.	B
Bayern Munich (Germany)	1984–90	Won five domestic titles in six seasons but lost its only European Cup final.	B
PSV Eindhoven (Netherlands)	1985–92	Captained by Ruud Gullit, among others, this team won six of seven domestic titles, one European Cup, and one treble.	B
Red Star Belgrade (Yugoslavia)	1987–92	Won three straight Yugoslav titles and four in five seasons, with one European Cup.	B
AC Milan* (Italy)	1987–96	Over nine seasons, *Gli Immortali* (the Immortals), captained by the legendary Franco Baresi, won three of nine European Cup/Champions League finals while winning five Italian titles and two Intercontinental Cups. It went unbeaten in 1991–92 during a 58-match streak. But this team finished third and fourth in Italy in two seasons and finished one season with no trophies. Its peak Elo rating also failed to crack the top fifteen.	C
Olympique de Marseille* (France)	1988–93	Captained by Didier Deschamps, this team won five straight French Ligue 1 titles (but had to forfeit one after a bribery scandal) and became the first French team to win the Champions League.	C

TEAM	DATES	COMMENTS	DQ CODE
Barcelona (Spain)	1990–94	Captain Andoni Zubizarreta's team won four straight Spanish titles and one Champions League in two finals appearances.	B
Ajax (Netherlands)	1993–98	Won four of five Dutch titles, including three straight, plus one Champions League in two finals appearances when Danny Blind was captain. It finished fourth in the league in 1996–97.	B
Juventus (Italy)	1994–98	Won three of four Italian titles and one Champions League title with two runner-ups.	B
Manchester United* (England)	1995–2001	Captained primarily by Roy Keane, this team won five English titles and two FA Cups and made it to at least the quarterfinals of the Champions League in all but one season, winning it once in a season where it completed the first-ever English treble. But by failing to win a second Champions League, it couldn't match the records of other elite teams.	C
Bayern Munich (Germany)	1998–2003	Won four of five German titles, two German Cups, and one Champions League in two finals appearances.	B
Real Madrid (Spain)	1999–2003	Won two of four Spanish titles and two Champions Leagues but finished third and fifth in the Spanish league.	B

TEAM	DATES	COMMENTS	DQ CODE
Boca Juniors (Argentina)	2000–04	Won three of four Copa Libertadores titles with one runner-up and two Intercontinental Cups but only two of ten possible domestic titles.	B
Internazionale (Italy)	2005–10	Javier Zanetti's team won five domestic titles and one Champions League in a season with a treble of trophies, but failed to add a second Champions League title.	B
Bayern Munich (Germany)	2012–16	Captain Philipp Lahm's club team won four Bundesliga titles and one Champions League among several other titles.	B
Football: Women's International			
Germany*	2003–07	Won two straight World Cups behind captains Bettina Wiegmann and Birgit Prinz but won only a bronze medal in the '04 Olympics.	B
United States*	2012–15	Won one Olympic gold medal and one World Cup, and won or drew 91 percent of its matches under captain Christie Rampone but fell short of the record of the 1996–99 U.S. team.	B
Handball: Men's International			
Sweden	1998–2002	Won three consecutive European titles and one world championship.	B

TEAM	DATES	COMMENTS	DQ CODE
Handball: Women's International			
Denmark*	1994–2000	Won two Olympic gold medals and two European titles under Karen Brødsgaard and Janne Kolling but failed to truly dominate the sport. It lost two of three world championships and finished tenth in the 2000 European Championship.	B
Ice Hockey: Men's International			
Canada	1920–32	Won four Olympic gold medals and six straight World Championships but rarely played outside those competitions.	A
Soviet Union*	1963–72	Won three straight Olympic gold medals and nine straight World Championships against amateurs but lost a series against Canada's best NHL players in 1972.	B
Ice Hockey: National Hockey League			
Ottawa Hockey Club	1903–06	Held the Stanley Cup for four years under captain and coach Alf Smith.	B
Toronto Maple Leafs	1946–51	Captained by Syl Apps and Ted Kennedy, this team won four NHL titles in five seasons but fell short of the record of five straight.	B
Detroit Red Wings	1949–55	Took four NHL titles in six years and won or drew 77 percent of its games under captains Sid Abel and Ted Lindsay.	B

TEAM	DATES	COMMENTS	DQ CODE
Montreal Canadiens	1964–69	Jean Béliveau's team won four NHL Stanley Cups in five seasons, one win short of the record.	B
Montreal Canadiens*	1975–79	Won four straight Stanley Cups and won or drew an unrivaled 86 percent of its games behind captain Yvan Cournoyer but failed to match the record of five consecutive titles.	B
New York Islanders	1979–83	Denis Potvin's team won four straight Stanley Cups, one shy of the record.	B
Edmonton Oilers	1983–90	Wayne Gretzky and Mark Messier led this team to five Stanley Cups in seven seasons, falling short of the record of five in five.	B
Rugby League			
St. George Dragons* (Australia)	1956–66	Won a world-record eleven consecutive domestic titles under captains Ken Kearney and Norm Provan, but rarely played teams from abroad and were soundly beaten in 1962 by an English team.	A
Wigan Warriors* (England)	1986–95	Captained at the outset by the great Ellery Hanley, this team won a record seven English titles and three of five World Club Challenges at a time when England dominated the sport of rugby league. Yet it failed to make the '89 Club Challenge final and fell short of St. George's world record of eleven consecutive domestic titles (see page 291).	B

TEAM	DATES	COMMENTS	DQ CODE
Rugby Union: Men's International			
New Zealand All Blacks	1961–69	Led at the outset by captain Wilson Whineray, this team lost two matches in nine years with a streak of seventeen straight test wins. It played before the World Cup era and failed to match the records of later All Blacks teams.	A
Volleyball: Men's International			
Soviet Union*	1977–83	Led by Vyacheslav Zaytsev, this team won one Olympic gold medal, two straight world titles, two straight World Cups, and four consecutive European titles (once without conceding a set). But many top teams boycotted the 1980 Olympics.	A
Italy	1990–98	Won one World Cup, six World League titles, and two European titles under captain Andrea Gardini but failed to win an Olympic gold medal.	B
Brazil*	2002–07	Won one Olympic gold medal, two World Cups, two World Championships, and five World League titles behind captain Nalbert Bitencourt but did not surpass the achievements of the Soviets (see above).	B
Volleyball: Women's International			
Soviet Union	1949–60	Won three World Championships and four of five European titles before women's volleyball was an Olympic sport.	A

TEAM	DATES	COMMENTS	DQ CODE
Japan	1962–68	Won one Olympic gold medal, two World Championships, and two Asian titles behind captain Masae Kasai but failed to match the record of Cuba.	B
Soviet Union	1968–73	Lyudmila Buldakova's team won two Olympic gold medals, one World Championship, one World Cup, and one European title.	B
Water Polo: Men's International			
Hungary	1926–38	Won two of three Olympic gold medals and five European titles in a row before the World Cup and World Championship era.	A
Hungary*	1952–64	Captained by the great Dezső Gyarmati, this team won three Olympic gold medals and three straight European titles but played in an era when international tournaments were few and far between.	A
Hungary	1973–79	Won one Olympic title, two European titles, one World Cup, and one World Championship but failed to dominate the sport.	B
Yugoslavia	1984–91	Won two Olympic gold medals, two World Cups, and one European title behind captain Igor Milanović, but failed to equal the success of the earlier Hungarian water polo dynasty.	B
Italy	1992–95	Won one Olympic gold medal, one World Championship, one World Cup, and two European titles, but many top teams did not compete in the '92 Olympics.	A

TEAM	DATES	COMMENTS	DQ CODE
Water Polo: Women's International			
Netherlands	1987–93	Won three European titles, four biennial World Cups, and one World Championship before women's water polo became an Olympic sport.	A
United States*	2007–16	Won two straight Olympic gold medals, two World Cups, and eight of ten World League titles under captain Brenda Villa and her successor, Maggie Steffens. In the summer of 2017, the team won its second consecutive World Championship, but had not yet matched the Dutch record of four straight World Cups.	B

Acknowledgments

Writing a book about the world's greatest teams has made me a thousand times more appreciative of my own.

It begins with my brilliant, gorgeous, and altogether Captain Class wife, Christy Fletcher, who not only pored over drafts but never hesitated to roll up her sleeves and wrestle every logistical monster that came along—all while building a thriving business and quarterbacking the lives of two busy, bright, adorable kids. She has taught me more about doggedness, selflessness, emotional control, principled dissent, functional leadership, and practical communication than I knew there was to learn.

Gus and Sylvie soldiered on for long stretches with boundless good humor despite minimal input from Dad (who is delighted to finally start making up for this). My brother Max planted these seeds by charging into sports and letting me tag along, while my mother, Linda, prevailed upon me to get more sleep and liven up my language. Helene and Vincent McCarren offered heaps of warmth and insight; Anita Fussell gladly hopped on a plane whenever things got sticky; and the indestructible Janet Ebora kept everything humming along, always with a smile. I never had the chance to discuss this project with my father, Jack L. Walker, who died when I was 19. He devoted his career as a political scientist to studying the relationship between circumstances and behaviors and to finding ways to speak out for the overlooked. He had a passion for sports and for bringing analytical rigor to complicated subjects. I've tried my best to follow his lead.

Everybody needs good editors—especially an editor. The remarkable talent cluster behind this book includes Andrew Goodfellow in London, Ben Ball in Melbourne, and Miguel Aguilar in Barcelona, who made these pages better in myriad ways. The incomparable Andy Ward at Random House nearly killed me with that wicked blue pen of his, but I'm so glad he did. He is a genius, a mensch, and a Tier One captain tip to tail. I would join any team he assembled.

My natural wonder of an agent, Elyse Cheney, pushed me toward the goal line with her laser-like focus on solutions, while Alex Jacobs and Natasha Fairweather translated these ideas into many different languages and sporting cultures. The sure-footed Andrew Beaton dug through archives, crunched numbers, conducted interviews, and tracked down obscure books about Hungarian water polo without showing any *visible* signs of distress. Colleagues Joshua Robinson, Matthew Futterman, and Ben Cohen provided contacts, read drafts, and agreed to slip random questions about captains into their own interviews. The resourceful Ben Phelan kept my facts straight, and Neal Bascomb and Beth Rashbaum shored up my structure. Thanks to Maria Braeckel, Gina Centrello, Kelly Chian, Andrea DeWerd, Benjamin Dreyer, Susan Kamil, Leigh Marchant, Cindy Murray, Kaela Myers, Joe Perez, Tom Perry, and Amelia Zalcman at Random House in New York—and Sarah Bennie, Shantelle David, and Anna Mrowiec at Ebury in London—for seeing potential in this project and handling every detail with patience and panache.

A far-flung crew of translators, agents, editors, fixers, and media professionals helped me navigate the globe. They include: Gilian Trelles in Havana; Cristiana Coimbra in Rio; Chemi Torres in Barcelona; Philippe Tournin and Pauline Lambertini in Paris; Ana Rivera and Juan Camilo Andrade in Madrid; Alan Samson and Benjamin Miller in London; Rhona Macdonald in Glasgow; Peter Sherrard in Dublin; Martin Hägele in Munich; Lawrence West in Melbourne; Jon Earle, Tim Bent, Tahiri Viñas, Gary Springer, Eric Souffer, Sabrina Carrozza, and Jacqueline Frajmund in New York; Dave Kaplan at the Yogi Berra Museum & Learning Center; Jim O'Brien in Pittsburgh; Meredith Geisler in Washington; Liz Lauffer in Vermont; and Charlotte Simcock at the New Zealand consulate.

So many friends and colleagues provided guidance and support: Reed Albergotti, Al Anspaugh, Rachel Bachman, Dan Barbarisi, Diane Bartoli, Ken Bensinger, Carl Bialik, Elizabeth Bernstein, Sharon and John David Box, Dana Brown, Jeremy Brown, Scott Cacciola, Susan and Ken Cain, Jim Chairusmi, Joanna Chung, Kevin Clark, Jon Clegg, Rich Cohen, Elisha Cooper, Brian Costa, Jonathan Dahl, Jared and Talie Diamond, Nando Di Fino, David Enrich, Ken Fletcher, Alix Freedman, Sara Germano, Paul Gigot, Sylvie Greenberg, Rick Hahn, Sloan Harris, Chris Herring, Ashley Huston, Jodi Kantor, Aditi Kinkhabwala, Monica Langley, Byrd and Alanna Leavell, Ron Lieber, Joanne Lipman, Lorne Manly, Gabriele Marcotti, Joe and Noel Mihalow, Chad Millman, Bruce Nichols, Cian O'Carroll, Vanessa O'Connell, Bruce Orwall, Matt Oshinsky, Jim and Karen Pensiero, Tom Perrotta, Ann Podd, Brad Reagan, Brad Roaman, Matt Schuetze, Andrea Schulz, Eben Shapiro, Aimee Shieh, Mike Sielski, Warren St. John, Scott Stein, Bob Sutton, Adam Thompson, Don Van Natta, Nikki Waller, and John Williams. The crew at Hu Kitchen, the morning shift at the Jade Hotel, Maury Rubin at City Bakery, and Bianca at The Market in Greenport kept me from developing scurvy. Thanks to Aldo's, Joe Café, and Think Coffee for letting me loiter, and to the 1211 AOA security team for never questioning what I was doing alone in a dark office at five A.M.

The best team I've ever played for is the *Wall Street Journal*. I'm deeply grateful to Gerry Baker for giving me leave to do this and continuing to champion our sports coverage even when the Giants were 6–10, and for the Tier One leadership and support of Rebecca Blumenstein, Christine Glancey, Almar Latour, Will Lewis, Neal Lipschutz, Alex Martin, Rupert Murdoch, Matt Murray, Jim and Karen Pensiero, and Paul Steiger among many others. Mike Miller has been a rock of wisdom and good counsel during our long, madcap journey together, and Darren Everson, Geoff Foster, Derick Gonzalez, and Kevin Helliker manned my oar splendidly during my absence from the sports department. Dennis Berman kept me motivated with his early-morning mantras, and Jason Gay forced me to laugh—and also to think—harder than I ever have. Thanks to my page-one collaborators Dagmar Aalund, Mike Allen, Beth Blackshire, Rick Brooks, Madeline Carson, Carrie Dolan, Sam Enriquez, Phil Izzo, Dan Kelly, Jill Kirschenbaum, Emma Moody, Sarah Morse, Todd Olmstead, Mitch Pacelle, Allison Pasek, and Steve Yoder for their astute suggestions and emergency copyedits.

I'll end with a heartfelt thanks to two extraordinary colleagues: Robert Thomson, the world's greatest mentor, whose contagious enthusiasm, intellectual firepower, abundant humor, and indecipherable riffs on Aussie rules football have changed me profoundly for the better; and Matthew Rose, the *Journal*'s tireless, visionary enterprise editor, who invited me into his splendid orbit and then covered my back as I scrambled to finish this project. I'm proud to say that the better half of my brain is an extension of theirs.

Bibliography

WATCH LIST

Barça Dreams: A True Story of FC Barcelona. Entropy Studio, Gen Image Media, 2015.

Bill Russell: My Life, My Way. HBO Sports, 2000.

Capitão Bellini: Herói Itapirense. HBR TV, 2012.

Carles Puyol: 15 Años, 15 Momentos. Barça TV, 2014.

Dare to Dream: The Story of the U.S. Women's Soccer Team. HBO Studios, 2005.

Die Mannschaft (Germany at the 2014 World Cup). Little Shark Entertainment, 2014.

England v Hungary 1953: The Full Match at Wembley. Mastersound, 2007.

Fire and Ice: The Rocket Richard Riot. Barna-Alper and Galafilm Productions, 2000.

Height of Passion: FC Barcelona vs. Real Madrid. Forza Productions, 2004.

Hockeyroos Win Gold (2000 Olympic Final). Australian Olympic Committee, 2013.

Inside Bayern Munich. With Owen Hargreaves. BT Sport, 2015.

Legends of All Blacks Rugby. Go Entertain, 1999.

Les Experts: Le Doc (French handball at the 2009 World Championships). Canal+ TV, 2009.

Les Yeux Dans Les Bleus (France in the 1998 World Cup). 2P2L Télévision, 1998.

Mud & Glory: Buck Shelford. TVNZ, 1990.

Nine for IX: The 99ers. ESPN Films, 2013.

Of Miracles and Men. (Soviet hockey at the 1980 Olympics). ESPN Films 30 for 30, 2015.

Pelé: The King of Brazil. Janson Media, 2010.

Pelé and Garrincha: Gods of Brazil. Storyville, BBC Four, 2002.

Puskás Hungary. Filmplus, 2009.

Red Army (Soviet hockey). Sony Pictures Classics, 2014.

Tim Duncan and Bill Russell Go One on One. NBA.com, 2009.

Tim Duncan: Inside Stuff. NBA Inside Stuff, ABC, November 2004.

Weight of a Nation (2011 New Zealand All Blacks World Cup campaign). Sky Network Television, 2012.

Yogi Berra: American Sports Legend. Time Life Records, 2004.

SUGGESTED READING

Abrams, Mitch. "Providing Clarity on Anger & Violence in Sports." *Applied Sports Psychology*. January 7, 2016.

Ambady, N., and R. Rosenthal. "Half a Minute: Predicting Teacher Evaluations from Thin Slices of Nonverbal Behavior and Physical Attractiveness." *Journal of Personality and Social Psychology* 64, no. 3 (2003).

Balague, Guillem. *Pep Guardiola: Another Way of Winning*. London: Orion, 2012.

Ball, Phil. *Morbo: The Story of Spanish Football*. London: WSC Books, 2011.

Barra, Allen. *Yogi Berra: Eternal Yankee.* New York: Norton, 2009.

Berra, Yogi, and Edward E. Fitzgerald. *Yogi: The Autobiography of a Professional Baseball Player.* New York: Doubleday, 1961.

Berra, Yogi, and Dave Kaplan. *You Can Observe a Lot by Watching: What I've Learned About Teamwork from the Yankees and Life.* Hoboken, N.J.: Wiley, 2008.

Blount, Roy, Jr. *About Three Bricks Shy . . . And the Load Filled Up.* Pittsburgh: University of Pittsburgh Press, 2004.

Burns, James MacGregor. *Leadership.* New York: Harper & Row, 1978.

Buss, A. H. *The Psychology of Aggression.* New York: Wiley, 1961.

Cain, Susan. *Quiet: The Power of Introverts in a World That Can't Stop Talking.* New York: Crown, 2012.

Canetti, Elias. *Crowds and Power.* New York: Farrar, Straus & Giroux, 1962.

Carrier, Roch. *Our Life with the Rocket: The Maurice Richard Story.* Toronto: Penguin Canada, 2001.

Charlesworth, Ric. *The Coach: Managing for Success.* Sydney: Macmillan, 2001.

Cooper, Cynthia. *She Got Game: My Personal Odyssey.* New York: Warner Books, 1999.

Cruyff, Johan. *My Turn: A Life of Total Football.* New York: Nation, 2016.

Davidson, Richard J., and Sharon Begley. *The Emotional Life of Your Brain: How Its Unique Patterns Affect the Way You Think, Feel, and Live—and How You Can Change Them.* New York: Hudson Street Press, 2012.

Davis, Willie. *Closing the Gap: Lombardi, the Packers Dynasty and the Pursuit of Excellence.* Chicago: Triumph, 2012.

DeVito, Carlo. *Yogi: The Life & Times of an American Original.* Chicago: Triumph, 2008.

de Wit, Frank, L. Lindred Greer, and Karen Jehn. "The Paradox of Intragroup Conflict: A Meta-Analysis." *Journal of Applied Psychology* 97, no. 2, March 2012.

do Nascimento, Edson Arantes. *Pelé: The Autobiography.* London: Simon & Schuster, 2006.

Dweck, Carol. *Mindset: The New Psychology of Success.* New York: Ballantine, 2007.

Ferguson, Alex. *Managing My Life.* London: Coronet, 2000.

Ferguson, Alex. *My Autobiography.* London: Hodder & Stoughton, 2013.

Ferguson, Alex, and David Meek. *A Will to Win.* London: Andre Deutsch, 1997.

Ferguson, Alex, and Michael Moritz. *Leading: Learning from Life and My Many Years at Manchester United.* London: Hodder & Stoughton, 2015.

Fetisov, Viacheslav, and Vitaly Melik-Karamov. *Овертайм* (Overtime). Moscow: Vagrius, 1998.

Fox, Dave, Ken Bogle, and Mark Hoskins. *A Century of the All Blacks in Britain and Ireland.* Stroud, U.K.: Tempus, 2005.

Gal, Reuven. *A Portrait of the Israeli Soldier.* Westport, Conn.: Greenwood Press, 1986.

Gittleman, Sol. *Reynolds, Raschi and Lopat: New York's Big Three and the Great Yankee Dynasty of 1949–1953.* Jefferson, N.C.: McFarland & Co., 2007.

Goldblatt, David. *Futebol Nation: The Story of Brazil Through Soccer.* New York: Nation, 2014.

Goleman, Daniel. *Emotional Intelligence.* New York: Bantam, 1995.

Goleman, Daniel. *Social Intelligence: The New Science of Human Relationships.* New York: Bantam, 2006.

Goleman, Daniel, Richard Boyatzis, and Annie McKee. *Primal Leadership: Unleashing the Power of Emotional Intelligence.* Boston: Harvard Business Review Press, 2013.

Golenbock, Peter. *Dynasty: The New York Yankees 1949–1964.* Englewood Cliffs, N.J.: Prentice Hall, 1975.

Gordon, Alex. *Celtic: The Awakening.* Edinburgh: Mainstream, 2013.

Goyens, Chrys, and Frank Orr. *Maurice Richard: Reluctant Hero.* Toronto: Team Power Publishing, 2000.

Hackman, J. Richard. *Collaborative Intelligence: Using Teams to Solve Hard Problems.* Oakland, Calif.: Berrett-Koehler, 2011.

Hackman, J. Richard. *Leading Teams: Setting the Stage for Great Performances.* Boston: Harvard Business Review Press, 2002.

Halberstam, David. *Playing for Keeps: Michael Jordan & the World He Made.* New York: Broadway, 1999.

Hawley, Patricia H., Todd D. Little, and Philip Craig Rodkin, eds. *Aggression and Adaptation: The Bright Side to Bad Behavior.* Mahwah, N.J.: Erlbaum, 2007.

Hebert, Mike. *Thinking Volleyball: Inside the Game with a Coaching Legend.* Champaign, Ill.: Human Kinetics, 2014.

Howitt, Bob. *A Perfect Gentleman: The Sir Wilson Whineray Story.* Auckland: HarperCollins, 2010.

Hughes, Simon. *Red Machine: Liverpool FC in the 1980s.* Edinburgh: Mainstream, 2013.

Hunter, Graham. *Barça: The Making of the Greatest Team in the World.* London: Backpage Press, 2012.

Iacoboni, Marco. *Mirroring People: The New Science of Empathy and How We Connect with Others.* New York: Farrar, Straus & Giroux, 2008.

Ibrahimović, Zlatan, and David Lagercrantz. *I Am Zlatan: My Story On and Off the Field.* New York: Random House, 2014.

Jehn, K. A., and E. Mannix. "The Dynamic Nature of Conflict: A Longitudinal Study of Intragroup Conflict and Group Performance." *Academy of Management Journal,* April 2001, vol. 44, no. 2.

Keane, Roy, and Roddy Doyle. *Roy Keane: The Second Half.* London: Weidenfeld & Nicolson, 2014.

Keane, Roy, and Eamon Dunphy. *Keane: The Autobiography.* London: Penguin, 2002.

Kelly, Stephen F. *Graeme Souness: A Soccer Revolutionary.* London: Headline, 1994.

Kerr, James. *Legacy: What the All Blacks Can Teach Us About the Business of Life.* London: Constable & Robinson, 2013.

Körner, Torsten. *Franz Beckenbauer: Der Freie Mann.* Frankfurt: Scherz, 2005.

Lahm, Philipp, and Christian Seiler. *Der Feine Unterschied* (The Subtle Difference). Munich: Kuntsmann, 2011.

Lainz, Lluís. *Puyol: La Biografía.* Barcelona: Córner, 2013.

Lazenby, Roland. *Michael Jordan: The Life.* New York: Back Bay, 2014.

Leary, Mark R., Richard Bednarski, Dudley Hammon, and Timothy T. Duncan. "Blowhards, Snobs, and Narcissists: Interpersonal Reactions to Excessive Egotism." In Kowalski, Robin M., ed., *Aversive Interpersonal Behaviors.* New York: Plenum Press, 1997.

Lisi, Clemente A. *The U.S. Women's Soccer Team: An American Success Story.* Lanham, Md.: Scarecrow Press, 2010.

Lister, Simon. *Supercat: The Authorised Biography of Clive Lloyd.* Bath: Fairfield Books, 2007.

Longman, Jere. *The Girls of Summer: The U.S. Women's Soccer Team and How It Changed the World.* New York: Harper, 2000.

Lowe, Sid. *Fear and Loathing in La Liga: Barcelona, Real Madrid, and the World's Greatest Sports Rivalry.* New York: Nation, 2014.

Maraniss, David. *When Pride Still Mattered: A Life of Vince Lombardi.* New York: Simon & Schuster, 1999.

McCaw, Richie. *The Real McCaw: Richie McCaw: The Autobiography.* London: Aurum Press, 2012.

McFarlane, Glenn, and Ashley Browne. *Jock: The Story of Jock McHale, Collingwood's Greatest Coach.* Melbourne: Slattery Media Group, 2011.

Melançon, Benoît. *The Rocket: A Cultural History of Maurice Richard.* Montreal: Greystone, 2009.

O'Brien, Jim. *Lambert: The Man in the Middle.* Pittsburgh: James P. O'Brien, 2004.

O'Connor, Ian. *The Captain: The Journey of Derek Jeter.* New York: Mariner, 2011.

Pascuito, Bernard. *La face cachée de Didier Deschamps* (The Hidden Side of Didier Deschamps). Paris: First Editions, 2013.

Pentland, Alex. "The New Science of Building Great Teams." *Harvard Business Review,* April 2012.

Pomerantz, Gary. *Their Life's Work: The Brotherhood of the 1970s Pittsburgh Steelers, Then and Now.* New York: Simon & Schuster, 2013.

Ponting, Ricky, and Geoff Armstrong. *Ponting: At the Close of Play.* London: HarperCollins, 2013.

Puskás, Ferenc. *Puskás: Captain of Hungary.* Stroud, U.K.: Tempus, 2007.

Reynolds, Bill. *Rise of a Dynasty: The '57 Celtics.* New York: New American Library, 2010.

Rooney, Dan, David F. Halaas, and Andrew E. Masich. *Dan Rooney: My 75 Years with the Pittsburgh Steelers and the NFL.* New York: Da Capo Press, 2007.

Rotunno, Ron. *Jack Lambert: Tough as Steel.* Masury, Ohio: Steel Valley Books, 1997.

Rouch, Dominique. *Didier Deschamps: Vainqueur dans l'âme* (Didier Deschamps: Conquering Soul). Paris: Editions 1, 2001.

Russell, Bill, Taylor Branch, and Alan Hillburg. *Second Wind: The Memoirs of an Opinionated Man.* New York: Ballantine, 1980.

Russell, Bill, and David Falkner. *Russell Rules: 11 Lessons on Leadership from the Twentieth Century's Greatest Winner.* New York: Dutton, 2001.

Russell, Bill, and Alan Steinberg. *Red and Me: My Coach, My Lifelong Friend.* New York: Harper, 2009.

Shelford, Buck, and Wynne Gray. *Buck: The Wayne Shelford Story.* Auckland: Moa, 1990.

Smith, Sam. *The Jordan Rules.* New York: Pocket Books, 1993.

Stremski, Richard. *Kill for Collingwood.* Sydney: Allen & Unwin, 1986.

Tarasov, Anatoly. *Настоящие мужчины хоккея* (The Real Men of Hockey). Moscow: Physical Culture and Sport, 1987.

Tavella, Renato. *Valentino Mazzola: Un Uomo, un giocatore, un mito.* Turin: Graphot Editrice, 1998.

Taylor, Rogan, and Klara Jamrich, eds. *Puskas on Puskas: The Life and Times of a Footballing Legend.* London: Robson Books, 1997.

Torquemada, Ricard. *Fórmula Barça: Viaje Al Interior de un Equipo Que Ha Descubierto la Eternidad*. Valls, Spain: Lectio, 2013.

Waugh, Steve. *Out of My Comfort Zone: The Autobiography*. Melbourne: Penguin, 2005.

Whalen, Paul J., et al. "Human Amygdala Responsivity to Masked Fearful Eye Whites." *Science* 306, no. 17 (December 2004).

White, Jim. *Manchester United: The Biography*. London: Sphere, 2008.

Wilson, Jonathan. *Inverting the Pyramid: The History of Football Tactics*. London: Orion, 2008.

Writer, Larry. *Never Before, Never Again: The Rugby League Miracle at St. George 1956–66*. Sydney: Pan Macmillan, 1995.

Zitek, Emily M., and Alexander H. Jordan. "Technical Fouls Predict Performance Outcomes in the NBA." *Athletic Insight*, vol. 3, no. 1 (Spring 2011).

Index

An asterisk (*) denotes a Tier One (Greatest) team.

ABOUT THE AUTHOR

SAM WALKER is the *Wall Street Journal*'s deputy editor for enterprise, the unit that directs the paper's in-depth page-one features and investigative reporting projects. A former reporter, columnist, and sports editor, Walker founded the *Journal*'s prizewinning daily sports coverage in 2009. He is the author of *Fantasyland*, a bestselling account of his attempt to win America's top fantasy baseball expert competition (of which he is a two-time champion). Walker attended the University of Michigan. He lives in New York with his wife and their two children.

@SamWalkers